*Praise for*

# BECOMING EPIC

"For leaders, professionals, or anyone ready to make a lasting impact, *Becoming EPIC* offers more than inspiration—it delivers a blueprint for transformation. Dr. Kutz's voice is both motivational and deeply grounded, guiding readers toward a life where they are not only successful but profoundly fulfilled."

**Marshall Goldsmith**, PhD, *New York Times* bestselling author of *The Earned Life*, *Triggers*, and *What Got You Here Won't Get You There*

"*Becoming EPIC* delivers powerful leadership insights, seamlessly connecting ancient wisdom with modern-day challenges. Matt's ability to weave spiritual, emotional, and practical leadership into a cohesive guide sets him apart as a thought leader across industries. Having read every leadership book he has written, I can confidently say this is Matt Kutz's most transformative work yet. Whether you are aspiring or experienced, *Becoming EPIC* is a must-read that will inspire leadership growth at every stage!"

**Dr. Trevor M. Bates**, President, Mercy College of Ohio

"Personal growth and self-reflection aren't just ideas; they are verbs that require action. *Becoming EPIC* highlights the vulnerabilities we all face, while creating a path toward personal and professional betterment. Through his own challenges, Dr. Matt Kutz brings a perspective and clarity on navigating life and leadership's most difficult situations. From goal setting to relationship building to the true meaning of success, this is a must-read for those looking at becoming the best version of themselves."

**Dr. Corey Tremble**, Director of Athletic Training and Rehabilitation, Miami Marlins baseball club

"In this book, Dr. Kutz unveils through his own humanity the principles that cause good leaders to become great leaders. *Becoming EPIC* will challenge you to change when everything within you resists it, primarily because you realize being a leader isn't about you; it's about becoming the best version of you to inspire others. Developing as a leader never stops unless you settle for mediocrity. This book will either push you out of the rut of mediocrity or accelerate your leadership growth in ways you didn't know were possible. A must-read for leaders and aspiring leaders."

**Bo Salisbury**, Founder, Kingdom Culture International

"In an age of exalting victimhood, it is refreshing to find resources pointing to victorious outcomes in our complex human experience. Matt Kutz captures this thought in giving us a blueprint to live an epic life like King David. Matt's own journey opens insightful windows into this very path. I thoroughly enjoyed this book and recommend following Matt's process of overcoming our adversities and turning them into winning strategies."

**J.C. Alzamora**, President, LifeFlow Missions

"In a world where the pursuit of greatness is often overshadowed by the mundane and the mediocre, *Becoming EPIC* by Dr. Matt Kutz offers not just a road map but a transformative philosophy for those who seek to break free from the status quo. This book challenges its readers to rise above the ordinary and embrace a life of excellence, purpose, and impact. But what sets Dr. Kutz's work apart is not merely its focus on achievement—it is his emphasis on the core values that underpin true greatness. With his profound insight and clear vision, Dr. Kutz offers a guide that is not just for individual transformation but for societal change. This book is a call to action for those who are ready to embrace the EPIC within themselves. If you are ready to elevate your life beyond mediocrity, to live with purpose, and to lead with impact, then this book is for you."

**Dr. Ron Courson**, Executive Associate Athletic Director–Sports Medicine, University of Georgia

MATTHEW R. KUTZ, PhD

Foreword by Marshall Goldsmith

# BECOMING EPIC

*How* Excellence, Perception, Inspiration, *and* Compassion Can Be *a* Remedy *for* Mediocrity

amplify
an imprint of Amplify Publishing Group

www.amplifypublishinggroup.com

*Becoming EPIC: How Excellence, Perception, Inspiration, and Compassion Can Be a Remedy for Mediocrity*



**For more information, please contact:**
Amplify Publishing, an imprint of Amplify Publishing Group
620 Herndon Parkway, Suite 220
Herndon, VA 20170
info@amplifypublishing.com

Library of Congress Control Number: 2025910817

CPSIA Code: PRV0725A

ISBN-13: 979-8-89138-699-0

Printed in United States

*To my sons, Nathan and Jonathan.*

*You both are quickly becoming EPIC!*
*It has been my honor to be your dad. Words*
*cannot express how proud I am of you both!*
*You have been a great example to me of how to*
*practice the standards of Excellence, Perception,*
*Inspiration, and Compassion.*

*Keep becoming EPIC!*

# CONTENTS

## PART 3: ON INSPIRATION



## PART 4: ON COMPASSION



## PART 5: ON BECOMING

# FOREWORD

In *Becoming Epic: How Excellence, Perception, Inspiration, and Compassion Can Be a Remedy for Mediocrity*, Dr. Matthew Kutz offers a profound journey into self-mastery and purposeful living. This is not just another book about success; it's a road map for those committed to transcending superficial achievements in favor of personal growth and true fulfillment. Matt presents a powerful framework centered around the four maxims of Excellence, Perception, Inspiration, and Compassion, each crafted to foster resilience, inner strength, and meaningful progress.

What makes *Becoming EPIC* especially compelling is Matt's willingness to share the trials that shaped his perspective, most notably his battle with cancer. With unflinching honesty, he recounts how this life-altering experience forced him to redefine what it means to live fully and to excel, not by society's standards, but by his own. This personal touch transforms the book from a theoretical self-help guide into a relatable, empathetic companion for anyone facing adversity. Matt illustrates that true excellence is not about avoiding hardship but about leveraging those experiences to strengthen our resolve, sharpen our focus, and deepen our compassion for others.

Each chapter in *Becoming EPIC* invites readers to reflect on their values, reconsider their goals, and challenge their assumptions. Matt makes it clear that personal growth is an active, intentional process—a journey that requires patience, discipline, and self-compassion. Through practical exercises, mindset shifts, and actionable advice, he encourages readers to not only aspire, but to act.

*Becoming EPIC* is both a guide and a challenge. Matt empowers readers to push beyond the comfortable confines of "good enough" and to envision a life where excellence is the baseline. In a world often obsessed with shortcuts and instant gratification, this book stands as a refreshing reminder that the most meaningful growth happens gradually, with every choice and every small act of dedication. The EPIC mindset is not just a method for self-improvement; it's a lifelong commitment to living with purpose and integrity.

For leaders, professionals, or anyone ready to make a lasting impact, *Becoming EPIC* offers more than inspiration—it delivers a blueprint for transformation. Matt's voice is both motivational and deeply grounded, guiding readers toward a life where they are not only successful but profoundly fulfilled. This book is a valuable companion for anyone willing to do the work, embrace change, and become the most "epic" version of themselves.

**Dr. Marshall Goldsmith,** Thinkers50 #1 Executive Coach and *New York Times* bestselling author of *The Earned Life*, *Triggers*, and *What Got You Here Won't Get You There*
2025

*Whatever your hand finds to do, do it with all your might, for in the realm of the dead, where you are going, there is neither working nor planning nor knowledge nor wisdom.*

Ecclesiastes 9:10

# PROLOGUE

Few people have lived a life as epic as David. Not many lives have captured the imaginations of people across so many diverse cultures and traditions like David, the shepherd boy turned giant slayer, poet, and king. His story, mostly chronicled in the Old Testament's 2 Samuel, continues to inspire and challenge us, transcending time and becoming a symbol of overcoming mediocrity to become epic. Not only is he the quintessential giant slayer, renowned for facing and defeating the undefeated giant warrior, Goliath, but David's exploits and attitude earned him a place in the lineage and ancestry of The Messiah.

David's journey from humble beginnings to legendary status is not just about facing giants—it's about the many battles he fought, both externally and internally, that reveal the mastery of becoming excellent, perceptive, inspired, and compassionate.

David is perhaps most famously known for his battle with Goliath, the undefeated Philistine warrior, where he showed that giants are not as unbeatable as they seem. Malcolm Gladwell's book *David and Goliath* highlights this story as an example of how perceived weaknesses can actually be strengths. Goliath was a giant weighed down by size and heavy armor. David, small and nimble, armed only with a sling, refused to wear armor that was bulky and clumsy. He turned what seemed to be his disadvantage, his size and lack of military experience, into his greatest weapon. His victory was not just an act of bravery, but it was one of *perception*—David saw what others couldn't. He understood that the battle would not be won by brute strength but by skill, speed, and faith. His perception also proved valuable as he invested his life into training an iconic band of warriors, eventually known as his mighty men, who themselves became giant slayers. But before that they were described as "distressed, in debt, and discontented" (1 Samuel 22:2). This was a motley crew. However, David's perception saw something in them others could not.

David's victory and his unparalleled leadership launched him into prominence, but it was far from the only notable aspect of his life. He was a man of many roles—capable shepherd, fierce warrior king, and killer of lions and bears. He was a brilliant psalmist and poet, infamous lover, mentor of men, devoted friend, and father of Solomon, the man who possessed legendary wisdom, hallmarks of *inspiration*. His friendship with Jonathan, the son of King Saul, exemplifies the maxim of *compassion*. Despite Jonathan's rightful claim to the throne, David and Jonathan shared a bond that transcended personal ambition. David's compassion for his friend allowed him to remain loyal even in the face of Saul's attempts to kill him.

Yet, David's life was also marked by flaws and failures. He was not perfect—far from it. In fact, it is this very imperfection that made his story so powerful and relatable. Like all of us, David struggled with his weaknesses. He was an adulterer and arranged the murder of another man to cover up his crime. He was a father who failed to discipline his son, Absalom, who would later rebel against him. He was a man of violent temper, prone to making decisions in anger. His beginnings were humble, even painful—he was forgotten by his father and brothers, likely the bastard son of an illicit love affair, and for much of his youth, he was overlooked and ignored.

David could easily have been defined by these failures. He could have remained the adulterer, the murderer, the absentee father, and the man abandoned by others. Yet, what made David truly *epic* was his ability to repent—not merely in the sense of asking for forgiveness, but in the truest sense of the word: changing his mind. The word "repent" comes from the Greek word *metanoia*, meaning to "change one's mind." Repentance is more about faulty thinking than faulty behavior. David's greatness came from his willingness to turn away from his mistakes and change his way of thinking. This lifestyle of repentance, this ability to *change*, is what set him apart and allowed him to grow through his failures.

One of the most famous examples of David's repentance is found after his adultery with Bathsheba. When the prophet Nathan confronted him with the parable of the rich man who stole a poor man's lamb, David, filled with righteous anger, declared the rich man deserved death. Nathan's response, "You are that man," struck David to his core. In that moment, David didn't harden his heart or justify his actions—he repented. He changed his mind, he started thinking differently, and as a result, he was restored. This act of repentance was not just a one-time event but a continual process in David's life. His ability to change his thinking, again and again, allowed him to be known as "a man after God's own heart."

David's life reminds us that becoming EPIC—that is, practicing *Excellence, Perception, Inspiration,* and *Compassion*—is a journey. It requires a willingness to grow, to learn from failures, and to change course when necessary. *Excellence* isn't achieved by being perfect, but by constantly striving toward the best version of yourself, as David did in every stage of his life. *Perception* is about seeing what others cannot, like David's insight into Goliath's weaknesses or his understanding of the need for repentance. *Inspiration* is found throughout the psalms David wrote—songs of worship, lament, and hope that continue to inspire millions. And *Compassion* is shown in David's relationships, his loyalty to Jonathan, his mercy toward Saul, and his grief for Absalom, even after his rebellion.

David's life was truly epic not because he was without fault but because he overcame his faults and grew through them. Each of us, like David, has the potential to live an epic story. It's not about avoiding failure; it's about how we respond to it. The secret to David's greatness—and to ours—is found in the ability to change, unlearn and relearn, to see beyond the moment, and to think differently than we do now.

To live an epic life is to believe that no matter where we start, or how many times we fall, the future will be greater than anything we can currently see or understand. Becoming EPIC is within reach for all of us if we are willing to embrace life as a journey, committing to be excellent, perceptive, inspired, and compassionate. Then, like David, we must be willing to change our thinking, grow from adversity, and want to become more than we ever imagined possible.

# INTRODUCTION: THE BEGINNING

It all began with a phone call. I didn't know it then, but that conversation would change the course of my life and career. On the other end of the line was a senior executive from a Fortune 500 company, inviting me to speak to his team about a concept I'd coined in my research: contextual intelligence.

As our phone conversation progressed, the executive explained how he'd stumbled upon my article. "I was at an event at Stanford University's business school," he said, "where our CEO was receiving the Man of the Year Award. Warren Bennis, the legendary leadership scholar, introduced our CEO and mentioned that one of the reasons for his success was his 'contextual intelligence.'"

He continued, "I had never heard that term before. I literally wrote it on a napkin, stuck it in my pocket, and later Googled it. An article you wrote on contextual intelligence was at the top of the list. When I read it, I was floored—I'd never encountered anything like it. It felt like you had discovered the 'it factor' in leadership that so many have been searching for."

He then told me about his team's process: when they find something compelling, they study it, make notes, put it away for six months, and then revisit it. If it still resonates, they know they've found something powerful. "Your article passed our six-month test," he said, "and I want you to come and speak to us about it."

Little did I know that his division alone generated $16 billion in revenue and that the individuals I would be presenting to were among the smartest minds in global business services. His invitation both excited and overwhelmed me. I was a college professor with no corporate leadership experience, and here was a top executive in a multinational Fortune 500 corporation, telling me that his team—some of the smartest people in the world—wanted to learn from me. Up to that point, my biggest accomplishment was completing a textbook and climbing the academic ladder. I had no idea what I was walking into or how I would even begin to prepare.

"Bring your A-game," he advised, "because if you don't engage them, you won't make the impact I think you could." *What's his idea of an "A-game?"* I thought.

With trembling hands, I accepted, but I was deeply intimidated. I asked him, somewhat sheepishly, "Would it be alright if I used my dissertation slides? They're academic, but it's where the concept of contextual intelligence began."

He said, "No," and warned me not to present academic mumbo jumbo or his team would eat me alive. So, I immediately began refining my material. But only because they agreed to pay me what I thought was an exorbitant fee, which I later found out was spare change for them.

When the day arrived, I drove to their global headquarters. My nerves were already on edge, compounded by the fact that my car—a '94 Honda Accord with peeling paint and a zip-tied side mirror—was far from the Bentleys and Mercedes Benzes lining the executive parking lot. I decided to avoid the executive garage entirely, parking instead in a nearby paid lot on the street catty-corner to their global headquarters. My anxiety only grew as I navigated layers of tight security to reach the C-suite, where I encountered more luxury and sophistication than I'd ever imagined.

The executive led me to a sleek, futuristic room he proudly called their "hologram room." The walls and floors were stark white, and in each corner were high-tech 3D cameras that projected holographic images. "This room alone cost a million dollars," he said, explaining they had sixteen such rooms worldwide to simulate face-to-face meetings. I was awestruck and intimidated by their investment in cutting-edge technology.

We finally reached the conference room, where the six team members and an additional guest—the director of their corporate university—were waiting. The presence of the director, who managed one of the top corporate training programs globally, added to my nerves. As I adjusted my suit, bought hastily off the rack, I glanced at the director's wrist and noticed his watch—an Omega, likely worth more than my car and possibly half a year's salary. Imposter syndrome flooded over me, but there was no backing out now.

Fifteen minutes into my presentation, a hand went up. It was the director of the corporate university, and he didn't have a question; he had a comment. "Dr. Kutz," he began, "obviously, you're nervous." Yup, "you're nervous," were the first words I heard from the group. If you ever do public speaking, you know that when your nerves are affecting the audience it's not a good thing. I was failing, which only heightened my anxiety. He continued, "But let me tell you something. What you've shared about contextual intelligence so far is the best leadership concept I've ever heard, and we hear and explore every possible angle on leadership; yet, this stands out."

He suggested we take a break. *Really?* I thought. We had only been at it for fifteen minutes, and already they wanted a break. I realized they didn't need the break, I did. I gratefully accepted, using the opportunity to collect myself and get some amazing food from the grazing station in the lobby of the executive suites. When we reconvened, the director of the corporate university told me, "This is a game-changing concept, and we want to spend the rest of the time exploring how to integrate it into our organization."

For the next three hours, we dove deep into contextual intelligence. We talked about my ideas, my theories around it, the constructs that supported it, and even the biblical basis of the concept from the Old Testament's Tribe of Issachar. They asked probing questions I hadn't considered, giving me insights that helped refine the concept further. By the end of the meeting, I realized that the time and effort I'd poured into preparation had paid off. I left that room with a sense of purpose I hadn't felt before and a clearer vision for how contextual intelligence could shape leadership in real-world settings. I also began to realize this idea had the potential to impact more than just leaders or businesses. The director told me, as I was leaving, something that has stuck with me ever since. He said, "If I had known about this concept and its principles seven years ago, I wouldn't be divorced right now." WOW! That was the first time I realized I had a potentially great idea, but I didn't know how to leverage it yet.

After the meeting, the director offered to walk me to my car. I declined because I didn't want him to know I hadn't used the parking pass they sent me. For a moment, I considered standing by a random car to let him believe it was mine, but then I realized, with my luck, I might pick his car to stand by. Then I would be crazy too. So, he just walked me out to the lobby; as we walked, he encouraged me to secure legal protections for my work and intellectual property. "In two weeks, we're moving forward with this," he said. "You can either benefit or get taken advantage of. I hope you'll take my advice."

The magnitude of his words struck me. I went home with renewed focus and began to prepare like never before. I hired an attorney, filed for intellectual property rights and copyright, and set up the foundational work for what would become the framework of my concept of contextual intelligence and a reputation as an award-winning author and corporate trainer. From that point forward, I validated what I had always assumed: the journey to excellence always begins with preparation.

As our relationship developed, the company invited me back and even asked if I'd written a book on contextual intelligence. When I admitted I hadn't, they encouraged me to start one. So, I did. I self-published it, and they bought several hundred of the first copies off the press. They warned me that when others heard of what they were doing with this, they would come calling, so I should get a website and other logistics in place. They weren't wrong. Within that first year and a half, I had sold 3,000 copies and my first three clients were other corporate giants. Most people spend their entire careers trying to get into companies like the ones I worked with.

They also suggested creating a tool to measure contextual intelligence in leaders, leading me to develop the Contextual Intelligence Profile™. That tool went on to become a validated instrument, and that original self-published book eventually won the Leadership Book Award for Innovation and Cutting-Edge Perspective. Eventually, it was purchased by a formal publishing house and, over a decade later, is still helping leaders worldwide. I also recently renewed the contract to write an updated and revised edition.

This journey would never have been possible without the depth of preparation that went into my initial research, learning to ask the right questions, writing and rewriting, and the foundational framework. Preparation enabled me to get my idea published in an academic journal—a place where "good ideas often go to die." That publication helped me introduce my idea to leaders in some of the world's most prestigious companies.

Looking back, I realized that preparation is the cornerstone of excellence. I wasn't initially ready for that Fortune 500 boardroom or the global platform my work would eventually reach, but preparation gave me the courage to step into it. Every small effort, every moment of hard work invested, prepared me for the opportunity that ultimately changed my life.

In the journey toward becoming EPIC, preparation isn't optional; it's essential. It's the commitment to show up ready, no matter how intimidating the circumstances, and it lays the groundwork to becoming EPIC.

**FIGURE 1: EPIC LOOP**

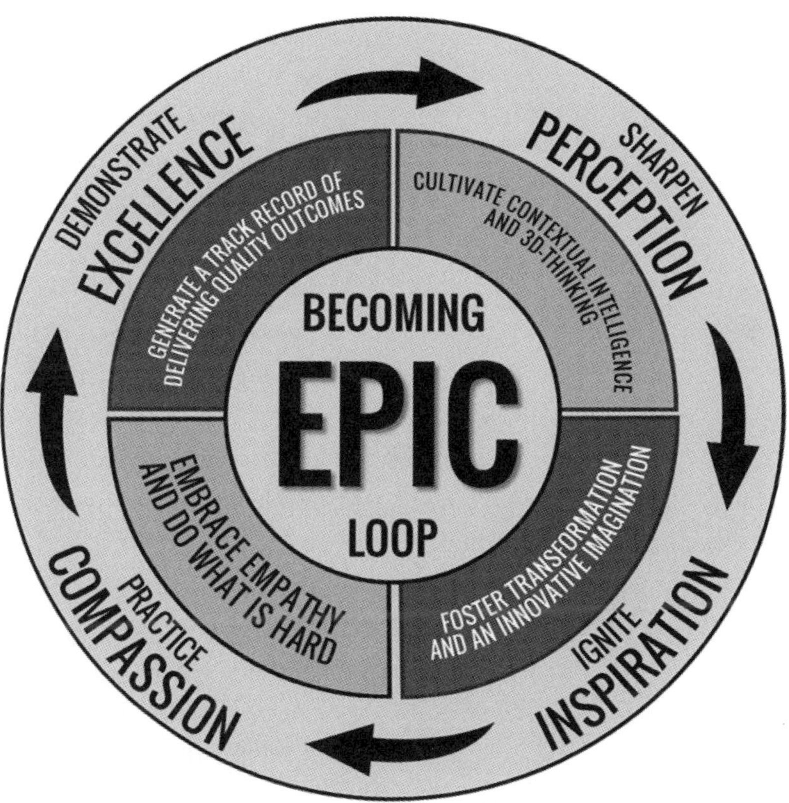

# 1

# THE PATH TO MASTERING YOURSELF

In today's world, success is often defined by external achievements: wealth, status, accolades, or the number of social media followers we have. But true success isn't about what we accomplish outwardly—it's about who we become along the way and how we become that person. Lifelong personal development forms the foundation for any lasting success, transcending professional titles, accomplishments, or material gain. It's about conquering yourself, changing your mind, controlling your actions, and developing your relationships all with the intention to live a life of meaning and fulfillment.

Whether you're looking to excel in your career, improve your relationships, or simply lead a more purposeful life, the journey starts from within. When you take the time to invest in personal growth, you're not just improving yourself—you're creating a ripple effect that impacts everyone around you. When you become better, the people around you become better.

The sports world is full of historical icons and athletes who validate this reality. It is well-observed among fans, players, and coaches that high-caliber athletes elevate the level of play of the others on their team. The same is true in the corporate world and the world of relationships. When you work hard to improve your performance and conquer your defeating mindsets, the people around you will also elevate their performance. Leadership guru John Maxwell refers to this as the law of the lid. In his book *The 21 Irrefutable Laws of Leadership*, Maxwell states that a person's leadership ability is the "lid" that determines their level of effectiveness. In other words, an organization or individual's success is limited by the capacity of those around them. Please, don't let your limited capacity be the reason someone else does not succeed. If your ability is low, it acts as a lid that keeps the potential for others' success capped, no matter how talented or motivated the people around you are. To raise the overall potential of an organization, team, or individual, you must continuously improve.

The journey toward personal growth has been more than just a series of professional ambitions or academic achievements for me. It has been profoundly shaped by one of the most significant and unexpected challenges of my life: my battle with advanced metastatic prostate cancer.

In November 2023, I was diagnosed with an aggressive form of prostate cancer that had already metastasized to my bones and lymph nodes. While initially paralyzing, it ultimately became the moment that brought my life, my work, and my sense of purpose into sharp focus. As a college professor, leadership consultant, and thought leader in contextual intelligence, I had always pursued excellence. But cancer forced me to look deeper, to reassess what excellence really meant, and to explore new perspectives on life, success, and fulfillment.

Through the darkest days of treatments—surgery, radiation, and ongoing hormone therapy—I began to develop a framework that I now call the **EPIC Mindset:** a way of approaching life through the lenses of **Excellence, Perception, Inspiration,** and **Compassion.** These four principles didn't just help me battle cancer—they helped me thrive. I am convinced they can help you too. They became the foundation of how I approach every challenge, whether personal or professional. And in this book, I want to share these principles with you.

## WHY PERSONAL GROWTH IS THE KEY TO SUCCESS

Personal growth isn't just a buzzword or a trendy concept. It's a lifelong commitment to becoming the best version of yourself. The process of personal growth involves self-awareness, continuous learning, deep spirituality, and intentional action. It means reflecting on where you are, understanding where you want to be, and making deliberate choices to bridge that gap. Becoming your future self is possible, but you must be EPIC to do it!

One of my favorite authors, Dr. Benjamin Hardy, outlines in his book *Be Your Future Self Now: The Science of Intentional Transformation* the idea that who you are today is not fixed, and that your future self can be intentionally shaped by the actions and decisions you make now. I believe that you can become your future self by bringing your best identity out of the future into the present. Hardy argues that to achieve meaningful growth and success, you must clearly envision your ideal future and then align your present behavior with that vision, making deliberate changes to become your future self. By setting goals, clarifying outcomes, adopting new habits, and making choices that reflect who you want to become, you can transform your current self into a person capable of living the life you aspire to. Do not underestimate the power of intentionality and forward-thinking when becoming your future self.

Success, in its truest sense, is a byproduct of dying to self. Personal growth may seem paradoxical. True growth comes only when your current self-identity dies and old habits are left behind. When you focus on growing as a person, it will cause you to realize the best place that growth occurs is in the ground—planted like a seed. I don't mean a literal death, but a spiritual one. Success (i.e., growth) naturally follows when you die to your ambition and give up self-promotion. You become better equipped to handle challenges, more resilient in the face of adversity, and more capable of building meaningful relationships. The habits you develop, the mindset you cultivate, and the way you approach life all determine the trajectory of your success. As you are now, that can't be done.

My cancer diagnosis was the ultimate test of this philosophy. Before that moment, I had achieved what some would call success—awards, advanced degrees, leadership positions, influence, and a solid career. But cancer stripped all of that away and left me with a new challenge. I had to dig deep and redefine what success meant for me. Was it continuing to chase achievements, or was it something more meaningful? Could I find a way to excel even when my physical body was fighting for survival? That's when I realized that becoming my future self wasn't just a nice idea; it was essential. My future self was vibrant, vigorous, healthy, and alive!

This type of growth is key because it builds the foundation for everything else. It doesn't matter how high you climb or how much you achieve if you don't have the emotional resilience, clarity, or spiritual strength to sustain it. Success that's not rooted in this type of growth is often fleeting. That's why conquering self is the ultimate pathway to true and lasting success.

## THE FOUR MAXIMS OF A LIFE WELL LIVED

In this book, we will explore the four maxims that form the foundation for a life of purpose, fulfillment, and success: **Excellence, Perception, Inspiration,** and **Compassion.** I believe these maxims are interconnected, and together they create a balanced and holistic approach to becoming who you were meant to be. Mastering each of these areas will enable you to unlock your full potential and lead a more impactful life.

As I faced cancer and its ongoing treatments, these four maxims became my guiding lights. They reminded me of what mattered most, kept me grounded, and helped me push forward. Let me walk you through how these principles have shaped my life—and how they can shape yours too.

### Excellence

Excellence isn't about being perfect or outperforming others—it's about determining to be the best version of yourself. It means setting high standards and committing to continuous improvement in everything you do. Excellence is a habit, a mindset, and a way of life. It's about showing up every day with intention, putting in the effort to grow, and giving your best in every situation. Excellence begins with a desire to win and the determination to pursue victory. No one sets out to compete in a race with the intention of losing. The countless miles of training, blisters, and leg pain would all be wasted otherwise. When we decide to run a race, we do it to win! The reward for excellence isn't always immediately manifested. Sometimes the benefits of excellence are not realized until much later.

For me, excellence became less about achieving goals and more about showing up with integrity and discipline, even on the hardest days. During my cancer treatments, there were days when I couldn't control the outcome—whether it was the effectiveness of a therapy or how my body would respond. But what I could control was my commitment to showing up as the best version of myself, whatever that looked like in the moment. Some days, excellence meant pushing through fatigue to work on my projects; other days, it meant honoring my need for rest and recovery.

When you pursue excellence, you begin to see the power of small, incremental improvements. Excellence is an iterative process! Excellence isn't achieved overnight—it's the result of consistent effort, discipline, and focus over time. It is about trying, adjusting, trying again, adjusting again, and repeating that pattern until excellence is recognized. In the long run, the pursuit of excellence leads to mastery in both your personal and professional life. Excellence will eventually provide opportunities for you that you once thought impossible. Excellence is a better credential than experience or academic achievements. Excellence eventually becomes an example others aspire to.

### Perception

Perception is about how you see and understand the world around you. It's the ability to go beyond the surface, to read between the lines, and to pick up on subtle cues that others might miss.

Perception is right discernment. Being perceptive allows you to make better decisions, navigate complex situations, and build stronger relationships. Perception is about where you set your mind. If you set your mind to focus on the immediate issues of your current situation, you are more likely to get frustrated and lose focus and clarity.

I have always loved the proverb that says, "There is a way that seems right to a man, but its end is the way to death." Perception requires closely examining those things that seem (or feel) right. Many times, those are misleading and ultimately take you in the wrong direction. To perceive accurately often means to look beyond or past the opportunity right in front of you and to plan for the obstacles that are "down the road" that may hold you up from becoming your ideal self. It is often the lack of perception that lures us into pursuing the convenient opportunity directly in front of us.

As I navigated my cancer journey, perception took on a whole new meaning. I had to become acutely aware of my body, my emotions, the world around me, and what I would need from my future self. I learned to read my energy levels, interpret medical advice, and understand my emotional responses to both good and bad news. It taught me to be more spiritually discerning and acutely aware of the condition of my soul—my mind, will, and emotions. Perception also helped me reframe my situation—not as a tragedy, but as an opportunity to grow, to learn, to unlearn, and to share my journey with others in a way that could inspire hope.

Perception isn't just about being observant—it's about cultivating self-awareness and contextual intelligence. It's about seeing situations from multiple perspectives, challenging your own biases, and staying open to new insights. When you become more perceptive, you gain clarity and insight that enable you to handle life's challenges with greater wisdom.

### Inspiration

Inspiration is the fuel that drives creativity, passion, and purpose. It's the spark that ignites your motivation and keeps you moving forward, even in the face of obstacles. Innovation and creativity are the outcomes of inspiration. It doesn't strike at the whim of the Muses. Inspiration obeys you as you conquer your thoughts and defeat undesirable imaginings.

During my treatments, there were times when inspiration felt far away. But I learned that inspiration isn't about waiting for the perfect moment—it's about creating it. I began to cultivate inspiration in small ways, whether it was through journaling, finding moments of beauty in nature, or reflecting on the reasons why I wanted to keep going. Inspiration wasn't always a big, bold feeling; sometimes it was a quiet but steady reminder that life, even with its challenges, is worth engaging in fully.

Learning how to cultivate inspiration means knowing how to tap into your inner creativity. The spirit within you is stronger than the situation around you. When you realize this, you can find inspiration in everyday moments of life. That's living an inspired life. It's about connecting with your purpose, aligning your actions with your values, and staying energized by the things that matter most to you.

### Compassion

Compassion is the foundation of meaningful relationships and personal fulfillment. It's the ability to connect with others on a deep level, to understand their pain, and to offer kindness and empathy. But compassion isn't just about showing care for others—it's also about doing hard things.

In Steve Magness's great book, *Do Hard Things: Why We Get Resilience Wrong and the Surprising Science of Real Toughness*, he challenges traditional ideas of toughness and resilience, offering a unique perspective on mental strength and how to cultivate it. Magness argues that real toughness isn't about brute force, pushing through pain, or ignoring emotions, but rather, it's about understanding when to persist and when to adapt. He emphasizes the importance of self-awareness, emotional regulation, and flexibility in achieving long-term success. Magness provides strategies for developing resilience, handling stress, and overcoming challenges by embracing discomfort in a smart, thoughtful way. Magness promotes a balance between mental toughness and self-compassion to help individuals perform their best, especially under pressure.

Compassion implies the idea of feeling sorrow for someone in grief or suffering with or alongside someone. In its original Latin it is a compound word: *com*, meaning "with" or "alongside of," and *passion*, meaning "to suffer." While not traditional, it is not too large a stretch to understand compassion as being intentional about doing the hard thing now; it might be painful, but it leads to long-term benefits. The compassionate thing is to help others, and to decide to suffer a little bit today so that you don't have to suffer as much tomorrow.

Cancer forced me to learn self-compassion in ways I hadn't before. It taught me that pushing through isn't always the answer—sometimes, the most compassionate thing you can do for yourself is to rest and live to fight another day, which is hard with deadlines and undone projects pressing in on you. I also found that showing compassion to others—whether through sharing my story, offering encouragement, or simply being present—brought immense healing, both to myself and those around me. Compassion is two-fold. It means to suffer with others and to do the hard things now so that it's easier later. Practicing foresight manifests when we have compassion for our future selves as well!

True compassion requires strength, courage, and vulnerability. It's about being present with others, even in difficult moments, and offering support without judgment. Compassion also means doing the hard thing and setting healthy boundaries, knowing when to give and when to protect your own well-being.

## HOW TO USE THIS BOOK TO TRANSFORM YOUR LIFE

This book is your road map to transformation. Each chapter will dive deep into one of the four maxims, providing you with practical strategies, mindset shifts, and actionable steps you can take to master each area. By the end of this journey, you'll have a comprehensive toolkit for living a more purposeful, fulfilled, and successful life.

Here's how to get the most out of this book:

1. **Read with an open mind**: Be willing to challenge your current beliefs and perspectives. Personal growth requires a willingness to change, and this book will push you to think differently about yourself and the world around you.
2. **Take action**: This isn't just a book to read and put on the shelf—it's a guide for transformation. Don't just read the content; take the time to apply what you

learn. Personal growth happens through action, and each chapter is designed to help you make meaningful changes in your life.

3. **Reflect regularly:** Personal growth is a process, and reflection is a key part of that process. Take time after each chapter to reflect on how the concepts apply to your life and what changes you need to make. Consider keeping a journal where you can write down your thoughts, insights, and progress as you work through the principles in this book.
4. **Be patient with yourself:** Becoming EPIC doesn't happen overnight. Be patient with yourself as you work through the challenges and embrace the changes that come with personal growth. Just as I learned through my cancer journey, there will be ups and downs, but each step forward is progress, no matter how small.
5. **Revisit the content:** As you grow and evolve, the lessons in this book will take on new meaning. Come back to the chapters that resonate with you the most and continue to refine your understanding of the four maxims as you move forward on your journey. Becoming EPIC is a lifelong pursuit, and these principles will support you at every stage.

The journey toward mastering yourself through Excellence, Perception, Inspiration, and Compassion is not a straight path. It's filled with twists, turns, and unexpected challenges. But through those challenges, you can discover the strength, resilience, and clarity that allow you to lead a life of greater purpose and fulfillment.

Remember, this book is more than just words on pages—it's a blueprint for living an EPIC life. The more you invest in your personal growth, the more you'll see the results reflected in every area of your life. By embracing the principles of Excellence, Perception, Inspiration, and Compassion, you'll not only achieve success, you'll thrive in a way that feels deeply meaningful.

As you move through this book, let my journey be a reminder that adversity doesn't have to define you—it can refine you. You can access the power to create a life of purpose, joy, and fulfillment, regardless of the adversity you face. With EPIC thinking as your guide, you can overcome anything and live a life that truly matters.

2

# THE DANGERS OF MEDIOCRITY

I have aways been inspired by this quote from Robert Brault, "We are kept from our goals not by obstacles but by a clear path to lesser goals." Mediocrity is a big problem. It is a plague of pandemic proportions. Andrew Carnegie said, "People who are unable to motivate themselves must be content with mediocrity, no matter how impressive their other talents." So many talented people are settling for partial achievement because of fear of not measuring up or failing. As we saw in the prologue, David's brothers and other soldiers suffered from mediocrity. They were afraid they wouldn't measure up and it paralyzed them. Being EPIC is about embracing risk and accepting the possibility of trying and failing.

Mediocrity is not just a barrier to becoming EPIC; it can have profound effects on those around you and their motivation and morale, and it can even stress the body itself. Choosing to remain in a mediocre state can lead to a range of psychological and physiological problems, leaving you unmotivated, disconnected, and unhealthy.

Being mediocre is not the same as being satisfied with the status quo. Both involve resistance to growth, yet they operate in slightly different ways.

## MEDIOCRITY: ACCEPTING "GOOD ENOUGH"

Mediocrity stems from the idea of being "halfway up the mountain"—neither striving for excellence nor failing, but instead operating in a state of moderate quality. A mediocre person is not bad, but they are not good either. It carries with it the connotation of being lukewarm. No one enjoys anything served lukewarm; it often makes you gag. Either be hot or cold, bad or good, but don't try something with the intention to do just enough to not be bad—don't half-ass life!

As a twenty-five-year college professor, I have seen my fair share of students who consistently turn in average work despite being capable of more, because they don't want to put in the extra effort. They aren't failing, but they aren't excelling either. They've accepted "good enough." They live by the old adage: Cs get degrees.

Mediocrity is about individual effort and mindset. It's a personal choice to not push for your best. People who are mediocre focus on being slightly better than some but are afraid to push themselves to excel. Mediocrity is often self-imposed and manifests when someone has the potential to achieve more but chooses not to.

## STATUS QUO: PRESERVING THE CURRENT STATE

Keeping the status quo, on the other hand, refers to maintaining existing systems, structures, or norms. The status quo is about external conditions, resisting change or innovation, and sticking with what already exists. It's less about individual effort and more about the overall environment or the system in place. Keeping the status quo happens when people or organizations stick with familiar practices or policies, often out of fear of the unknown, conservatism, or lack of vision.

For example, a company continues to use outdated technology in its operations because it's what they have always done, even though more efficient options exist. The company avoids change due to fears of disruption and cost, choosing to maintain the current system.

The status quo reflects a collective or systemic resistance to progress or change, whereas mediocrity is a personal or individual mindset of accepting less than your full potential. Both are bad; mediocrity is worse.

## THE INTERSECTION OF MEDIOCRITY AND STATUS QUO

Mediocrity can sometimes contribute to maintaining the status quo. When individuals accept mediocrity, they may be less likely to push for change or improvement, both for themselves and within larger systems. Conversely, an environment that rigidly maintains the status quo can encourage mediocrity, as it signals that striving for excellence or change is not valued or rewarded. Both concepts, though different, can contribute to stagnation in personal growth and hinder you becoming EPIC.

## EROSION OF MOTIVATION AND MORALE

One of the biggest dangers of mediocrity is its gradual erosion of motivation. When you settle for mediocrity, you no longer strive for higher goals, and over time, you lose the drive to push beyond your current state. This erosion of motivation leads to complacency, where the status quo becomes acceptable, even if it isn't fulfilling.

Morale suffers in this state. Whether it's in the workplace, in personal projects, or in relationships, settling for mediocrity dulls the sense of accomplishment and meaning that comes from pursuing excellence. You start to feel disengaged, and this disengagement affects not only how you feel about yourself but also how others perceive you. Mediocrity fosters an environment where people settle for less, and that resignation often spreads like a virus, infecting those around them. In teams, workplaces, and families, mediocrity lowers the collective spirit and drive.

In organizations, mediocrity kills innovation and enthusiasm. Employees who feel stuck in mediocre roles or who see their leaders tolerating mediocrity often feel unmotivated. This can lead to lower productivity, lack of engagement, and a decline in overall morale, as the environment becomes one where people don't feel challenged or appreciated for striving for their best.

### Effects on the Human Body

Interestingly, mediocrity doesn't just affect the mind—it has tangible effects on the body as well. When we remain in a state of mediocrity, we are likely to engage in patterns of stress, poor habits, and physical stagnation. Here's how mediocrity manifests in the body:

1. **Increased stress:** Living in a mediocre state often leads to dissatisfaction and unspoken frustration. This can result in chronic stress, as you feel trapped between

wanting more and accepting less. Chronic stress raises cortisol levels, which can lead to a weakened immune system, increased blood pressure, and a host of other physical ailments.

2. **Physical stagnation:** Mediocrity in your personal life often leads to physical stagnation. You may stop challenging yourself physically, resulting in poor fitness habits. Sitting in a sedentary lifestyle without the drive to push yourself can lead to weight gain, muscle atrophy, and cardiovascular issues.
3. **Mental health issues:** The long-term impact of remaining in a mediocre state can also lead to depression and anxiety. When people feel they are not reaching their potential, this gap between where they are and where they want to be creates an ongoing sense of dissatisfaction. Over time, this can lead to depression, as mediocrity dulls the excitement and passion for life. Similarly, anxiety can arise from knowing that you're capable of more but feel trapped by your own comfort and fear of failure.

### Mediocrity Stalls Creativity

Mediocrity not only stalls personal growth but also stifles creativity and innovation. The comfort of "good enough" means you're less likely to take risks, explore new ideas, or push the boundaries of what's possible. Creativity thrives in environments where people are encouraged to experiment and innovate, but mediocrity creates a climate where these qualities are discouraged.

When you settle into a mediocre mindset, you lose the curiosity that drives discovery and creativity. You become content with routine and the familiar, which leads to a lack of original thinking. This stifles innovation and the creative solutions you can bring to your career, relationships, and pursuits.

## THE REMEDY TO MEDIOCRITY

The first remedy to mediocrity is excellence. If mediocrity is settling for the middle, excellence is the relentless pursuit of mastery in everything you do. Excellence is not about perfection but about striving to be the best version of yourself, continuously learning and pushing your limits.

Excellence demands significantly more from you than mediocrity does. It requires commitment, discipline, risk-taking, and the willingness to face challenges head-on. When you pursue excellence, you reject the notion of "good enough" and instead commit to giving your best effort, regardless of the circumstances. You become focused on growth, not just outcomes, understanding that excellence is a journey rather than a destination.

### Gaining Clarity Beyond the Middle

Perception is the second EPIC maxim that counters mediocrity by sharpening your self-awareness and helping you recognize where you've settled. To break free from this state, you need clarity about where you are and where you want to go.

Perception allows you to see beyond the surface of your circumstances. It helps you identify the areas where you are coasting or staying safe. When you develop perception, you become more attuned to the patterns in your life that keep you from pursuing greatness. With improved perception, you can challenge your own assumptions and beliefs about what is possible. Instead of accepting mediocrity as the norm, you begin to see the untapped opportunities for growth and improvement.

### Fueling the Desire to Climb Higher

Mediocrity often sets in when we lose our sense of purpose and motivation. Without inspiration, the third remedy, the desire to strive for more fades, and it becomes easy to settle for less. Inspiration is the fuel that drives us to move beyond mediocrity. It reignites our passion and gives us the energy to keep climbing the narrow path up the mountain, even when the path is difficult and hard to find.

Inspiration doesn't have to come from grand, life-changing moments; it can be found in the small, everyday reminders of what we're capable of. Whether it's a story of someone overcoming adversity, a new idea that sparks creativity, or simply a moment of reflection, inspiration pushes us to move forward.

Without inspiration, mediocrity becomes the default state because there's nothing driving you to go beyond the ordinary. But when you're inspired, you're willing to take risks, make bold choices, and stretch beyond what you thought possible. Inspiration challenges mediocrity by showing you that there is something greater to strive for—something worth the effort.

### Kindness as a Pathway to Growth

The fourth remedy to mediocrity is compassion. At first glance, compassion might not seem like a remedy to mediocrity, but it plays a crucial role in breaking free from the middle ground.

Self-compassion allows you to be kind to yourself when you fall short of your own expectations. Many people settle for mediocrity because they fear failure or criticism. They stay in the middle because it feels safer than reaching for something higher and potentially falling short.

However, when you practice self-compassion, you give yourself the freedom to fail, learn, and grow. You recognize that mistakes are part of the journey, and they don't define your worth or other people's worth. Agreeing to show compassion for yourself opens the door to taking risks and striving for excellence without the fear of harsh self-judgment. It also allows you to show kindness to others, fostering an environment of growth and support, rather than competition and judgment.

Compassion challenges mediocrity by creating a space for vulnerability and learning. When you know that it's okay to stumble, you're more willing to take the first step toward the peak of the mountain.

### An EPIC Cure for Mediocrity

Mediocrity, with its illusion of comfort and safety, prevents people from realizing their full potential. But the EPIC maxims—Excellence, Perception, Inspiration, and Compassion—provide the remedy. These values encourage you to pursue more, gain clarity about your purpose, stay motivated, and show kindness to yourself and others.

Breaking free from mediocrity means rejecting the middle ground and committing to the lifelong climb toward your fullest potential. By embracing these maxims, you can overcome the inertia of mediocrity and live a life of purpose, growth, and fulfillment.

PART 1

# ON EXCELLENCE

3

# THE NATURE OF EXCELLENCE

Excellence is one of the most powerful and transformative principles in life. When you commit to pursuing excellence, you're not just aiming for a short-term goal or a fleeting achievement; you're engaging in a lifelong journey toward being the best version of yourself. But what does it really mean to exhibit excellence, and how does it differ from the relentless pursuit of perfection? In this chapter, we'll explore what excellence looks like in practice, why it's essential to distinguish it from perfectionism, and how cultivating a growth mindset and setting your own standards can lead to a fulfilling and successful life.

Excellence has always been a driving force for me. In fact, my parents went out of their way to ensure I embraced a spirit of excellence. Whether in my professional work as a professor, consultant, and speaker, or personally as a husband, father, or neighbor, I've always tried to pursue excellence with determination and focus.

Perhaps nothing illustrates my parents' relentless insistence on excellence more than when I called in sick to work one afternoon as a sophomore in high school. I was feeling a fever coming on, so after lunch I went to the school nurse who recommended rest. I called my boss at the department store I worked at and told her I was sick and needed to call off from my after-school shift. No problem; I had a great reputation as a hard worker, so I had earned some credit, and besides, one of the older guys wanted more hours anyway. I went home and took a nap on the sofa. Sometime later, my dad came home from work and walked right by me napping on the couch. A few minutes later he came back and asked, "Aren't you supposed to be at work?"

I innocently said, "Yeah, but I don't feel well, so I called in sick." He bit his tongue and walked back into the kitchen. I didn't think anything of it. A couple minutes later I realized he wasn't biting his tongue, he was loading his verbal canon.

He came back and read me the riot act. I am not exaggerating to say he had me convinced if I didn't go to work the world would stop spinning on its axis and fall out of the galaxy, hurtling toward the sun to be consumed and ending all life in the universe. You see, Kutzes don't quit; when we give our word, we honor our word, even to our own hurt. And unless I was on my literal deathbed, I would be there. Showing up to work was an issue of integrity. There were plenty of people who needed good work and couldn't get it, so I was not even allowed to entertain the idea of not working if I was at all physically able. My dad made me apologize, tell my boss I was fully recovered, and that I was coming in to finish my shift and would be there in fifteen minutes.

"No worries," she said. "Stay home; I found a sub for you."

Well, I told my dad, it was too late—she already had someone covering for me. "That's great," he said. "You can still go in and volunteer your time to make it easier on the guy you made sub for you." So, I had to go to work not feeling one hundred percent and work the rest of that shift for free! Joni, my boss, paid me anyway. I mistook work ethic for excellence. I know now that excellence always includes a strong work ethic; I also learned that it is possible to work hard without excellence.

From that day on I never missed a scheduled day of work, and for over thirty years I never missed work because I felt sick. I even passed kidney stones at work, refusing to go home early or miss a day. To me, excellence became something it was never meant to: a display of strength and the denial of weakness. I have also come to learn that this level of hubris not only hurts you, but it can get other people sick too. I am not advocating going to work sick. However, I am advocating that you should work at a commitment that you are obligated to keep for integrity's sake.

My journey with excellence took on a new dimension when I became a father in 2001. Being a husband had helped me prioritize "getting it right." But fatherhood forced me to realize I had to model the life I wanted for my son. So, the journey to excellence continued. I was challenged to up my excellence game again over two decades later when I was diagnosed with metastatic prostate cancer. That moment when the doctor looked me in the eye and confirmed the diagnosis, my entire world changed. Everything I thought I knew about success, about pushing myself to the limit, about giving my best effort—all of it had to be redefined. I thought I understood what it meant to be excellent, but cancer forced me to learn the true meaning of excellence in a way I never expected.

Excellence, I discovered, wasn't about never falling or always hitting my mark. It wasn't about perfect execution or flawless outcomes. It became about showing up, fully present, even when I felt weak, tired, or afraid. It meant only giving what I could each day, even if it wasn't the same level of output I'd once achieved. It meant acknowledging that sometimes excellence was found not in how hard I worked, but in how well I adjusted to my body's demands, how much I cared for myself and others, and how I balanced the relentless drive I'd always had with the new limitations I faced.

Now might be a good time to stop and consider what limitations you must overcome to take that step toward excellence. Get out a pen and paper and make a list of the attitudes, assumptions, and behaviors you believe are keeping you from excellence. Draw three columns on your sheet of paper and label each column: 1) attitudes keeping me from excellence, 2) assumptions I hold (or jump to) that blind me from clarity; and 3) behaviors that stifle my progress. Take your time, make a good list, and if you need others to help you, ask them! Once the list is completed, write down several things you can do to overcome what you have listed.

## WHAT DOES IT MEAN TO EXHIBIT EXCELLENCE?

Excellence isn't about achieving a specific outcome or being the best at everything you do. Instead, it's a mindset and an approach to life. It's about showing up consistently, giving your best effort, and striving to improve, no matter the task at hand. Excellence is about being fully engaged in the process, paying attention to the details, and always looking for ways to enhance your performance or understanding.

When I began cancer treatment, excellence meant something different than it had in the past. I had to let go of the idea that excellence was synonymous with high productivity or visible achievements. There were days when simply facing the uncertainty of the future and showing up for my family was the greatest act of excellence I could offer. In this new reality, excellence meant growth despite adversity. It meant being kind to myself and leaning on my friends when my body and mind were weak. It meant maintaining focus on what I could control: my mindset, my attitude, and my actions, no matter how small they seemed.

Nassim Nicholas Taleb's *Antifragile: Things That Gain from Disorder* introduces the idea of thriving and growing stronger under stress and adversity. Unlike fragile things that break under pressure, robust things that remain unchanged, or resilient things that bounce back to normal, antifragile things thrive and become stronger in chaos, unpredictability, and disorder.

In the context of excellence, antifragility encourages individuals to embrace challenges, volatility, and setbacks as opportunities for growth. It shifts the mindset from fearing failure or disruption to actively seeking out experiences that push one's limits and foster resilience. I refer to this as curating disruption. By curating disruption, individuals can continuously improve and achieve excellence not through avoiding difficulty but by learning to adapt, evolve, and grow stronger from every obstacle they face. Curating disruption is one thing; facing uninvited adversity is another. I learned that regardless of it being curated or uninvited, antifragility must occur.

Practicing excellence means committing to high standards, not because of external pressure or competition, but because you value growth and improvement. It's an internal desire that propels you to go beyond the minimal expectations, to challenge yourself, and to take pride in what you do. Whether you're working on a project, building a relationship, or taking care of your health, excellence involves a commitment to doing things with integrity, intention, and care; and when the unexpected happens, let it make you stronger. I am convinced that chaos is the package your potential arrives in.

## EXCELLENCE VS. PERFECTION: WHY THEY'RE NOT THE SAME

One of the biggest misconceptions people have is confusing excellence with perfection. While both concepts involve striving for a high standard, they are fundamentally different. Understanding the distinction between excellence and perfection can free you from the toxic pressures of perfectionism and allow you to focus on more meaningful growth. Perfection is not possible, but excellence is.

When I was young, I often flirted with perfectionism. I believed that to achieve excellence, I had to push harder and deliver more. I thought that excellence was about competition with others. But the adversity of life forced me to confront the limitations of that mindset. Well before the physical toll of treatments, fatigue, and the emotional weight of uncertainty, I learned I could no longer chase perfection. I had to learn that excellence isn't about flawless execution—it's about doing the best you can with what is in your hand right now.

Perfection is about trying to avoid mistakes and meet impossible standards. Perfectionists are often driven by fear—of failure, of criticism, of not measuring up. This leads to a mindset of rigidity, where any deviation from the perfect result is seen as a failure. Perfectionism often paralyzes people, making them afraid to take risks, try new things, or even complete tasks because they worry they won't meet some predetermined external standard.

On the other hand, excellence is about embracing mistakes and learning from them. I had to learn to let go of the idea that success meant pushing through at all costs. There were days when excellence meant resting, allowing my body to heal, and trusting that taking care of myself today would give me the strength to face tomorrow. I didn't want to learn that lesson, but my wife, Angie, made me learn it! Thanks, babe! Excellence is about aiming high but remaining flexible, knowing that growth comes from trial and error. Excellence is an iterative process.

Creative people understand the power of iteration. No one produces their best work the first time. Dr. Brené Brown describes the concept of the "shitty first draft" (SFD) in her book *Rising Strong*, where she shares about her work on vulnerability and creativity. She emphasizes that the initial version of anything we create—whether it's writing, a project, or a new idea—doesn't need to be perfect. The SFD gives you permission to produce a messy, imperfect first attempt, knowing that it's a necessary step in the creative process. Brown highlights that embracing the SFD allows us to get past our fear of failure or imperfection and take action, rather than getting stuck in overthinking or self-doubt. It's a way to silence the inner critic and make progress, recognizing that refinement and improvement come in later drafts. If we embrace the iterative process, we can bypass the perfectionism that leads to burnout and frustration, and deal in excellence, which leads to fulfillment and resilience.

When you let go of the need to be perfect and instead focus on doing your best and learning from each experience, you free yourself from unnecessary stress and open the door to greater growth and satisfaction.

## GROWTH MINDSET

At the heart of excellence is the growth mindset, a concept developed by psychologist Dr. Carol Dweck. A growth mindset is the belief that abilities, intelligence, and talents can be developed through effort, learning, and perseverance. However, before abilities can be developed, they must be desired. Without wanting to be better, growth cannot occur. This echoes the New Testament, where Paul urges his readers to "eagerly desire the better spiritual gifts." In contrast, a fixed mindset assumes that abilities are innate and unchangeable—that you either have a certain talent or you don't.

The normal path of life and the things we accomplish along the way challenge the growth mindset. In fact, it is often what we achieve that hinders us the most. We begin to believe our own internal monologue. The monologue that says this—and not that—is what I am good at. So, we double down on whatever "this" is, allowing ourselves to be deceived into believing that "that" is something to avoid. The reality is that success in one area does not mean success in another area is impossible or even hard.

Cancer tested my growth mindset in ways I never anticipated. It forced me to confront the reality that there were many things beyond my control—the progression of the disease, the side effects of treatment, and the uncertainty of outcomes. But what I could control was my attitude and my commitment to learning and adapting throughout the process. I couldn't change my diagnosis, but I could change how I responded to it. Every day since has been an opportunity to grow in some small way, whether that was mentally, emotionally, or spiritually.

People with a growth mindset see their adversity as opportunities to learn and improve. They're not afraid of failure because they understand that setbacks are part of the iterative learning process. Instead of being discouraged by obstacles, they see them as chances to develop new skills or refine existing ones. This mindset is critical to achieving excellence because it encourages continuous growth and improvement, rather than being fixated on static achievements.

Becoming excellent means recognizing that every challenge, every failure, and every success is a learning opportunity. The growth mindset also shifts your focus from external validation to internal growth. Instead of seeking approval from others or comparing yourself to their achievements, you focus on your own journey and your own progress.

A well-known example of the growth mindset leading to learning and innovation is the story of Netflix. In its early years, Netflix was a DVD rental service, competing against Blockbuster. When they introduced their subscription model and later explored streaming, they faced skepticism and challenges. However, instead of sticking to their initial business model, Netflix embraced a growth mindset, viewing setbacks and market shifts as opportunities to learn and evolve. This mindset led them to pivot to streaming content, invest in data-driven decisions, and eventually create original programming, which revolutionized the entertainment industry. Their willingness to innovate and adapt, rather than fear failure, transformed Netflix into a global leader in digital streaming and entertainment.

On the other hand, a classic example of a fixed mindset leading to failure is the downfall of Blockbuster. In the early 2000s, Blockbuster was the dominant video rental chain, but when Netflix approached them with a partnership opportunity to expand into online streaming, Blockbuster dismissed the idea, believing their existing business model was unshakable. They were fixed in their belief that their brick-and-mortar stores and the ubiquity of the DVD player were enough to maintain market dominance. This rigid mindset prevented them from even seeing the rapidly changing technology landscape, leading to their eventual bankruptcy while Netflix thrived by embracing innovation.

In my journey, the growth mindset wasn't just about physical healing—it was about how I could learn to live fully in the face of adversity. I had to adapt to a new normal, learn to listen to my body, and accept that some days would be better than others. But through it all, my growth mindset has allowed me to stay focused on the process of becoming stronger not just physically, but mentally, spiritually, and emotionally.

## SETTING YOUR OWN STANDARDS

One of the most important aspects of achieving excellence is setting your own standards. Before we face adversity, many of us often measure success by external markers—professional accolades, productivity, and accomplishments. But facing adversity forces us to redefine what success and excellence look like on a personal level.

Personal excellence doesn't mean trying to meet arbitrary benchmarks or comparing yourself to others. In fact, we mustn't compare ourselves to others. Comparison causes you to lose sight of reality. Personal excellence means taking ownership of your growth and progress, and deciding what excellence looks like in your life. For me, excellence became about living fully each day, nurturing my relationships, producing quality instead of a large quantity of ideas, and finding meaning in small moments of joy and connection. I am a big believer that each person should be the judge of their own actions and not compare themselves with others. When we do that, we can be proud of our accomplishments. In the end, each person must be responsible for themselves and not become a victim of envy or feelings of inferiority.

Setting your own standards means being honest with yourself about what matters most. For me, it wasn't about pushing through treatments or pretending everything was fine—it was about showing up authentically, even on the hard days, and doing what I could to contribute to my own healing and to the lives of those I love.

To set your own standards of excellence, start by asking yourself a few key questions:

1. What do I value most in life?
2. What areas of my life matter most to me, and where do I want to grow?
3. How can I align my daily actions with my long-term goals?

To me, excellence required showing up with integrity—whether that meant working on projects when I had the energy or resting and recharging when my body needed it. It also meant being present for my family and friends, sharing my experiences with others who could learn from them, allowing them to speak into my life what they were observing I needed, and staying committed to my personal growth despite adversity.

Excellence is a journey, not a destination. Excellence has never been about perfect outcomes—it's about the courage to grow, learn, and strive to be the best version of yourself, no matter what obstacles you face.

# 4

# THE ROADBLOCKS TO EXCELLENCE

Excellence is a journey paved with obstacles, both external and internal. Whether you're dealing with challenges in your personal life, your career, your health, or external stressors, roadblocks can make the pursuit of excellence daunting. Life has a way of forcing us to confront many of the roadblocks that we'll discuss in this chapter—perfectionism, fear of failure, and the temptation to settle for comfort. But excellence isn't about ignoring these roadblocks; it's about learning how to overcome them.

In this chapter, we'll dive into some common mistakes that can sabotage the journey to excellence, the myths that mislead us, and the limiting beliefs that hold us back. We'll explore how these barriers quietly shape our decisions, diminish our confidence, and keep us from reaching our full potential. By recognizing and addressing these obstacles, we can clear the path toward growth, unlock new opportunities, and move closer to the excellence we are capable of achieving.

## MISTAKES THAT SABOTAGE YOUR JOURNEY TO EXCELLENCE

### Perfectionism: The Enemy of Progress

In my professional life, whether it was writing books, delivering lectures, treating athletes, or consulting with organizations, I tried to hold myself to high standards. Nothing wrong with that. I wanted everything I did to be excellent. But I didn't always understand the difference between perfectionism and excellence. Perfectionism is a very sharp double-edged sword that makes it easy to cut yourself. It can push you to work hard, but it can also paralyze you, making you afraid to take risks or even finish tasks.

When I was diagnosed, perfectionism became a huge obstacle. Especially when it came to treatment options. I wanted guarantees. I wanted perfect treatments and I wanted my healthcare team to be perfect. No mistakes. After all, my life was at stake. I learned early on not to hold myself to perfect standards. Likewise, integrity dictated that I not hold my doctors to perfect standards either.

There were days when I simply didn't have the energy to be the version of myself I thought I needed to be. My work, my relationships, and my health all felt like they were slipping out of my control. I had to learn that excellence didn't mean perfection. Achievement was being redefined before my eyes, and it wasn't easy to accept. At times I had to prove this adversity didn't control me—I controlled it. I was deceiving myself. Who was I kidding? I couldn't, and you can't, simply think your adversity away. Perfectionism is a form of self-deceit that masquerades as confidence.

We all must let go of the self-limiting belief that doing things error free is a possible outcome. Instead, we need to redirect our efforts toward making progress, no matter how small. This shift in mindset allowed me to regain momentum, both in my recovery and in my work. I stopped letting the fear of being found out as a fraud, which is the central lie of perfectionism, hold me back.

Steve Jobs was known for his relentless pursuit of excellence, but early in his career, that pursuit was often tied to perfectionism. His desire for flawless products led to frustrations and delays at Apple, which ultimately led to his dismissal from the company he founded. However, when Jobs returned to Apple in 1997, he had learned from his earlier mistakes. Instead of letting perfectionism stifle progress, he focused on creating excellent products—ones that balanced innovation with functionality. Jobs realized that waiting for perfection could prevent good ideas from reaching the market, and that excellence was about improving through iteration. The iPhone, which redefined the tech industry, wasn't perfect in its first iteration, but it evolved into one of the most successful products because Jobs prioritized progress over perfection. Sometimes a good idea with flaws is better than no idea at all!

## THE DANGER OF MULTITASKING

I used to pride myself on being able to juggle multiple projects at once. I was involved in teaching, consulting, writing, service to my church, and public speaking—all while managing my personal and family life. Multitasking felt like a badge of honor, but it was diluting my effectiveness. In fact, one of the biggest obstacles to excellence is multitasking. Dr. Paul Hammerness and Margaret Moore, authors of *Organize Your Mind, Organize Your Life: Train Your Brain to Get More Done in Less Time*, say that multitasking increases the chances of making mistakes and missing important information and cues. Multitaskers are also less likely to retain information in working memory, which can hinder problem-solving and creativity.

After my diagnosis, my ability to multitask disappeared. Treatments left me fatigued, mentally and physically. I had to decide: either continue trying to juggle everything or focus on one thing at a time and do it well. I did my best to always choose the latter, and it taught me a valuable lesson—excellence requires focus. FOCUS is Following One Course Until Successful. Multitasking scatters your energy and attention, but when you home in on one task, you can achieve excellence in that area before moving on to the next.

This principle applies in every area of life. Whether you're leading a team or working on personal development, success comes from focusing your efforts on what matters most, not trying to do everything simultaneously.

As President of the United States, Barack Obama had to juggle multiple national and international crises—from the 2008 financial meltdown to complex foreign policy issues. Early in his presidency, Obama learned that multitasking on such a vast scale could lead to inefficiency. His administration began to focus on a few key priorities—revitalizing the economy, passing healthcare reform, and ending wars in Iraq and Afghanistan. By narrowing his focus to what mattered most, Obama was able to lead his administration to significant accomplishments, rather than be overwhelmed by the sheer number of issues on his plate. The point is excellence also requires learning which things to take off your plate and not merely realizing that your plate is too full.

**Settling for Comfort**

Cancer forced me to face discomfort head-on. There were days when the mental anguish made me want to retreat, to take the easy way out, to avoid any "normal" challenges. But I quickly learned that true excellence isn't about choosing comfort—it's about choosing growth, even when it's difficult. Excellent people simply decide to do hard things. Sometimes, the hard thing is to rest or just do one thing at a time. Sometimes being excellent means choosing the option with the highest risk of making me look bad if it fails. And other times, it requires us to make the choice that no one else sees and that we dread doing. Like getting up at some god-awful early morning hour to run or hit the gym.

Before my diagnosis, I often sought challenges that played to my strengths. But during my illness, I had to confront the reality that the biggest challenges are often the ones we don't choose. I didn't get to pick this battle, it chose me; but I did get to choose how I faced it. Excellence meant accepting the discomfort and pushing through it, rather than retreating into comfort and ease.

I believe this principle applies to all of us. When we settle for what's easy or familiar, we miss out on the growth that comes from stepping outside our comfort zone. True excellence requires embracing the challenges that stretch us, even when they are uncomfortable.

Richard Branson, the founder of Virgin Group, is known for embracing challenges. His willingness to take risks and step into discomfort has led to many of his greatest successes. Branson's decision to start Virgin Atlantic in 1984—going head-to-head with established airlines—was seen as risky. Yet, he leaned into the challenge, believing that disruption was necessary for growth. His willingness to face difficult situations directly, rather than settle for comfort in his existing businesses, helped him build a global empire across multiple industries.

Comfort zones are called that for a reason—they are comfortable, familiar, and often peaceful and non-problematic. Why would I choose to disrupt that? Only a crazy person would, right? The fact is disruption is essential for growth. Without disruption our comfort causes atrophy. In human physiology atrophy is the deterioration of muscle tone, size, and strength. If we do not disrupt comfort with selected resistance, what I call curated disruption and what exercise scientists call progressive overload, we will eventually be unable to move at all. In other words, our comfort can kill us and eventually become our tomb. Excellence requires the choice to do hard things.

Take my story for example. Securing tenure and earning the rank of full professor is a milestone few reach and even fewer willingly leave behind. I'd spent eighteen years climbing the academic ranks, pouring everything I had into teaching, research, and service. Years of late nights, meticulous documentation, and justifying my worth to a tenure committee. For anyone who's been through it, you know the feeling: the stress, the scrutiny, and the constant doubt, as if at any moment someone might say, "You're just not good enough."

After years of jumping through hoops and enduring the hypercritical lens of external reviewers, I finally made it. And let me tell you, nothing quite matches the satisfaction of landing tenure and full professor status. That role is as close as academia comes to a "forever" job. For most people, tenure is the ultimate safety net, and achieving it is the finish line where they can finally settle in. Most people breathe a sigh of relief and enjoy the security they've worked so hard to achieve.

But then there's me—the person who decided to leave it all.

A few years after securing full professor rank, an opportunity presented itself that was as enticing as it was terrifying. I had the chance to build something from scratch with a colleague who shared a vision to push our profession forward: a brand-new, self-funded doctoral program. The role offered none of the security and all of the risk—no tenure, no guarantees, and all the unknowns that come with a new program. And I had a lot to lose.

Leaving tenure for a clinical faculty role without that coveted safety net was not a decision I made lightly. It was probably one of the toughest decisions I've ever faced. It wasn't just about walking away from a stable income; it was about stepping away from an identity I'd built over years, from a life with predictable patterns, and from the well-respected, coveted role of "tenured professor." There were so many factors swirling in my mind—security, reputation, my family's future. But beyond the doubt and fear, one thing stood out: the drive to do something meaningful.

The truth is, as cushy as tenure can be, there's a point where comfort becomes a ceiling. And staying in my role just because it was safe began to feel stifling. My colleague and I had a vision to create a program that could break new ground in our field, recruiting students and creating content that could challenge the status quo and make a real difference.

So, I did it. I left tenure behind and jumped headfirst into the world of uncertainty. There's a special kind of thrill (and nausea) that comes from starting something with no guarantees, and in this case, knowing we'd be self-funded only heightened the stakes. But taking that risk meant I could live out my commitment to the profession and genuinely push it forward in ways I couldn't from within the traditional structure.

Now, looking back, I know it was the right decision. I'm in a role that constantly challenges me, surrounded by students and colleagues who inspire me. Every day, I get to create content that doesn't just fill a curriculum but advances our profession and leaves a mark on the students who will carry it forward. As risky as it was, the move paid off in more ways than I could have imagined.

Taking the hard road isn't always the easiest or the most rational choice, but it's often the most rewarding. The lesson here? Sometimes, walking away from your comfort zone and embracing the unknown can lead you to exactly where you're meant to be.

## COMMON MYTHS ABOUT EXCELLENCE

### Myth #1: Excellence Means Being the Best

Early in my career, I believed that excellence meant being the best. I measured success by how I compared to others. But when I faced cancer, I realized that excellence had nothing to do with *being* the best; it had everything to do with *doing* my best. In competitive running there is the concept of a personal record (PR). The PR is an incredible illustration for overcoming this myth. I am a recreational runner. I have run countless 5Ks, several 10Ks, four triathlons, and two half-marathons. I enjoy running not for the sake of running, but because I found it fosters creativity for me. I do not run because I am fast or because I have endless stamina. In fact, I have never finished any of my races in first place. I have never even crossed the finish line first in my age or weight groups. But I also have never lost a race. I am not competing against the other runners. I am competing against my previous times. Being the overall best and reaching my personal best are very different things. I run for

PRs, and when I set a new PR you would think I just won an Olympic gold medal. On those days, I didn't win the overall races, but I did my best and that is excellent work!

In my personal and professional life, I stopped worrying about outperforming others and started focusing on whether I was making progress toward becoming the best version of myself. Some days, excellence meant being the best father and husband I could be, even if that meant temporarily stepping back from professional ambitions. Other days, it meant finding small wins in my treatment and recovery. Eventually, excellence became personal, not competitive.

When Satya Nadella took over as CEO of Microsoft, the company had lost some of its competitive edge in the tech world. Instead of focusing solely on beating competitors like Apple and Google, Nadella emphasized a new definition of excellence within Microsoft's culture. He focused on continuous improvement, learning, and innovation, encouraging employees to embrace a growth mindset. This cultural shift allowed Microsoft to regain its position as a leader in cloud computing and software development. Nadella's leadership demonstrated that excellence isn't about being the best, but about fostering an environment where everyone strives to improve and innovate.

### Myth #2: Excellence Is Only for the Naturally Gifted

It's easy to believe that only those with natural abilities or talents can achieve great things. That is definitively untrue. Excellence is about persistence, resilience, and the willingness to learn, unlearn, and relearn—not about natural talent or God-given ability.

There were days when I didn't feel strong or capable, but by focusing on small, incremental progress, I was able to redefine what excellence meant for me. This mindset shift allowed me to continue making meaningful contributions to my work and my family, even in the face of life-threatening adversity.

Abraham Lincoln's journey to the presidency was filled with setbacks, including multiple election losses, business failures, and personal tragedies. For example,

- He was defeated in the race for Illinois state legislator in 1832.
- He started a business only to see it go under. It was a store in New Salem, Illinois. His partner died and he could not sustain the business.
- He lost his run for Congress in 1843 and again in 1848.
- He lost his bid to become a U.S. Senator in 1855.
- He ran for Vice President of the U.S. in 1856 and lost.
- He again ran for the U.S. Senate in 1859 and lost yet again.

Lincoln wasn't seen as the most gifted politician of his time, but his persistence, resilience, and ability to grow from failures (antifragility) led him to become one of America's most iconic leaders. His excellence didn't come from natural talent; it came from his relentless commitment to growth, even in the face of seemingly innumerable failures.

### Myth #3: Excellence Is Measured by Constant Success

One of the most pervasive myths about excellence is the belief that it requires you to succeed constantly. Many people think that to be excellent, you must always win, always meet your goals, and always beat setbacks. However, this mindset is not only unrealistic but also counterproductive. Excellence is not about a flawless track record; it's about how you respond to failure and adversity. The journey toward excellence will involve missteps, failures, and challenges. The difference between those who achieve excellence and those who don't is their ability to learn from failure, adapt, and keep pushing forward.

I learned as a young man that excellence was not in avoiding setbacks, but in how I adapted to them. Each challenge became an opportunity to refocus, adjust my mindset, and find new ways to grow. As a father, I reiterated this mindset to my sons by constantly preaching that failure could be a badge of honor, but only if they didn't repeat the same failure.

Thomas Edison is a prime example of someone who debunked the myth that excellence requires constant success. Known for inventing the light bulb, Edison famously failed thousands of times before reaching his breakthrough. Instead of viewing these failures as a lack of excellence, Edison saw them as steps on the path to success. His ability to embrace failure as part of the process is what ultimately led to his groundbreaking achievements. Edison's story reminds us that excellence is about persistence and learning from mistakes, not one achievement after another.

## LIMITING BELIEFS THAT HOLD YOU BACK

There are four limiting beliefs that keep you from engaging in the journey toward excellence. Those beliefs tell you that you're not good enough, you have to be perfect or it's no use trying, you don't have the time or energy needed, and you're not specialized enough. Let's debunk each of these in turn.

### Limiting Belief #1: "I'm Not Good Enough"

The feeling of not being good enough is one of the most insidious roadblocks to excellence. After my diagnosis, there were moments when I felt like I wasn't good enough, strong enough, or spiritual enough to handle the physical and emotional toll of cancer treatment. But I realized that excellence isn't about feeling "good enough" all the time—it's about showing up, even when self-doubt creeps in. The fact is on my own I am not good enough. But I believe I have been given the grace to press in and boldly ask God for more grace when I am feeling inadequate. Feeling inadequate is par for the course when facing adversity, but becoming a victim of that feeling of inadequacy is something you cannot allow.

By focusing on the progress I could make each day, I was able to push past this limiting belief. I may not have felt "good enough" in the traditional sense, but I knew that showing up with courage and resilience was a form of excellence in itself.

### Limiting Belief #2: "I Need to Be Perfect to Succeed"

I have written a lot about perfectionism already. The "ism" makes it a type of religion, a religion that is a limiting belief. We have to learn to believe the right things. Part of being human is not intuitively knowing what limiting beliefs we hold on to. We learn what those are over time and with help. Left unchecked, our internal monologue will try and distract us from identifying our limiting beliefs. To get past that, we must ask ourselves the question posed by the Prophet Isaiah, "Whose report will I believe?" Reports are the internal stories or narratives we tell ourselves. There are other reports or narratives we can believe that can be found with the help of others—reports that are motivating and encouraging. The "report" of perfectionism whispers in your ear that you will never be good enough and that you do not have the capacity to do adequate work. Perfectionism breeds imposter syndrome.

Imposter syndrome and the belief that "I need to be perfect to succeed" are deeply intertwined, often reinforcing one another in a cycle of self-doubt and fear of failure. Imposter syndrome is the persistent feeling that you are a fraud or unqualified, despite evidence of your accomplishments and abilities. People who struggle with imposter syndrome believe that they have somehow deceived others into thinking they are competent, and they live in fear of being "found out."

This feeling of being an imposter frequently aligns with the limiting belief that you need to be perfect to succeed. The expectation of perfection puts immense pressure on individuals to constantly meet impossible standards, and any small misstep or perceived failure can trigger intense feelings of inadequacy.

### Breaking the Imposter Cycle

To overcome both imposter syndrome and the belief that perfection is necessary for success, it's important to recognize that excellence and growth come from learning, not from flawless execution. Accepting that everyone makes mistakes and that progress is built on learning from your imperfection is key to breaking free from this limiting belief.

When you let go of the need for perfection, you create space for self-compassion and personal growth. By doing so, you can start to see yourself not as an imposter but as someone with a growth mindset who is capable of learning, growing, and succeeding through effort and hard work, rather than through the impossible pursuit of perfection. Imposter syndrome is not a weak adversary. Breaking the burden of believing you are an imposter is not for the faint of heart. In chapter 19 we will explore the nuances of imposter syndrome in much more detail.

### Limiting Belief #3: "I Don't Have Enough Time"

Another limiting belief that holds many people back from pursuing excellence is the notion that they don't have enough time. The demands of life—work, family, personal responsibilities—can make it feel impossible to dedicate time to improving, mastering a skill, or achieving excellence in a particular area. Many people believe that unless they can commit large blocks of time, there's no point in starting.

This belief can be incredibly limiting because it prevents you from making progress, even in small, manageable ways. The truth is excellence is achieved through consistent, focused effort over time, in bite-sized attempts, not through marathon sessions of work or practice. Even short, daily efforts can compound into significant improvements over weeks, months, or years.

When I was going through cancer treatment, I often felt that my time and energy were severely limited. There were days when I could only dedicate a few minutes to personal growth or professional work. Initially, I thought that without substantial time, I couldn't make a meaningful impact. But I soon realized that excellence isn't about the quantity of time—it's about the consistent effort. Small, consistent actions, even when time is short, are what lead to lasting progress. In fact, this book is a product of taking less than an hour a day during my thirty-seven days of radiation to write just 1,000 words per day. Do small things too; they eventually turn into something big!

In 2015 I started on a journey to lose weight. I had recently seen a picture of myself at my sister's wedding that alarmed me. I needed to lose weight. That reality was compounded by a not-so-great doctor appointment. You know the kind, where your doctor wants you to cut out salt and fats and start taking blood pressure (BP) and cholesterol medicines. Well, I wasn't having it. He didn't even suggest I diet and exercise. It was straight to the medications. When I challenged him on it, he relented, and we agreed on a six-month checkup. The deal was if I lost the weight and my numbers checked out, we'd be good. If at six months my numbers were still high, I'd take the medications. Well, six months came, and I had lost over thirty pounds, and my BP and cholesterol were within normal limits.

The point is my goals were bite-sized. I didn't change much at all in the beginning. I just started by walking a few times a week and keeping a food log. Without changing what I ate, I simply reduced the number of calories I ate in a day. I stopped eating when I reached my predetermined calorie limit. It was working. With relatively little effort, I achieved something significant. But it didn't happen overnight or in one grand gesture. That walking turned into jogging, and then into running. Over the years, mind you, I began running in 5Ks, 10Ks, triathlons, and half-marathons. I lost an additional 30 pounds. All by taking very small steps that didn't take huge amounts of time or major commitments.

Elon Musk, the CEO of Tesla and SpaceX, is known for managing multiple high-stakes companies while also investing time in new projects. Despite having what appears to be an overwhelming workload, Musk is able to focus on what's most important by managing his time in highly efficient ways. He breaks his day into five-minute blocks and prioritizes tasks based on their impact. Musk's ability to manage his time effectively and break tasks into small, focused efforts demonstrates that excellence is possible even when time is limited and external demands are great.

**Limiting Belief #4: "I Am Not Specialized Enough"**

Another roadblock to excellence is over specialization. In today's world, there's a pervasive belief that to achieve excellence, one must specialize early, commit deeply to a narrow field, and pursue advanced mastery through intense focus. While this approach has merit in certain domains, David Epstein, in his book *Range: Why Generalists Triumph in a Specialized World*, challenges the idea that specialization is the only path to excellence. Epstein argues that generalists—those who explore a wide range of interests and acquire diverse skills—are often better equipped to solve complex problems and achieve success in an unpredictable world. This reminds me of the iconic proverb about being a jack of all trades and how it is often misquoted. You may be surprised to learn that the actual quote has always been, "A jack of all trades is a master of none, but oftentimes better than a master of one."

Epstein's research reveals that generalists tend to excel in environments that require creativity, adaptability, and the ability to connect ideas across disciplines. They possess the broad knowledge necessary to innovate, offering perspectives that specialists may miss. In this context, excellence doesn't come from burrowing into one field but from synthesizing knowledge from many areas, allowing for a more holistic understanding of the world and greater capacity to approach challenges with novel solutions.

## THE POLYMATH ADVANTAGE: UNLOCKING VERSATILITY

Waqas Ahmed, in his book *The Polymath: Unlocking the Power of Human Versatility*, expands on this idea by exploring the concept of polymaths—individuals who cultivate expertise in multiple areas. Ahmed's work argues that human versatility, the ability to learn and thrive across various domains, is not only achievable but necessary in our fast-paced, interconnected world. He demonstrates how polymaths throughout history—from Leonardo da Vinci to Benjamin Franklin—exemplify that broad intellectual curiosity and a commitment to diverse learning are key drivers of excellence. In fact, thought leaders often become so because they can integrate multiple fields and disciplines, making connections and seeing possibilities others do not.

Both Epstein and Ahmed emphasize that excellence is not confined to narrow specialization. Instead, it can emerge from a broader pursuit of knowledge across disciplines, which enhances creativity, problem-solving, and adaptability. The polymathic mindset, much like Epstein's generalist approach, encourages us to embrace curiosity and view learning as a lifelong, multidimensional process.

## EMBRACING RANGE ON THE PATH TO EXCELLENCE

The idea that excellence can be achieved through versatility and generalization is critical to our understanding of what it means to become EPIC. While specialization has its place, especially in certain technical or scientific fields, the broader world rewards those who can pivot, adapt, and synthesize knowledge from diverse sources.

By exploring multiple disciplines, gaining experiences in varied contexts, and connecting seemingly unrelated ideas, generalists often excel in leadership, innovation, and creative problem-solving. In this way, being excellent isn't just about depth; it's also about breadth. Generalists and polymaths don't shy away from learning across fields; they embrace it, and this diversity of knowledge fuels their ability to achieve greatness.

Excellence through range allows for versatility, creativity, and adaptability, which are crucial in a complex world. Excellence doesn't always require narrow specialization—it can also emerge from the wide-reaching curiosity that fuels brilliance.

## OVERCOMING THE ROADBLOCKS TO EXCELLENCE

Overcoming the roadblocks to excellence doesn't happen overnight, nor does it come without effort. But by recognizing and addressing these obstacles—whether it's perfectionism, multitasking, avoiding challenges, myths, or limiting beliefs—you can clear the path to your own personal growth and success.

My battle forced me to confront many of these roadblocks head-on. I had to redefine what excellence meant to me, learn to focus on progress over perfection, and embrace challenges rather than shy away from them. It wasn't always easy, but the experience has been transformative.

Excellence is not about being the best or never making mistakes. It's about antifragility, showing up, and giving your best effort regardless of the circumstances. It's about growth and learning from every experience, no matter how painful or challenging.

The same lessons can be applied to leadership and personal development. From Steve Jobs and Satya Nadella to Abraham

Lincoln and Richard Branson, we see that excellence isn't tied to natural talent or a flawless track record—it's about persistence, iteration, focus, and a commitment to continuous improvement.

As you move forward on your journey to becoming excellent, remember that the roadblocks you encounter are not signs of failure—they are opportunities to grow, learn, and evolve. By facing these challenges with courage and determination, you can overcome the obstacles that stand in your way and unlock greater potential. Lean into life and believe that you can be excellent.

5

# PRACTICAL STRATEGIES FOR EXHIBITING EXCELLENCE

Exhibiting excellence isn't an abstract concept; it's a process that requires deliberate effort and strategic thinking. Excellence is a choice. Talking about being excellent is empty and shallow. Excellence is demonstrated through actions, not words. In this chapter, we'll explore practical strategies for setting high but realistic standards, making incremental improvements, and developing habits that lead to long-term success. By integrating these practices, you'll be able to turn excellence from an ideal into a reality.

## HOW TO SET HIGH BUT REALISTIC STANDARDS

Excellence begins with setting high standards for yourself, but those standards need to be realistic. If your goals are too lofty or unattainable, you'll quickly become discouraged, which can lead to frustration or burnout. On the other hand, if your standards are too low, you'll never push yourself to achieve your full potential. There is a very thin line between a standard of excellence that is too high and one that is too low. Finding that line takes trial and error and honest reflection. In the doctoral program I teach at Florida International University, we have a word we frequently use with our students when they reach their first obstacle in pursuing academic excellence: **PIVOT**. To us at Florida International University's athletic training department, to PIVOT means to Persevere, Improvise, Visualize, Overcome, and Transform. Reaching excellence requires the ability to PIVOT.

PIVOT provides a powerful framework for setting high but realistic standards of excellence. Here's how each element supports this process:

1. **Persevere:** Perseverance helps you stay committed to your high standards, even when faced with challenges. It reminds you that setbacks are part of the journey, and it encourages persistence, ensuring you don't lower your standards due to temporary obstacles.
2. **Improvise:** Excellence often requires flexibility. Improvising means adapting when things don't go as planned. This helps you maintain your high standards without being rigid, allowing for adjustments when necessary, which keeps your goals realistic.
3. **Visualize:** Visualization allows you to see the desired outcome with clarity instead of certainty, helping you align your efforts with your goals. By envisioning what success looks like, you can set ambitious yet achievable standards with a clear picture of where you're headed.
4. **Overcome:** This aspect requires commitment to overcoming obstacles that might lower your standards. By

acknowledging challenges and working to conquer them, you maintain your high standards while ensuring they are grounded in reality.

5. **Transform:** Transformation is about growth and becoming someone new. Allow obstacles to change more than just what you think; let them change how you think. This ensures that your standards of excellence evolve over time, aligning with your growth and development. It reminds us that what was excellent yesterday may be mediocre today.

Taken together, these five aspects of PIVOTing help you set standards that push you to grow while also being adaptable and realistic, supporting your path to excellence.

High but realistic standards strike a balance between challenging you and being within your reach. Here's how to set standards that elevate you without overwhelming you:

1. **Align your standards with your values:** Excellence starts with understanding what matters most to you. If your goals and standards don't align with your core values, you'll never find the motivation to pursue them. Take time to reflect on your long-term vision and what excellence looks like in the areas of life that contribute to that vision—whether that's your career, relationships, health, or personal development.
2. **Break down large goals:** Instead of setting vague or massive goals like "be the best in my field," "lose 100 lbs. by summer," or "become a billionaire," break

them down into actionable steps. For example, if excellence in your career means becoming a leader in your industry, set a high standard like "learn a new skill each month" or "mentor two junior colleagues." These smaller goals are measurable and attainable, giving you clarity and motivation. In my award-winning book *Contextual Intelligence: How Thinking in 3D Can Help Resolve Complexity, Uncertainty, and Ambiguity*, I describe the difference between goals and outcomes. One of the things that keeps people from breaking down their goals successfully is not understanding the fundamental differences between goals and outcomes. Most of the time the goals we pursue are actually outcomes of some other behavior. Examine your goals to discover what the prerequisite behaviors are to them occurring. Doing that is the same as breaking down lofty goals.

For example, imagine you set the lofty goal to get promoted at work. This is actually an outcome. It is the outcome of consistently improving your leadership skills, taking on challenging projects, or mentoring junior colleagues. These are the behaviors that lead to the outcome of promotion. Instead of declaring getting a promotion as the goal, work toward becoming a better mentor, and over time, the outcome you initially wanted, promotion, becomes a reality.

By identifying and focusing on these prerequisite behaviors, you break down the larger outcome into actionable, achievable steps—making success more likely.

3. **Make your standards flexible:** Life is unpredictable, and rigid standards can lead to disappointment. It's important to be adaptable, allowing for changes in circumstances without losing sight of your long-term goals. Your journey toward excellence will evolve, and your standards should evolve with it. Remember to PIVOT.

Nelson Mandela's life is a powerful testament to setting high yet realistic standards. During his fight against apartheid in South Africa, Mandela set an incredibly high standard: the complete dismantling of institutionalized racial segregation. His vision wasn't simply to oppose injustice; it was to transform the entire system into one that embraced justice for every person. However, Mandela also understood that achieving this vision would take time, patience, and strategic thinking. After being imprisoned for twenty-seven years, Mandela emerged not as a man seeking revenge but as a leader committed to reconciliation and nation-building. His standards were high, but he balanced them with a realistic approach to building unity and peace through diplomacy, not through violence or radical change.

Mandela maintained a long-term vision and set realistic, incremental goals that gradually moved South Africa toward peaceful transformation. Through negotiations, he secured the release of political prisoners and worked tirelessly with former adversaries to dismantle apartheid, all while keeping his ultimate vision intact.

Mandela's ability to combine high standards with practicality made him an exemplary leader.

## THE POWER OF INCREMENTAL IMPROVEMENT

One of the most effective strategies for exhibiting excellence is the practice of incremental improvement. The idea is simple: instead of trying to make quantum leaps, focus on small, consistent improvements over time. This approach leverages the power of compounding, where even small gains made regularly can lead to significant progress. It also allows for dramatic growth despite the size of the implemented improvement. It doesn't always happen, but in a complex system—and life and human organizations are complex systems—it can happen where large or dramatic changes have little to no effect. It can also happen where small, seemingly minor tweaks result in tremendous impact. Think of the butterfly effect. Julius Caesar said, "It is easier to find men who will volunteer to die than to find those who are willing to endure pain with patience."

Consider the Japanese philosophy of Kaizen (meaning "continuous improvement"), which is often applied in business and manufacturing but is equally powerful for personal growth. By focusing on making 1 percent improvements every day or week, you'll see exponential growth over time.

Here are a few ways to harness the power of incremental improvement:

1. **Focus on small wins:** Every small improvement counts. Whether it's writing 200 words a day for a book or committing to a ten-minute workout, these small actions build momentum and help you achieve

excellence over time. In 2014, Admiral William McRaven popularized this ideal with his now viral commencement speech at University of Texas on making your bed every morning.

2. **Celebrate progress:** Recognizing and sometimes celebrating your small wins keeps you motivated and engaged. Excellence isn't about one big achievement: it's about the steady accumulation of small, meaningful progress along the way.
3. **Iterate and adjust:** As you make progress, take time to reflect on what's working and what isn't. Excellence requires adaptability, and small incremental improvements allow you to course correct as needed without the pressure of massive change.

In his acclaimed book, *Psycho-Cybernetics*, Maxwell Maltz compares this process to how a ballistic missile operates. A missile doesn't travel in a straight line to its target—it constantly makes tiny adjustments along the way, correcting its course every time it veers off track. Because the adjustments are small and occur immediately when its sensors signal a wrong trajectory, they appear to be going in a straight line. Similarly, your journey toward excellence involves regular self-assessment and slight recalibrations, ensuring you stay aligned with your goals even if you momentarily drift.

Bill Gates demonstrated the power of incremental improvement. As the cofounder of Microsoft, Gates didn't set out to create a tech giant overnight. Instead, he and his team continuously improved their software products step by step, releasing new versions of Microsoft Windows and Office, each better than the last.

Gates understood that innovation comes from relentless dedication to improving on previous versions. Microsoft's success wasn't built on perfection in the first attempt, but on the willingness to iterate and to keep refining, testing, and improving products based on user feedback and market demands.

Gates and his team embraced a mindset of intentional iteration. By continually releasing software updates and listening to customer feedback, Microsoft was able to stay ahead in the rapidly evolving tech industry.

## MASTERING ONE KEY AREA AT A TIME

A common mistake people make when pursuing excellence is trying to excel in too many areas at once. This diffuses your focus and makes it harder to achieve meaningful progress in any single area. Instead, simplify and work on mastering one key area at a time.

Serena Williams is one of the greatest athletes of all time, and her career exemplifies the principle of mastering one key area at a time. From a young age, Serena and her sister Venus focused on honing their tennis skills, with their father strategically emphasizing different aspects of their game as they developed. Throughout her career, Serena focused on mastering specific skills: her powerful serve, her aggressive baseline play, and her mental toughness. Each of these elements became a pillar of her dominance in the sport. Instead of spreading herself thin by trying to excel in multiple areas at once, Serena methodically built her strengths, adding layers of excellence as she progressed. Similarly, Kareem Abdul Jabar tells how his legendary coach, John Wooden, would insist that excellence started with learning how to put on socks and tie their shoes to avoid blisters. Wooden's famous insistence on perfecting the fundamentals of the game was the bedrock for excellent play.

To master one area at a time:

1. **Identify your priority area:** Whether it's your career, a personal skill, or an aspect of your health, choose one key area where you want to focus your efforts. This doesn't mean neglecting other areas, but it does mean that your primary energy and resources are directed toward mastering this particular aspect of your life at this point in time. Only after excellence is established in this area can you move on to another.
2. **Set specific, measurable goals:** Once you've identified your priority area, set clear, actionable goals. For example, if you want to master public speaking, your goal could be to deliver one presentation per month or join a speaking club like Toastmasters to improve your skills.
3. **Commit to hard work over superficial wins:** Excellence requires focus and commitment. By limiting distractions and dedicating time to deliberate practice, you'll achieve mastery faster than if you were juggling multiple priorities. Excellence is built through sustained attention and effort in a single area.

## HABITS OF EXCELLENCE

It almost sounds too simple, but consistency is the key to long-term excellence. Developing habits that support your goals ensures that you're taking action every day, no matter how small, toward achieving excellence. Habits make the pursuit of excellence automatic and ingrained in your daily routine, freeing you from relying on willpower alone.

James Clear's *Atomic Habits* delves deeper into how small, consistent actions can lead to profound and lasting changes. The core idea of the book is that it's not massive shifts that transform behavior, but tiny habits that compound over time. Clear explains that habits are the building blocks of our success, and by making small improvements each day—what he calls "atomic" changes—we can eventually experience significant, compounding results. In addition to his Four Laws of Behavior Change: Cue, Craving, Response, and Reward, Clear also introduces the concept of identity-based habits, emphasizing that to truly change, you must focus on who you want to become, not just on what you want to achieve. For instance, instead of setting a goal to run a marathon, focus on becoming a runner. This shift makes habits part of your identity, which helps sustain long-term change. Additionally, Clear discusses the power of habit stacking (linking new habits to existing ones) and the two-minute rule (starting a new habit by doing a version of it that takes only two minutes, making it easier to stick to).

Overall, Clear teaches that small, manageable actions, when repeated consistently, can lead to extraordinary personal and professional growth. By focusing on process over outcomes and making habits part of your identity, you can build systems that naturally lead to success. To develop the habit of excellence, I recommend you:

1. **Start small:** Building habits begins with small, achievable actions. If your goal is to get healthier, start with

a habit like drinking water first thing in the morning or doing ten minutes of exercise each day. Small habits are easy to implement and can be scaled up over time.

2. **Use triggers and cues:** Habits are easier to establish when they are tied to specific triggers or cues in your environment. For example, if you want to build a habit of journaling each morning, place your journal in a conspicuous place where it's the first thing you see in the morning.
3. **Measure your progress:** You will only ever get what you measure. Keep a habit tracker to monitor your consistency. For me, this takes the form of a forty-day calendar-like sheet where each of the forty boxes has four smaller check boxes in them. I call it the 4x40 challenge, where I do four things for forty days. Each day, I check off each of the four things as I do them. Visual reminders of your progress reinforce the habit and help you stay motivated. The satisfaction of seeing your progress builds meaningful momentum.

## BUILDING A ROUTINE FOCUSED ON PROGRESS

Establishing a routine that supports your goals is crucial to maintaining consistent effort toward becoming EPIC and practicing excellence. A well-structured routine helps you prioritize the most important activities and eliminates the guesswork about what to focus on each day. To build a routine that fosters progress:

1. **Prioritize key tasks:** Identify the most critical tasks that contribute directly to your goals and make those

tasks the cornerstone of your routine. If excellence in your field requires skill development, dedicate time each day or week to deliberate practice or learning.

2. **Time block your day:** Use time blocking to schedule periods of focused work on your most important activities. For example, set aside specific hours in the morning when your energy is highest to work on your priority tasks, then use the afternoon for less demanding activities like naps.
3. **Create routines for productivity:** Develop routines that signal the start and end of your work periods. This could be something as simple as starting the day with ten minutes of prayer or ending your work session with a spiritual meditation. These routines create a sense of flow and help you maintain focus.

## BREAKING GOALS DOWN INTO MANAGEABLE STEPS

I mentioned earlier in this chapter that breaking down large goals is important. I want to revisit that here and dive deeper. One of the most effective ways to ensure progress toward excellence is by breaking larger goals into manageable steps. When goals are too big or vague, they can feel overwhelming and discourage action. By dividing them into smaller, actionable tasks, you make the journey toward excellence more approachable and achievable.

Research on goalsetting has revealed some counterintuitive findings. One such finding is to be careful of how often, and to whom, you state your goals. We are used to setting up accountability partners when it comes to goal setting—someone who knows what we want to do and helps keep us on track. Sounds great, right? Well, it doesn't always work that way. Researchers have found that telling people your goals may unintentionally deter you from working toward those goals. In 2009, Peter Gollwitzer, a Professor of Psychology at NYU, and his colleagues reported that the simple act of publicly sharing your goal can make you less likely to do the work to achieve it, especially if that goal is closely tied to your identity. The study found that when people announce their intentions or goals, they often receive social recognition and validation, which creates a premature sense of accomplishment. This feeling of satisfaction can reduce the motivation to put in the necessary work to achieve the goal. Gollwitzer's research suggests that when we share our goals with others and receive praise or congratulations for merely having the goal, it tricks our brains into thinking we've already made progress. This can decrease our drive to take further action. To break down your goals:

1. **Describe the big picture:** As we learned from Stephen Covey, begin with the end in mind. So, start by clearly describing your long-term goal. This could be what Jim Collins calls a BHAG (Big Hairy Audacious Goal) in his book *Built to Last: Successful Habits of Visionary Companies*. But you must embrace the *long-term* nature of the big picture. Do not fool yourself into believing it is closer than it really is. For example, if you want to write a New York Times bestselling book, be prepared to write a lot of books that aren't best sellers, or that aren't even any good. Remember, it's the big picture that inspires you, but it's the little things that move you forward.

2. **Create smaller milestones:** Break the big picture outcome into bite-sized milestones. If writing a book is the goal, the milestones might include outlining the chapters, writing 500 words per day, or completing one chapter per month.
3. **Focus on the next step:** Don't get overwhelmed by the entire process. Instead, focus on the next small step you can take today. Completing each step builds momentum and brings you closer to your overall goal.
4. **Keep some goals personal:** Be mindful of to whom and of how much you share your goal. Don't sabotage your path to excellence by believing the kudos you receive from people impressed by your goals and action plans are actually progress. Sharing too much may be detrimental.

## OVERCOMING SETBACKS ON YOUR PATH TO EXCELLENCE

Setbacks are an inevitable part of any journey toward excellence. How you respond to these setbacks will determine whether you continue to grow or become discouraged. The key is to reframe failures and challenges as opportunities to learn and improve, rather than as roadblocks to your success.

### Reframing Failures as Opportunities to Grow

Thomas Edison is famously quoted as saying, "I have not failed. I've just found 10,000 ways that won't work." This mindset captures Edison's approach to invention and innovation. Throughout his career, Edison experienced countless failures in his pursuit of developing groundbreaking technologies like the electric light bulb. However, he never viewed failure as a negative outcome. Instead, he saw each failure as a necessary step toward success.

Failure doesn't have to be the opposite of success—it can be an integral part of the journey. When you experience setbacks, view them as the gift of feedback rather than a verdict on your ability. This mindset allows you to benefit from your mistakes and use them as steppingstones toward excellence.

1. **Analyze the setback:** When you encounter a failure or setback, take time to reflect on what went wrong and why. In fact, you can do that before the setback. A premortem is a strategic thinking technique used to anticipate potential problems and challenges before a project or plan is implemented. Unlike a postmortem, which analyzes what went wrong after a failure, a premortem involves imagining that your goal has already failed and then working backward to identify the reasons for its failure. Understanding the root cause helps you avoid repeating the same mistakes.
2. **Focus on what you can control:** While you can't control every outcome, you can control your response to setbacks. Focus on the actions you can take moving forward to continue improving, rather than dwelling on the failure itself.

## STAYING RESILIENT THROUGH CHALLENGES

Resilience is the ability to bounce back from setbacks and continue pursuing your goals despite adversity. Developing resilience is essential for developing and maintaining excellence. Practice self-compassion: When you face challenges, it's easy to be overly critical of yourself. Instead, practice self-compassion by recognizing that setbacks are a natural part of the learning process. Keep your long-term vision in mind: During difficult times, it's important to stay connected to your long-term goals. Remember why you're pursuing excellence in the first place, and let that vision motivate you to keep going, even when the path gets tough.

## TURNING EXCELLENCE INTO A DAILY PRACTICE

Exhibiting excellence is a continuous process that requires focus, dedication, and strategic action. By setting high but realistic standards, embracing incremental improvement, and developing consistent habits, you can make excellence a part of your everyday life. Remember, the path to excellence is not about being perfect—it's about making steady progress, overcoming setbacks, and staying committed to your goals.

6

# ACHIEVING EXCELLENCE IN EVERY AREA OF LIFE

Excellence is often thought of as something reserved for one specific area—perhaps your career, an athletic pursuit, or personal hobbies. But true excellence permeates every area of life. It isn't just about achieving success in your job or reaching a personal milestone; it's about showing up fully and striving for growth and mastery in every role you play—whether as a husband or wife, a parent, a colleague, or simply an individual striving for personal fulfillment.

In this chapter, we will explore what it means to achieve excellence in several key areas: personal relationships, career or business, health and self-care, spiritual discipline, and the delicate balance between knowing when to focus and when to let go. There are more areas of course. Life is very complex, but these areas are often the foundation on which life is built. By understanding how excellence looks in each area, you can work toward living a more fulfilling life.

## EXCELLENCE IN YOUR PERSONAL RELATIONSHIPS

Relationships are at the heart of human existence. Whether they're with friends, family, or a lover, the quality of our relationships deeply impacts our sense of well-being and happiness, which directly impacts our state of excellence. Exhibiting excellence in your personal relationships doesn't mean being perfect—it means being present, empathetic, and committed to fostering the growth and well-being of those around you.

### Be Present and Engaged

One of the most critical components of excellence in relationships is being present. In a world filled with distractions, it can be easy to have conversations while your mind is elsewhere. Excellence in relationships requires you to be fully engaged when interacting with others. This means putting down your phone, turning off distractions, and truly listening to the person in front of you. This is easier said than done. The dopamine hit we receive from our smart devices is as addictive as opium. In the long run, that leads to anxiety and chronic disease from the cortisol and dopamine rollercoaster.

When you're fully present, you show the other person that they matter and that their thoughts and feelings are valuable. Being present builds trust and deepens connections. It is a very high form of respect, and respect sits at the core of healthy relationships. In a world full of distractions, offering someone your undivided attention can feel like a rare and meaningful gift, strengthening bonds in ways that words alone cannot.

### Practice Empathy

Empathy is a cornerstone of excelling at relationships. It's not just about understanding the words someone is saying but also identifying with their emotions and perspective. To practice empathy, take the time to attentively listen to their feelings, not just their words. Try to place yourself in the other person's shoes. Reflect on how they might feel or why they might have the perspective they do, even if it differs from your own. Here are a few practical tips for fostering the kind of empathy that leads to excellent relationships.

1. **Actively listen:** Give your full attention when someone is speaking. Put away distractions, maintain eye contact, and show you are present through nonverbal cues like nodding or leaning in. Avoid interrupting or formulating your response while they are talking.
2. **Validate their feelings:** Acknowledge the emotions they express, even if you don't fully agree with their point of view. Simple statements like, "That sounds really difficult" or "I can understand why you'd feel that way" demonstrate that their feelings are seen and respected.
3. **Ask open-ended questions:** Encourage deeper conversation by asking questions that invite them to share more, such as "Can you tell me more about that?" or "How did that make you feel?" This shows you care about their experience and are genuinely curious.
4. **Put yourself in their shoes:** Take a moment to imagine yourself in their situation. Consider how you might feel if you were facing similar circumstances. Reflect

on their background, values, and life experiences that may shape their current emotions or decisions.

5. **Mirror emotions, not just words:** Pay attention to their tone, facial expressions, and body language. Respond with emotional sensitivity, matching your reaction to their mood. If they are excited, share their enthusiasm. If they are upset, respond with gentleness and calm.
6. **Practice patience and suspend judgment:** Empathy often requires resisting the urge to immediately offer solutions or critiques. Be patient and let them express themselves fully before you respond.
7. **Follow up:** Show ongoing care by checking in with them later about the issue or topic they shared. A simple "I was thinking about what you said the other day—how are you feeling now?" can reinforce your support.

### Commit to Growth and Vulnerability

Excellence in relationships also requires a commitment to growth and vulnerability. Every relationship will encounter challenges, and how you handle those challenges can determine the depth and success of the connection. Being vulnerable means being honest about your feelings, admitting when you're wrong, and having difficult conversations. It's about being open to growth, both as an individual and as part of a partnership. My wife Angie and I made a commitment to each other over two decades ago that we would set aside time and money to actively engage in at least one marriage enrichment activity each year. By God's grace we have done that, and those incremental steps for twenty-plus years have resulted in a marriage we are both proud of. We are not perfect; our conflict culture is what marriage gurus John and Julie Gottman call volatile. Two volatile temperaments in the house make for some exciting conversations.

Take, for instance, the time early in our marriage—on our third wedding anniversary—when we got into a very public and loud argument. We took a weekend trip to one of our favorite cities, Cincinnati, to celebrate. To our delight, right outside our hotel was an amazing summer festival. The streets were full of life and laughter, with many restaurants, music, and vendors. We set out to find a nice place to eat dinner. Well, I was more interested in exploring and Angie was more interested in eating. When I casually dropped my wallet and keys into her purse—she lost it. Epic meltdown. That mindless inconsiderate act was just enough to trigger a volatile reaction, which I gladly reciprocated. Without going into all the details, we ended up in a screaming match in the middle of the festival. We are sure people thought it was an impromptu theater production. People were stopping and watching as we were yelling and screaming, pointing fingers at each other. Eventually, this led to Angie dropping her purse in the middle of the street, with all our money, the car keys, my wallet, and hers. She walked off in one direction and I, the other, leaving the purse there in the middle of the street, and every five feet or so we'd turn back to yell at each other.

Eventually we wised up and realized someone could make off with the purse and we'd be in no position to stop them. So, we rendezvoused back at the purse. We picked it up and walked into the nearest restaurant. After we ate, we laughed, apologized to each other and had a great evening. To this day we wonder how many people in that crowd would have lost a bet about us being divorced by now.

Our commitment to an excellent marriage and growth has helped us curb our volatile defaults to be open and vulnerable to each other. We have learned firsthand that excellence in relationships isn't about avoiding conflict—it's about embracing conflict as a gift that refines us and teaches us how to better practice respect, understanding, and a willingness to grow.

## EXCELLENCE IN YOUR CAREER OR BUSINESS

Excellence in your career or business is often the most visible form of success. It's where hard work, calling, talent, and ambition come together. However, just like in relationships, achieving excellence in your career doesn't mean perfection; it means striving for continuous improvement, building resilience, and pursuing meaningful work.

### The Mastery Mindset

In the professional world, those who achieve excellence have a mastery mindset. They aren't content with just doing the bare minimum; they seek to master their craft, whether they're artists, entrepreneurs, or corporate leaders. Developing this mindset involves:

1. **Commitment to self-determined learning (something education scholars call heutagogy):** Seek opportunities that teach you the skills you need to get where you want to be. Curate your own learning, whether through formal education, mentorship, or self-study.

Mastery is never static—it's a lifelong pursuit and it requires an acute sense of what you need to learn next to become excellent at what you do.

2. **Deliberate practice:** Excellence always springs from focused, intentional practice. Identify the key skills you need to excel in your field (or desired field) and dedicate time regularly to improving them.
3. **Embracing feedback as a gift, not criticism:** Seek feedback from colleagues, supervisors, or customers, and use them all as tools for growth. Those who excel are always looking for ways to improve, even when the feedback is tough to hear. Never make excuses for feedback you don't like. Own it.

## Build Antifragility and Adaptability

The road to excellence is rarely smooth and never linear. Challenges, failures, and setbacks are inevitable. What sets those who achieve excellence apart is their antifragility and ability to grow from setbacks. When things don't go as planned, don't give up—reassess, adjust, and try again. Remember to PIVOT (Persevere, Improvise, Visualize, Overcome, and Transform).

Disruption is inevitable. Planning and expecting everything to go as intended is naïve. I am not implying you shouldn't plan; that is also naïve. I am also not suggesting you should always have a plan B or C in place. I am saying that excellence always requires pivoting and while we should plan as strategically as possible, it is wise to know the unexpected will alter your trajectory. Don't let those disruptions take you off course. Use the detour to learn something new as you reroute back to your original destination. Grow and improve from the disruption.

### Find Meaning in Your Work

Excellence in your career also requires you to find meaning in your work. This doesn't mean every job needs to be a passion project, or that you must love every aspect of your job—to that I would say, "Grow up!" But it does mean aligning your professional life with your values and purpose. When you find meaning in your work—whether through the impact you make, the relationships you build, or the growth opportunities available—you're more likely to give your best effort. Unfortunately, the complexity of work today makes finding meaning more difficult.

Research by David Rooke, from Harthill Consulting, reports that only 5 percent of healthcare clinicians have the meaning making capacity to draw significant value from their work. This study is talking about medical professionals, but I'd guess this is true of all of us. Translating that finding suggests that 95 percent of people don't know how to make meaning from their work.

Meaning making capacity is an intellectual and emotional convergence that involves these two parts of our brain working together to make sense of life events and relationships, with respect to self. It requires us to accurately assess our experiences, understand the significance of those experiences, and use that knowledge to make sense of our life.

Our jobs should be meaningful, but we should not expect them to give us all or even most of our meaning. We often expect our jobs to be fulfilling. As if *we* need something from it. The truth is that it needs something from us. Expecting your job to fulfill you is giving too much of our power away to a manager or a bureaucratic hierarchy. I believe, instead, we should be giving meaning to the people around us. Making meaning is a responsibility we bring to our work, not the other way around.

## EXCELLENCE IN HEALTH AND SELF-CARE

Perhaps the most transformative lesson that cancer taught me was the importance of excellence in self-care. Ironically, I am a licensed athletic trainer with a graduate degree in exercise science. I know the value of exercise and health. Before my diagnosis, like many high achievers, I often had a one-dimensional view of health, working out. For me that meant running—fast jogging really. But when faced with cancer, I had no choice but to confront this imbalance head-on and embrace health as more than just being physically active.

Excellence in health became a priority because, without it, nothing else mattered. I learned to listen to my body in ways I never had before. I couldn't power through fatigue or ignore the toll that treatment took on me. Excellence in health meant making conscious, deliberate choices to support my body's healing. This often meant walking instead of running and walking with a partner, my wife, instead of doing it alone.

I adopted a regular exercise routine that was gentle but consistent, focusing on staying active in ways that were sustainable. I also became more mindful about what I ate, ensuring that I nourished my body with non-processed, nutrient-rich foods to support recovery. Rest became a nonnegotiable part of my day—no longer a luxury, but a critical element of self-care. Being EPIC means managing recovery as well as activity.

### Mental and Emotional Well-Being

Excellence in health extended beyond the physical. It required me to take care of my mental and emotional well-being as well. Cancer brings with it an overwhelming emotional burden, and I had to learn to manage stress, anxiety, and fear in a healthy way. I started practicing prayer much more intentionally, allowing myself time each day to focus on the present and quiet the noise in my mind.

This wasn't just about surviving the disease—it was about thriving, mentally and emotionally, despite the challenges. I sought support from counselors and leaned on friends who had gone through similar experiences, finding strength in community. This holistic approach to health, where I valued mental and emotional well-being as much as physical recovery, became the foundation of my self-care. Any of us who are experiencing adversity need to realize that a proper balance between body, mind, and spirit is critical to becoming EPIC.

Take a moment to reflect on adversity. No doubt you have experienced some. How has it shaped you? How has it changed your perspective? Has that change been helpful or harmful?

## EXCELLENCE IN SPIRITUAL DISCIPLINE

For many, spiritual growth provides a foundation for navigating life's challenges and finding meaning and purpose. Spiritual discipline—whether through religious practice, meditation, mindfulness, or simply time for reflection—helps cultivate inner peace, resilience, and a sense of connection to something greater than oneself.

After my diagnosis, this aspect of life took on new importance. Facing the uncertainties of illness, I found that nurturing my spiritual life gave me strength, perspective, and a deeper sense of purpose. When I was younger, I read almost everything Richard Foster wrote, and my battle with aggressive prostate cancer brought me back to one of my favorite spiritual formation books, *Celebration of Discipline: The Path to Spiritual Growth.*

This classic text explores the importance of spiritual disciplines in deepening one's relationship with God and fostering personal transformation. Foster describes three categories of spiritual disciplines: inward disciplines (such as meditation, prayer, fasting, and study), outward disciplines (simplicity, solitude, submission, and service), and corporate disciplines (confession, worship, guidance, and celebration). I now needed all these disciplines to battle well and "stay strong," as they say. Foster emphasizes that these practices are not ends in themselves but tools for spiritual growth, leading to greater freedom, joy, and peace.

In my own journey I began to emphasize the inward discipline of prayer, the outward discipline of simplicity, and corporate discipline of community worship. Integrating Foster's ideas of discipline has helped me recover with grace and I believe they can help you too. Pick one or two from each category and begin to integrate them into your life and habits.

Just as physical health requires consistent effort, so does spiritual growth. Developing a regular spiritual practice—whether through prayer, meditation, reading sacred texts, or spending time with God—allows you to connect with your spirit and the world around you.

For me, prayer and the sacraments became integral to my routine, especially during my treatment. These practices gave me moments of stillness in a time of physical and emotional turbulence.

Through quiet reflection and prayer, I could process my fears, find peace, and remind myself of the bigger picture beyond the challenges I was facing. Here are a few tips to developing spiritual practices:

1. **Consistency is key:** Whether it's five minutes of meditation or daily journaling, commit to a regular practice that grounds you and helps you focus on developing your spirit.
2. **Create a space for reflection:** Designate a quiet space for spiritual practice. It can be a corner in your home, a spot in nature, or simply a time each day to pause and reflect.
3. **Start small:** If you're new to spiritual practice, begin with manageable steps, like starting each day with a moment of gratitude. Gradually build up your practice as it becomes part of your routine.

### Finding Meaning and Purpose

Spiritual discipline helps you find meaning and purpose in life's experiences, especially the difficult ones. My journey with cancer forced me to grapple with questions about life, death, and what truly mattered. Through my spiritual practice, I found meaning in the struggle. Instead of seeing cancer as a purely negative force, I began to see it as a catalyst for personal growth, clarity, deeper connections with others, and greater empathy.

Spiritual discipline can help you reframe life's challenges, providing you with the strength to face adversity and the insight to find purpose in it. Whether you connect with a religious tradition or not, cultivating your spiritual life adds richness and depth to your pursuit of excellence.

### Spiritual Disciplines

Reflect on your values and beliefs by spending time contemplating what gives your life meaning. What are your core beliefs? How do they guide your decisions and actions? Turn challenges into growth opportunities by using your spiritual practice to reframe difficulties in life. Rather than seeing adversity as something to avoid, look for the lessons and growth that can come from it. For example, we are told that Jesus was a man of sorrow and acquainted with grief. He Himself had to learn obedience through the things He suffered. If Christ had to suffer to learn, we are certainly not exempt from it.

### Cultivating Peace and Resilience

In a world filled with stress, uncertainty, and constant demands, having a spiritual foundation helps you stay grounded. It gives you a deeper sense of calm and the ability to weather storms with grace. For me, the practice of prayer was not just a tool for relaxation but a lifeline that helped me cultivate antifragility. During treatments, when my body felt weak, my spiritual practices strengthened my mind and spirit. It helped me face uncertainty with courage and stay hopeful even in the darkest moments.

### Connecting with Something Greater

One of the most powerful aspects of spiritual discipline is the sense of connection to something greater than yourself. Spiritual practice helps you step outside of your individual concerns and see the broader context of life. Battling cancer, I found solace in connecting with something greater than myself. This connection gave me strength, a sense of belonging, and a deeper purpose. Here are a few ways to connect:

1. **Explore faith:** If you're part of a faith tradition, deepen your understanding and connection to your faith. If you're not religious, seek spiritual practices that help you connect with the world around you. Most Americans claim to be Christians. The statistics are overwhelming. The United States boasts the highest number of Christians of any country in the world with 230,000,000 or 71 percent of the population. Yet many do not know the sacred and rich spiritual practices of their faith until it is too late.
2. **Spend time in nature:** Nature has a unique ability to inspire awe and connect us with God. Take time to be outside, whether for a walk in the park or quiet reflection in a natural setting. Excellent spiritual growth means being intentional and developing those spiritual disciplines identified earlier by Richard Foster.
3. **Engage in service to others:** One of the most profound ways to connect with something greater than yourself is through acts of service. Helping others brings you outside of yourself and creates a sense of purpose that few other things can achieve.

Excellence in life isn't just about outward achievements—it's about cultivating a strong inner life. Spiritual discipline helps you connect with your deeper identity, build resilience, and find meaning and purpose in your experiences, which is foundational to being excellent.

Cancer was not just a physical battle for me; it was a spiritual battle. My spiritual discipline gave me the strength to persevere, the peace to accept what I couldn't control, and the perspective to find meaning in adversity. In achieving excellence, don't neglect the spiritual dimension of your life. It is here that you will find the inner strength, clarity, and purpose to thrive in every other area of life.

## STRIKING THE BALANCE: WHEN TO FOCUS, WHEN TO LET GO

Perhaps one of the hardest lessons I had to learn was when to focus intensely on one area of life and when to let go. Adversity has a way of forcing you to let go of the things you can't control, and in doing so, it taught me the value of balance.

There were times when I had to give my full attention to my health—when treatments were intensive or my body needed rest and recovery. During these times, I allowed myself to focus on my well-being without guilt; that was hard, knowing that effort in other areas (like my career) would have to be paused. I didn't like it. It felt like admitting defeat. But that was a self-defeating belief. Life will often ask you to focus, unfocus, and refocus. Being excellent is about acknowledging those times and seasons, not ignoring them.

Excellence is about balance—knowing when to strive, rest, push forward, and let go. Cancer taught me that balance doesn't mean always giving equal attention to every area; it means being fully present and committed to what matters most in the moment. If you allow it, your adversity can teach you the same thing as well.

## A THOUGHT ON QUITTING

We've all heard this axiom: "winners never quit, and quitters never win." This is only partly true! Quitters never win—true. Winners never quit—false. There is an unmistakable paradox here. I am convinced that what we call "failure" is often quitting too soon. I am also positive that many of our failures come from holding on to something unnecessary too long. Becoming EPIC requires learning when it is time to let go.

Excellence is not about never quitting; it is about knowing *what* to quit and *when* something should be abandoned. Let go of your ego. Being a quitter is not the same as letting go of something that is holding you back.

Angela Duckworth's work on grit highlights the importance of perseverance and passion in achieving long-term goals, emphasizing that sustained effort often matters more than talent alone. In *Grit: The Power of Passion and Perseverance*, Duckworth argues for the value of quitting—but not in the way most people think. Rather than viewing quitting as a failure, she reframes it as a strategic decision that can sharpen focus and increase the likelihood of success. Duckworth distinguishes between quitting impulsively in the face of discomfort from letting go of pursuits that no longer align with one's strengths or long-term vision. In this sense, quitting becomes an essential part of perseverance, allowing individuals to redirect their energy toward more meaningful goals.

I love the story about Peter told in Luke 5:1–11, when he quit his profession to follow Christ. Peter, a skilled fisherman, had spent his life building his career and providing for his family. After an unsuccessful night of fishing, Jesus instructed Peter to cast his nets once more. The miraculous catch that followed opened Peter's eyes to Jesus' divine authority. When Jesus then called Peter to follow Him, Peter walked away from his boat and his nets; he left his livelihood behind to pursue a new, higher calling.

Peter's decision to quit fishing wasn't driven by failure or discouragement but by recognizing that his old life could hinder his greater purpose. Peter's choice to quit his job wasn't about abandoning hard work but about redirecting his perseverance toward a more meaningful mission. This shift ultimately allowed him to play a crucial role in the foundation of the early Church.

Peter's life highlights how "quitting," when done with intention and vision, can open the door to extraordinary growth and new opportunities. Peter is an example of a winner, who had the perception to quit the right thing at the right time.

## THE JOURNEY TO EXCELLENCE IN EVERY AREA OF LIFE

My journey, like yours, if you let it, reshaped my understanding of excellence. It's no longer only about outward success or ticking off achievements; it's about showing up fully in every area of life—relationships, career, health, spirituality—and doing so with presence, purpose, and balance.

Excellence isn't about having it all or being perfect in every role. It's about being present for the people who matter, finding meaning in your work, prioritizing your well-being, and knowing when to focus and when to let go. It's a lifelong journey, one that requires constant adaptation. In the end, becoming EPIC is more than pursuing excellence. The next aspect of EPIC living is about developing perception.

# PART 2

# ON PERCEPTION

# 7

# THE POWER OF BEING PERCEPTIVE

In the pursuit of growth, one trait often overlooked but crucial for success is perception. Dan Sullivan says that "our eyes only see, and ears only hear what our brain is looking for." Perception shapes the way we interpret the world around us, guiding our decisions, influencing our relationships, and helping us navigate complexity. Becoming more perceptive doesn't mean just observing more—it means deepening our understanding of the people and situations we encounter, becoming attuned to subtleties that others may overlook. This is what I call contextual intelligence, which I will unpack in the next chapter.

In this chapter, we'll explore the power of perception, why it matters, how it affects your decisions and relationships, and the key differences between perception and intuition. By the end, you'll have a deeper understanding of how honing your perception can transform not only how you see the world but how you respond to it.

## WHY BEING PERCEPTIVE MATTERS

Perception is the lens through which we view the world. It affects everything—how we see ourselves, how we interpret others' behavior, how we approach challenges, and even how we define success. At its core, perception is about leveraging hindsight, insight, and foresight (i.e., 3D Thinking). It's more than just seeing what's in front of you; it's about interpreting what you see through the lenses of the past, present, and future in a way that allows you to respond wisely and effectively.

Being perceptive enhances your awareness of the subtleties of human behavior and the intricacies of your environment. In both personal and professional settings, perception allows you to read between the lines, understand unspoken cues, and pick up on emotions or intentions that may not be explicitly stated. This heightened awareness provides valuable context and clarity, helping you make more informed decisions and avoid misunderstandings.

In my own journey, my ability to be perceptive grew significantly over time. Adversity, if you let it, tends to heighten your awareness of your emotions and fears. This can help you become more attentive to others and their pain. This awareness became a powerful tool for navigating personal relationships with empathy, and opportunities with wisdom.

The other side of the coin is also true. Sometimes, adversity can dull perception if you become too self-focused and introspective. In these cases, the opposite is true, and adversity blinds you to the needs and feelings of others. You should try and use adversity as an amplifier to others' needs instead of a drum drowning out their calls for help.

## ENHANCED DECISION-MAKING

Perception directly impacts decision-making. When you're able to perceive situations clearly—seeing them for what they truly are rather than what you wish them to be—you make decisions rooted in reality. This allows you to anticipate challenges, assess risks accurately, and seize opportunities that others might miss. This is a tremendous and often unfair advantage!

Leaders, in particular, benefit from strong perception. The ability to gauge the mood of a team, read the room during negotiations, or understand the broader dynamics of a situation can be the difference between success and failure. Being perceptive allows you to ask the right questions, seek the right information, and make choices that lead to better outcomes.

At its heart, perception is about understanding—not just situations, but people. By becoming more perceptive, you develop the ability to truly listen, to see beyond the surface, and to empathize with others. This creates deeper, more meaningful connections because you're able to relate to people on a more profound level.

In relationships, both personal and professional, being perceptive allows you to notice the little things that make a big difference—like recognizing when someone needs support or understanding when words don't match emotions. By seeing beyond what's immediately visible, you can respond with greater empathy and kindness, which strengthens your connections and relationships.

Perception doesn't just influence how you interpret the world—it actively shapes the decisions you make and the quality of your relationships.

Clearly perceiving situations can directly impact the choices you make. People with strong perception can see potential problems before they arise, notice opportunities others miss, and make decisions that are well informed and thoughtful.

For example, in business, a perceptive leader might sense tension in a meeting that others overlook. This leader would use that perception to adjust his or her approach, perhaps addressing concerns before they escalate into conflict. A perceptive decision-maker weighs not only the obvious facts but also the less tangible factors—like timing, emotions, and hidden dynamics—leading to choices that are more strategic and effective.

## THE R4 PROCESS™

One way to develop perception is to practice what I call the R4 Process. The R4 Process is described in detail in my book on contextual intelligence and consists of four phases of perceiving accurately. The four Rs are:

1. **Recognizing:** Recognize the subtle or nuanced shifts in your environment.
2. **Reordering:** Reorder any preestablished priorities you made before recognizing the subtle and nuanced shifts. Reorder the key metrics of success that you had predetermined before your interaction.
3. **Responding:** Respond to those new metrics of success with an adjusted list of what success means in light of the subtle changes you noticed.

4. **Reflecting:** Reflect on the accuracy of your perceptions of the previous three Rs.

Steve Jobs's effectiveness as a leader stemmed from his ability to perceive what customers wanted. His perception went beyond market research or focus groups. He had an uncanny ability to tap into the emotional and experiential needs of users, which helped shape iconic products like the iPhone and iPad. Jobs's decisions were often based on an acute understanding of human behavior and desire, which set Apple apart from its competitors. I believe Jobs's use of the four Rs—even if he never would have identified them as such—gave him the ability to see what others overlooked.

## PERCEPTION IN RELATIONSHIPS

In relationships, perception is the key to understanding others' emotions, needs, and motivations. When you're perceptive, you can recognize subtle cues—body language, tone of voice, or even silence—which can often reveal more than words. This ability to read between the lines helps you communicate more effectively and navigate complex emotions with grace and tact.

For example, a perceptive partner might notice that their spouse is stressed, even if they haven't said a word. Instead of waiting for a problem to escalate, the perceptive partner might offer support, address concerns, simply provide a listening ear, or, in some cases, be extra sensitive to their partner's triggers. This creates a sense of emotional safety and fosters trust in the relationship.

In professional settings, perception helps you build stronger, more effective teams. You'll notice when a team member is struggling, even if they haven't vocalized it, or when morale is low. By addressing these issues early, you can foster a more positive and productive work environment.

Oprah Winfrey's success isn't just due to her communication skills—it's her perception and empathy that have set her apart. Oprah has an extraordinary ability to read people's emotions and understand their deeper struggles, which allows her to ask the right questions and connect with her guests on a profound level. Her perceptive nature has enabled her to create trust and vulnerability in interviews, leading to authentic conversations that resonate with millions.

While perception and intuition are often used interchangeably, they are distinct qualities. Understanding the difference between them is essential for harnessing the power of perception.

## THE POWER OF OBSERVATION AND ANALYSIS

Perception is rooted in observation and analysis. It is more scientific and less mystical than many assume. It's about actively engaging with the world around you, noticing details, interpreting data, and making sense of what you see. Perception is a conscious process—you are aware of the cues, biases, and signals that inform your understanding of a situation. It requires mindfulness and attentiveness, and it's something that can be developed and sharpened over time.

For example, a perceptive person might notice a team member's body language during a meeting—perhaps they are avoiding eye contact or seem tense. The leader observes these details and uses that information to check in with the team member afterward, offering support or addressing any underlying issues.

Perception requires tacit knowledge. Tacit knowledge is an intuitive, experiential, and unspoken expertise that's difficult to articulate or document. It's a unique source of insight that is acquired through life experiences, training, and mindful interactions with others. Some people use the terms "wisdom" or "intuition" to describe tacit knowledge.

Intuition, versus direct observation, is more of an instinctual, subconscious process. It's that gut feeling you get when you know something is off, even if you don't have concrete evidence to back it up. Intuition often comes from experience—the brain rapidly processing past knowledge and experiences to arrive at a conclusion. It's what Daniel Kahneman, Nobel Laureate in behavioral economics calls *system 1 thinking*. This is thinking without going through a deliberate reasoning process.

In *Thinking, Fast and Slow*, Kahneman describes system 1 thinking as the brain's fast, automatic, and intuitive way of processing information. It operates effortlessly, relying on instincts, heuristics, and patterns to make quick judgments and decisions without conscious thought. System 1 thinking is what we use for everyday tasks like recognizing faces, reading emotions, or reacting to immediate situations, and it can be influenced by biases and emotions. While this type of thinking is efficient for routine decisions, it can also lead to errors or snap judgments because it often relies on gut feelings rather than careful analysis. Kahneman contrasts this with *system 2 thinking*, which is slower, more deliberate, and logical, used when deeper thought and analysis are required.

System 1 is essential for managing daily life but can be prone to mistakes when confronted with complex problems that need more careful reasoning. Intuition can be useful, but it's not always reliable because it operates without all the facts. It takes many shortcuts. It's essential to balance intuition with perception. While intuition may give you an immediate sense of a situation, perception helps you verify and understand the underlying causes of that feeling.

Both intuition and perception are valuable, but to make the most informed decisions, they need to work together. Your gut feelings (intuition) can alert you to something worth paying attention to, while perception allows you to gather data, analyze the situation, and arrive at a more informed conclusion. Becoming EPIC requires you develop your capacity to perceive and learn to accurately filter your intuition.

For instance, if you have an intuitive sense that a project is going off track, use your perceptive abilities to gather more information. Observe the behavior of your team, ask the right questions, and analyze the current state of the project, thereby validating or falsifying your intuition. By combining intuition and perception, you make decisions based on both instinct and evidence, and over time, you develop a richer ability to perceive.

## THE TRANSFORMATIVE POWER OF PERCEPTION

Perception is a skill that, when cultivated, can transform every area of your life. It deepens your relationships, enhances your decision-making, and gives you the ability to navigate complex situations with grace and wisdom. Whether it's sensing the emotions of a loved one, understanding the dynamics of a team, or interpreting the subtleties of a business deal, perception provides the insight needed to respond effectively and become EPIC.

As you continue your journey to becoming more perceptive, remember that this skill is developed through practice and awareness. Pay attention to the world around you—observe, analyze, and reflect. Practice the R4 Process. The more you hone your perceptive abilities, the better equipped you will be to achieve excellence in all areas of your life.

By understanding the difference between perception and intuition, and learning to balance both, you'll be able to make more informed, insightful decisions. The power of perception is a tool that can elevate your understanding of the world and your impact on it.

### KNOWING THE FINAL SCORE: A LESSON ON PERCEPTION

In my family, sports are as sacred as Sunday dinners. We're serious about our teams, and during football season, this means gathering around the TV for the big games. Thanks to the miracle of modern streaming, we often record games so we can start watching a little late—free from the interruptions of real-time schedules and endless commercial breaks. But there's one huge caveat: having to avoid spoilers.

One Saturday, we were watching a big game on about a two-hour delay. Not only was my family gathered around the TV, but several friends were over, amping up the excitement and energy in the room. We'd all been careful, staying off social media to avoid catching any glimpse of the final score. We wanted the thrill of watching it as if it were live, with every nail-biting moment intact.

Then, I made the ultimate rookie mistake. I casually picked up my phone during a lull in the game, and before I could even process what was happening, my ESPN app flashed the final score across the screen. Just like that, I knew how the game ended, and I was devastated that I'd spoiled it for myself. But I quickly realized that the others were still blissfully unaware of the outcome. So, I kept my face neutral and acted like nothing happened. I didn't want to ruin their experience.

Knowing the end of the game in advance had an unexpected effect on me. Within a few plays, our team's quarterback threw an interception—a "pick-six." Our team was suddenly behind, and you could feel the emotional tide in the room shift. Everyone around me went from excited to anxious, with visible distress as our team lost the lead. But here's the thing: I felt none of it. I was calm because I already knew that somehow, our team would turn it around. I just didn't know how.

Watching my friends and family ride the roller coaster of emotions, I realized something significant. My knowledge of the outcome made each setback bearable because I knew the final score. The interception didn't shake me because I had a broader perspective: victory was certain, even if the journey there looked messy.

And that's when it hit me—this is a powerful metaphor for life, especially when we're striving to be our best selves. What if we could hold that same assurance about who we are becoming?

In many ways, life is like that game, and we're like my friends, reacting to every setback as if it's the end of the story. But if we can see a clear picture of the person we want to become—our future self—then even when life throws us an "interception," we don't have to panic. We can trust that, ultimately, we'll reach the finish line we're meant to reach.

If you know in your core that you're on a path of growth and excellence, then temporary setbacks don't have to shake you. Like watching a recorded game when you know the final score, believing in the future version of yourself can bring a deep sense of calm.

When you have a clear picture of who you're becoming, you can face difficulties with the assurance that you're still moving toward that best version of yourself, even when things look bleak.

## THE POWER OF BELIEVING IN YOUR FUTURE SELF

Having a perception of the future you—like knowing the final score—can help you navigate difficult moments. When you trust in the person you're becoming and believe that your future self is a real person, even the biggest challenges don't feel quite as daunting. You'll still experience setbacks, but you won't feel like they define you or derail you.

### Building Confidence in Your Future Self

How can you develop a clear perception of your future self? Here are a few things to keep in mind:

1. **Visualize your best self:** Create a mental image of who you want to be. Imagine how that person would respond to setbacks, challenges, and even the small annoyances of daily life.
2. **Embrace setbacks as part of the process:** Knowing who you're becoming can give you the resilience to face obstacles without losing hope.
3. **Trust the transformation:** Remember, the seeds of your future self are already within you. Each challenge is helping bring that version of you to life.
4. **Stay committed to growth:** The journey of transformation is ongoing. Stay open to learning, to evolving, and to the discomfort that growth requires.

With a clear vision of your future self, you're not just reacting to life's disruptions; you're moving forward with the confidence that, no matter what, you're still on track to becoming the best version of yourself. Having a clear perception of who you are and who you are becoming makes life's setbacks much less intimidating and daunting. Just like watching that recorded game, you can face challenges with calm assurance, knowing that the final score is victory.

8

# PERCEPTION AND CONTEXTUAL INTELLIGENCE

Developing perception requires more than just skill or effort; it requires the ability to identify and understand the nuances of your environment. This is where contextual intelligence plays a crucial role in fostering better perception. Contextual intelligence (CI) is the capacity to recognize and navigate the complexity of different situations, environments, or contexts by integrating knowledge, perception, and intuition to make better decisions. Understanding the unique dynamics of each moment, identifying the variables affecting that moment, and adjusting your behavior to achieve a better outcome are how CI contributes to perception.

In this chapter, we'll explore Contextual Intelligence, the 3D Thinking Framework™, and the critical meta-skills that enhance perception. You'll understand how contextual intelligence can sharpen your ability to perceive the world around you to make better decisions and how to cultivate this crucial ability.

## UNDERSTANDING CONTEXTUAL INTELLIGENCE

In my research and work on contextual intelligence, I've described twelve behaviors organized around a framework I call 3D Thinking (hindsight, insight, and foresight). These twelve behaviors are fundamental to developing and applying contextual intelligence and help the development of perception.

### 12 Contextual Intelligence Behaviors

The twelve behaviors are practices and habits that allow you to navigate complex environments and make decisions attuned to the unique circumstances of each situation. These behaviors include:

1. **Change agent** – Demonstrates the courage to raise difficult and challenging questions that others may perceive as a threat to the status quo.
2. **Cognitive diversity** – Aligns diverse ideas by creating and facilitating opportunities for people with diverse backgrounds or experiences to interact in a nondiscriminatory manner.
3. **Communitarian** – Demonstrates involvement in community and civic responsibilities. Embraces civic obligations wholeheartedly.
4. **Consensus builder** – Demonstrates collaboration by convincing others of the value of a common or different point of view.
5. **Constructive use of influence** – Demonstrates the effective use of different types of power in developing and promoting an image.

6. **Critical thinker** – Connects disconnected ideas and experiences.
7. **Diagnosis context** – Interprets and responds to shifts or changes in one's surroundings, and can identify what contributed toward that shift.
8. **Future-minded** – Sees beyond contradictions (or obstacles) to a future others cannot yet see. Articulates that future to others clearly and succinctly.
9. **Influencer** – Demonstrates interpersonal skill by non-coercively affecting the actions and decisions of others.
10. **Intentional leadership** – Demonstrates awareness of and is proactive concerning their strengths and weaknesses.
11. **Mission-minded** – Recognizes how performance, attitude, and actions influence what others perceive to be true about the people or organizations they represent.
12. **Multicultural leadership** – Builds rapport with culturally and ethnically diverse individuals.

These twelve behaviors, when practiced simultaneously, help you see a more complete picture of any given situation and allow you to respond in ways that are more aligned with the context. These twelve behaviors are the building blocks to developing more accurate perception. Over time, consistently applying these behaviors sharpens your awareness, enhances decision-making, and helps you navigate complex situations with greater clarity and confidence.

## 3D THINKING: HINDSIGHT, INSIGHT, AND FORESIGHT

Three-dimensional (3D) Thinking is a framework that integrates three time orientations: the past, present, and future. These dramatically impact *how* you perceive things and *what* you are perceiving. These time orientations are referred to as hindsight, insight, and foresight. Each of them provides a different perspective on how to approach complex problems and decisions.

The twelve contextual intelligence behaviors fit into the 3D Thinking Framework. There are four behaviors in each of the three time orientations. The four hindsight behaviors are: consensus builder, constructive use of influence, critical thinker, and influencer. The four insight behaviors are: cognitive diversity, communitarian, mission-minded, and multicultural leadership. Lastly, the four foresight behaviors are: change agent, diagnosis context, future-minded, and intentional leadership.

### Hindsight

Hindsight is the ability to look at past experiences, decisions, and outcomes to gain valuable lessons and knowledge. It's about learning from the past without being sucked back into it. When applying hindsight, reflect on what worked and what didn't and use that information to inform your current decision-making.

As hindsight is developed it becomes more intuitive—though no less deliberate. You've heard that hindsight is 20/20, which means it is easier to understand a complex event after-the-fact, versus when it is being experienced. Once distanced from the event, the pattern emerges and makes more sense. Misinterpreting the past or looking at the wrong aspect of the past increases the probability of a mistake.

Unfortunately, many people inadvertently misuse hindsight by selectively remembering. Every single one of us is markedly predisposed to thinking errors like confirmation bias, hindsight bias, the availability heuristic, and other cognitive biases that keep us from remembering what actually happened. Unless we screen our hindsight through the perspectives of others or keep a detailed journal, it usually misleads us. When hindsight is used correctly, our past mistakes can be turned into valuable lessons.

For example, a leader who applies hindsight may recognize that a particular marketing strategy failed in the past because it didn't align with the current cultural climate. By learning from that mistake, they can avoid repeating it, or they can realize the cultural climate has shifted since then and that, with a few tweaks, it may work this time. Accurate hindsight sharpens your perception by allowing you to draw connections between past experiences and future needs.

### Insight

Insight is the ability to dial in to the present moment. It's about perceiving the underlying patterns and emotions that are at play in a current situation. Insight requires you to be fully present and aware of your own biases and the biases of other participants. When our insight is operating efficiently, it considers both explicit and implicit (or tacit) cues to form a more comprehensive understanding of what's happening. Insight is the product of hindsight and foresight. Insight is expressed by the equation H + F = I and can never be fully actualized without input from hindsight and foresight.

In personal relationships, insight might mean recognizing that a spouse's frustration isn't about the surface issue being blamed, but something deeper, such as the lack of feeling secure. Developing insight allows you to read between the lines and make sense of complex interpersonal dynamics, helping you respond in a way that leads to greater harmony and understanding.

For example, hindsight tells you these patterns of behavior and facial expressions mean something other than what is being explicitly communicated. Along with that is the knowledge of an upcoming event, requiring foresight, like the family vacation. Using hindsight and foresight generates the insight that your partner may be stressed about money and wondering how the vacation is going to be financed.

### Foresight

Foresight involves articulating future desires clearly and preparing for any obstacles to that future. It's the ability to project forward and imagine how current actions and decisions will bring the future to the present. While no one can predict the future with certainty, foresight enables you to assess potential scenarios, evaluate risks, and make informed choices that increase the likelihood of success.

Parents know how crucial foresight is. Parents who possess foresight can foresee the consequences of the choices their children make, allowing them to take preemptive action to mitigate negative outcomes or to capitalize on future opportunities. Foresight helps parents become proactive rather than reactive, which is key to navigating uncertainty.

My wife and I were very intentional about this when our kids were younger. We wanted them to make good choices and avoid the mistakes that we and many other kids made. We leveraged our foresight by telling them what was likely to happen and advising them to decide in advance how they should respond when those "predictions" came true. For example, drugs and alcohol at parties. When they were about eight or nine years old, long before they would be invited to these kinds of parties, we began to tell them that one day they will be at a party and be offered drugs or alcohol. We told them that the kids who decide to participate in that illegal activity do so not because they are bad kids, but because they didn't see it coming and panicked. Not wanting to be excluded, they will be reactive instead of proactive. So, I asked them to begin to think about what decision they will make when that opportunity occurs. I promised them it would occur.

From time to time over the years I would ask about it and reinforce how positive I was it would happen and not to be surprised by it. Well, time passed and, as they were popular athletes in school, that day came. Imagine their shock when they came home from a party where drugs were offered. They couldn't wait to tell me how right I was, and maybe they even thought I was a prophet. But they had already made their choice, so they enjoyed the party and were able to successfully refuse because they had expected it and already made their decision on how they would handle it.

When you are intentional about integrating hindsight, insight, and foresight, you create a powerful, multidimensional approach to navigating complex situations. It also helps foster perceptive ability. Three-dimensional thinking enables you to learn new lessons from the past, acutely understand the salient features of the present, and articulate the desired future—all essential elements of accurate perception.

## WHAT ARE META-SKILLS?

Meta-skills are emergent abilities that integrate hard and soft skills, forming a foundation from which new abilities and capacities emerge. They enhance and activate unknown or unrealized skills. CI wakes up these dormant skills, allowing individuals to contribute to a variety of contexts. These are higher-order skills and accelerate the development of new skills when the situation calls for them, but not before. Becoming proficient in meta-skills management requires a continual pursuit of hard and soft skills. The synergy of these two types of skills creates a new third set of meta-skills.

Meta-skills are overarching abilities that help you process information, solve problems, and adapt to new challenges. In short, they foster perception. They are not specific to one task or situation but apply broadly across different areas of life and work. Meta-skills enhance your ability to perceive and respond to the unique demands of different contexts.

Author Dr. Melis Senova states in a 2020 *Journal of Behavioural Economics and Social Systems* article of the same name, that "meta-skills are the key to human potential." Senova describes meta-skills, when present, as allowing us to "tolerate complexity, navigate ambiguity ..." (p. 137) and to see the totality of events and situations through their interconnections. Senova is a passionate advocate for realigning education to meet the needs of our complex modern era.

She claims that in an age where artificial intelligence and automation increasingly replace traditional roles, the need for meta-skills—such as creativity, leadership, emotional intelligence, agility, and resilience—has become essential. Perception requires moving beyond what can be learned through standardized knowledge.

She claims that today's workforce is still being trained for roles suited to past centuries, leaving them underprepared for modern, creative workplaces, which demand flexibility and innovative thinking. I agree. It's time to recognize and foster meta-skills—qualities that empower individuals to evolve, lead, and perceive reality as it is, not how we want it to be.

I have listed three central meta-skills that support the development of contextually intelligent perception: embracing complexity, leveraging synchronicity, and developing tacit knowledge.

### Embracing Complexity

The world is rarely simple, and achieving excellence requires you to be comfortable with complexity. Embracing complexity means recognizing that most situations involve multiple factors, layers of meaning, and competing priorities. Rather than trying to simplify everything, people with contextual intelligence embrace the intricacies and learn to navigate them effectively.

A helpful way to understand complexity is through the analogy of LEGO bricks and Play-Doh. Complicated problems are like LEGO sets—they may involve many pieces, but with the right instructions and effort, they can be disassembled and put back together predictably. Each piece has a clear function, and while the task may be challenging, there is a structured pathway to completion. When one colored brick is removed, a different color can replace it with minimal disruption to the other bricks. In contrast, complex problems resemble Play-Doh—once mixed, the colors cannot easily be separated or restored to their original form. Each individual color is forever changed by its being mixed with other colors. Complex situations are fluid, interconnected, and often resistant to linear solutions.

For example, in a corporate restructuring, a perceptive leader recognizes that the situation is more like Play-Doh than LEGO. It's not just about rearranging organizational charts; the process affects employee morale, company culture, and long-term strategy in unpredictable ways that are not always immediately observable. By embracing complexity, leaders can better anticipate the ripple effects of decisions, address the emotional and cultural components of change, and foster solutions that are adaptable rather than rigid. This mindset equips you to perceive the hidden dynamics that others might overlook and approach challenges with greater agility and depth.

### Leveraging Synchronicity

Synchronicity refers to the meaningful coincidences or alignments that occur in life. While it may seem abstract, learning to recognize and leverage synchronicity is a powerful meta-skill. It means paying attention to the seemingly unrelated events or signals that provide valuable insight or opportunity.

Leveraging synchronicity might mean recognizing that a conversation with a colleague on an unrelated issue unexpectedly provides the solution to a problem you've been facing at home. People with high contextual intelligence are attuned to these moments, noticing when things align in unexpected ways and seizing opportunities that others might overlook.

Carl Jung, the Swiss psychiatrist, coined the term "synchronicity" in the 1920s, though he would refine and elaborate on the concept over the next few decades. Jung's journey to defining synchronicity began with his fascination with the mysterious intersections between the inner and outer worlds—moments where a person's inner experience seemed to align uncannily with external events in a way that defied simple causation. This led Jung to explore the nature of meaningful coincidences, ultimately framing them as a phenomenon distinct from cause-and-effect, where two or more events occur together in a way that feels deeply significant.

One of Jung's most famous experiences with synchronicity involved a patient recounting a dream about a golden scarab, an ancient Egyptian symbol of transformation and rebirth. Just as she was describing the dream to him, a real scarab beetle appeared at the window, and Jung, feeling that this couldn't be a mere coincidence, opened the window to allow it in. This beetle was one of the European variety, known as a rose chafer, which bore a close resemblance to the Egyptian scarab. For Jung, the synchronicity of the beetle's appearance aligned perfectly with the emotional breakthrough his patient was on the brink of achieving.

To Jung, synchronicity meant that two events could be related not by cause but by meaning. He further collaborated with Nobel-winning physicist Wolfgang Pauli, whose work on quantum physics influenced Jung's thinking on how synchronicity might fit into a broader scientific framework. This cross-disciplinary dialogue convinced Jung that synchronicity wasn't a fringe idea but rather an essential part of understanding the mysteries of consciousness, time, and the collective unconscious.

Jung published his thoughts in his 1952 essay, "Synchronicity: An Acausal Connecting Principle." The term has since inspired thinkers in psychology, philosophy, and the arts, with many finding synchronicity a compelling way to frame life's most inexplicable coincidences. For Jung, synchronicity was a reminder that there are patterns to life's mysteries that reach beyond rational explanations.

### Developing Tacit Knowledge

Tacit knowledge is the unspoken, intuitive understanding that comes from experience. It's the kind of knowledge that's hard to put into words but is essential for making sound judgments in complex situations. Developing tacit knowledge requires a willingness to learn from experience, reflect on your actions, and internalize the lessons gained over time.

Michael Polanyi famously articulated this idea with the phrase, "We know more than we can tell." For example, a skilled surgeon might be able to perform complex procedures with precision, but the depth of their expertise—developed through years of practice—can't be fully explained in a textbook. They rely on tacit knowledge to make decisions in real time, sensing things that aren't explicitly taught.

Tacit knowledge is closely related to perception because it shapes how we interpret and respond to situations. Our perception of subtle cues, patterns, and contexts improves as we accumulate tacit knowledge, enabling us to make better judgments and decisions. In essence, tacit knowledge informs and refines our perception, allowing us to act with greater insight in complex or nuanced scenarios.

Tacit knowledge can be developed and even accelerated by curating new experiences. People open to experiencing new things and intentionally putting themselves in new or novel situations tend to develop tacit knowledge more quickly.

## THE CONNECTION BETWEEN CONTEXTUAL INTELLIGENCE AND BEING PERCEPTIVE

Contextual intelligence and perception are deeply interconnected. Being perceptive means more than just noticing what's happening around you—it involves understanding the context, why it's happening, and the potential impact of those interactions. Contextual intelligence enhances your perception by providing you with the tools to interpret and make sense of the subtleties in different environments. When you combine perception with contextual intelligence, you can:

1. **See beneath the surface:** You're not just observing what's happening; you're understanding the why behind it. Contextual intelligence gives you the deeper insight needed to read between the lines and grasp the full meaning of a situation.
2. **Adapt to different environments:** Perceptive people know how to adjust their behavior based on the context. Whether it's a boardroom meeting or a family gathering, contextual intelligence allows you to perceive the nuances of each environment and respond accordingly.
3. **Make wiser decisions:** Perception and contextual intelligence work together to improve your decision-making process. By perceiving the unique aspects of each situation and applying contextual intelligence, you can make choices that are aligned with both the present moment and the future.

**FIGURE 2: CONTEXTUAL INTELLIGENCE CIRCUMPLEX™**

## THE POWER OF CONTEXTUAL INTELLIGENCE IN ENHANCING PERCEPTION

Contextual intelligence is more than a tool for decision-making—it's a way of perceiving the world that allows you to navigate complexity, adapt to new challenges, and find clarity in ambiguity. Through 3D Thinking, the twelve CI behaviors, and the development of the three CI meta-skills, you can sharpen your perception and approach life's challenges with greater wisdom and precision.

By practicing contextual intelligence, you can deepen your understanding of the world around you, improve your relationships, and make decisions that are attuned to the unique circumstances of each situation. In doing so, you'll not only become more perceptive—you'll become more effective, adaptive, and resilient in your pursuit of becoming EPIC.

# 9

# OBSTACLES TO DEVELOPING PERCEPTION

Developing strong perception doesn't come without challenges. Common mistakes and misconceptions can cloud our awareness, limit our ability to perceive clearly, and make us miss important details or connections.

In this chapter, I will explore how to overcome obstacles to perception by highlighting examples from family life and leadership, showing how overcoming these roadblocks leads to greater clarity, stronger relationships, and better decision-making.

Throughout the distractions of life—being newlywed, having children, changing careers, cancer—I have come to deeply understand the concept of inattentional blindness, the tendency to not see what's right before us because we're too focused elsewhere. In times of adversity, this can make us miss moments of strength, connection, and insight because our minds are fixated on survival, fear, or uncertainty.

Inattentional blindness, also called perceptual blindness, is vividly illustrated by the famous "Invisible Gorilla" experiment conducted by researchers Christopher Chabris and Daniel Simons. In this classic study, participants were asked to watch a video of people passing a basketball and to count the number of passes made by players wearing white shirts. Midway through the video, a person in a gorilla suit walks into the scene, beats their chest, and then walks off. Astonishingly, nearly half the viewers didn't see the gorilla at all. Their intense focus on counting the passes blinded them to the unexpected presence of a gorilla walking right through the scene.

This experiment powerfully reveals how our attention can limit our perception, even when something as conspicuous as a gorilla is directly in front of us. When our mental "filters" are trained on one aspect of life, there's a real risk of missing the profound and meaningful things happening around us. This perfectly illustrates the now iconic quote from Stephen Covey, "We see the world, not as it is, but as we are …"

Early on, my thoughts centered on the unknowns of my diagnosis, and this narrow focus overshadowed any positives that were unfolding around me. The love and moments of profound clarity offered by friends and family were right there, but my mental lens was so narrowly focused on getting through each day that I hardly noticed them.

Inattentional blindness isn't just a quirk of the mind that can help us filter noise or prioritize urgent information; it's a barrier that prevents us from fully engaging with life's complexities. The New Testament offers a powerful illustration of this in the story of the two men on the road to Emmaus. In their grief from the aftermath of Christ's crucifixion and their subsequent loss of hope, they walked beside the resurrected Jesus without realizing who He was. They weren't expecting Him in that moment or even considering the possibility He could be alive. Their perception was constrained by their sorrow and expectations, showing how we too can become blind to the deeper meanings and opportunities present in the struggles that are occurring right in front of our eyes.

Reflecting on this has helped me to intentionally shift my perception. I've learned to look past the immediate uncertainty and search for opportunities, even in unexpected places. This broader view has revealed strengths I didn't know I had and connections I might have otherwise missed. True perception involves more than just seeing—it's about being open and aware, willing to look for what we might otherwise overlook.

## MISTAKES THAT BLOCK YOUR AWARENESS

### Mistake #1: Ignoring Feedback from Others

One of the most common mistakes that blocks perception is ignoring feedback from others. Feedback offers us an external perspective, an opportunity to see our blind spots and areas for improvement. Yet, we often dismiss it because it makes us uncomfortable or because we think we know better. Ignoring feedback prevents us from seeing the bigger picture and limits our ability to grow and adapt.

After my diagnosis, I faced this challenge head-on. I had always prided myself on being capable and self-reliant, and I thought I knew how to manage my health, career, and personal life. However, as the treatment progressed, I began receiving feedback that I wasn't as receptive as I should have been. I was withdrawing emotionally in an attempt to not let this disrupt my life or routines. I didn't know it then, but I wasn't focused enough on my mental and emotional well-being—just my physical recovery.

Initially, I brushed off these comments. I believed I could handle things on my own, and that pushing through would be enough. But as time went on, I realized that ignoring feedback was preventing me from healing—not just physically, but emotionally. I didn't even realize I needed emotional and mental healing. It wasn't until I actively started listening to the concerns of my friends and adjusting my behavior that I began to see a path forward that wasn't just about surviving but about finding balance and growth.

### How to Overcome This Mistake:

1. **Listen with an open heart and mind:** Allow others to offer their perspectives without jumping to conclusions, assuming you know where this conversation is heading, or defending your point of view. If they are perceiving something about your behavior or attitude, you must accept the fact that you did something to warrant their perception. Own it. Don't make excuses for it.
2. **Actively reflect on feedback:** Take time to consider the feedback you receive, even if it's uncomfortable or difficult to hear. Many times, feedback like this can be an incredible gift if we approach it with humility.
3. **Act on what you learn:** Adjust your actions based on the feedback you receive. This is perhaps easier said than done, but the rewards can be life changing. True

growth happens when you're willing to adapt your ideas and PIVOT.

**Mistake #2: Relying Too Much on First Impressions**

Another significant obstacle to perception is relying too much on first impressions. While first impressions can be powerful, they are often incomplete and based on superficial cues and confirmation bias. When you allow your initial judgment, a priori, to dictate your view of a person or situation, you may miss important information that emerges.

I've learned the hard way that first impressions can be misleading, especially when navigating something as complex as metastatic prostate cancer. At the beginning of my treatment journey, I formed quick judgments about the medical professionals I was working with. I felt that one of my doctors wasn't empathetic enough because of their direct and efficient communication style. This initial impression led me to doubt their ability to support me. But as time went on, I realized that this doctor's straightforward approach was what prompted me to take the necessary action I needed to start on my road to recovery. My initial judgment was clouded by my emotions, and I had missed the deeper level of care that they were providing through their expertise.

First impressions can also interfere with family dynamics. I remember meeting one of my son's new friends and immediately forming an opinion that they weren't a good influence. Based on a brief interaction, I concluded that this person was trouble. But as I spent more time observing their interactions, I realized that my first impression had been wrong. This child was loyal and supportive, and my initial reaction was based on my own biases and not accurate perception.

**How to Overcome This Mistake:**

1. **Suspend immediate judgment:** Resist the urge to form a solid opinion after a single encounter. Give situations and people time to reveal their true nature.
2. **Seek deeper understanding:** Ask questions and create multiple interactions over time to gather more context before reaching conclusions.
3. **Be willing to revise your view:** Accept that your first impression may not always be correct and be open to changing your perspective as more information becomes available.

**Mistake #3: Overlooking Subtle Cues**

Often, the most important elements of perception lie in the subtle, unspoken cues—the body language, tone of voice, or the context of a situation. Overlooking subtle cues can lead to missed opportunities for understanding, empathy, and insight. When we rush through life without paying attention to these details, we miss any deeper meaning behind people's words or actions.

It's easy to overlook subtle cues, especially in communication with children. My wife and I raised two boys and boys aren't always vocal about their struggles. But I noticed they were spending more time alone and seemed quieter than usual. If we had dismissed these subtle changes in behavior, we would have missed an opportunity to check in and offer support. By paying attention to these small cues, we were able to open a conversation that helped us navigate the situation together.

**How to Overcome This Mistake:**

1. **Slow down:** Take the time to observe body language, tone, and the environment. Small details can reveal a lot.
2. **Be present:** Practice being fully present in your interactions, so you're more attuned to the subtle dynamics of conversations.
3. **Ask follow-up questions:** If you sense something is off, ask clarifying questions to explore what might be happening beneath the surface.

## MISGUIDED PERCEPTION

Let's consider the all too familiar story of Jennifer, a Senior Account Manager and consultant known for her sharp instincts and ability to "read" clients quickly. When an eco-friendly fashion start-up approached her for help launching a new clothing line, Jennifer was confident she had this project in the bag. Grace, the clothing line's marketing director, stressed the importance of sustainability and connecting with ethically conscious millennials. Jennifer listened, nodded, and left the meeting believing she had a firm grasp of the project.

Jennifer's confidence rested on two major assumptions. First, she was a natural at perceiving the environment, something you either had or didn't—and she believed she had it. She had honed and refined her perceptive skills early in her career, so she didn't need to put extra effort into that now. Second, Jennifer was convinced that perceptive insights strike instantly. Based on the initial meeting, she felt she had Grace figured out.

Jennifer moved fast, crafting a campaign focused on partnering with popular influencers to promote the new clothing line. She didn't bother with follow-up questions or take time to research the brand's ethos or their competitors further. She trusted her gut and went with her first impression. Everything seemed straightforward to her.

However, a month into the project, Grace grew frustrated. The influencers Jennifer had chosen didn't align with her values, and the campaign felt generic, missing the authenticity and deeper ethical messaging Grace wanted. Grace finally reached out to Jennifer's management team, expressing her concerns. Jennifer was offended and taken aback—how could she have gotten it so wrong? Worse yet, how could her assessment be wrong?

The answer lay in Jennifer's misconceptions about perception. By believing that her ability to understand clients was a natural talent, Jennifer had neglected to put in the effort required to truly get to know Grace's needs. She hadn't done enough research on the sustainability movement or the specific needs of eco-conscious consumers. Worse, by assuming perception happens instantly, she had relied too heavily on her first impression of Grace's goals, failing to engage in follow-up conversations that could have clarified the brand's deeper mission.

Faced with the reality of her mistaken assumptions, Jennifer realized that perception isn't something that happens once and then remains static. She needed to approach perception as an evolving process, one that required constant attention and adjustment. Moving forward, she committed to changing her approach.

Jennifer learned that perception is a skill to be practiced, not an innate talent. Understanding the needs of others requires ongoing effort, reflection, and a willingness to adapt. She also realized that perception takes time. She needed to slow down and recognize that her first impression wasn't always the full picture. She started revisiting her campaign strategies regularly, asking more questions, and giving herself time to better understand the unique dynamics of each client.

## THE FIRST INSTINCT FALLACY

The First Instinct Fallacy is the mistaken belief that our initial response to a situation is always the most accurate or best choice, often leading us to rely on gut reactions rather than considering other possibilities or gathering additional information. This cognitive bias causes people to overvalue their first impressions or decisions, assuming that their immediate judgment is inherently superior. Our initial instinct can often be flawed, influenced by limited information, emotions, or unconscious biases.

For example, test-takers are often told to trust their first instinct when faced with tough multiple-choice questions on exams. The advice suggests that your first impulse—or gut reaction—is usually correct. However, research clearly indicates that this strategy can actually lower performance. Research has repeatedly shown that, in reality, test-takers are more likely to change an answer from wrong to right, which leads to better test scores.

This misconception persists because of a psychological bias. According to Justin Kruger, a psychologist at NYU Stern, people remember the times they change a correct answer to an incorrect one more vividly than when they change an answer from wrong to right. The frustration of "if only I had stuck with my gut response" sticks with us, while the positive instances of correcting a wrong answer are far less memorable because we tend to give ourselves the benefit of the doubt. This leads to the false belief that changing your initial answers usually harms performance, even though that has been disproven, and the opposite has been shown to be true. The lesson here is to not be afraid to critique your initial impression.

## MYTHS THAT LIMIT YOUR ABILITY TO PERCEIVE

In addition to behavioral mistakes, there are also myths that limit your ability to develop stronger perception. These myths create barriers, leading you to believe that perception is beyond your control or that it is something you can't improve over time.

### Myth #1: Perception Is an Inborn Talent

One of the most common myths is that perception is an inborn talent—something you either have or don't. Many people believe that some individuals are naturally gifted at perceiving things clearly, while others are not. This myth leads people to give up on improving their perception because they think it's a fixed ability.

Before my cancer diagnosis, I subconsciously subscribed to this myth. I believed that I was naturally good at understanding situations, and I didn't see the need to actively work on my perception skills. But cancer changed that. As I faced new, unfamiliar challenges, I realized that my natural ability wasn't enough. I had to actively develop my perception, learning to listen more deeply, observe more carefully, and adapt to new realities.

### How to Overcome This Myth:

1. **Adopt a growth mindset:** Recognize that perception is a skill that can be developed over time through practice and effort.
2. **Engage in reflective practice:** Regularly reflect on how you interpret situations and how you might improve your ability to perceive accurately. Try the R4 Process described earlier.
3. **Seek feedback:** Ask others how they perceive your ability to understand situations. Use their feedback to identify areas for growth.

### Myth #2: Perceptive Insights Strike Instantly

Another limiting myth is the belief that perception happens instantly—that you should immediately be able to grasp the full scope of a situation or a person. This myth can lead to frustration when your perception doesn't align with what is true. This type of incongruity is particularly harmful as it usually results in people assuming others are wrong or even "out to get them." Believing that perceptions strike you naturally can cause you to make snap judgments that are incomplete or inaccurate.

In my own journey, I've learned that perception takes time to develop. Adversity tends to be overwhelming. There is a flood of information and emotions. It was impossible to perceive everything clearly. I had to give myself the space to process the situation over time, allowing others close to me to help me perceive reality and allowing my perceptive capacity to evolve as I gathered more information and gained clarity about my treatment and life moving forward.

A great example of this can be found in the actions of Paul, told in Acts 15:36–40. Paul, preparing for one of his missionary journeys was asked about taking Mark as a companion. Paul refused. He believed, from one earlier interaction, that Mark would be detrimental to their mission. Paul was so sure of his hasty assessment that he broke friendship with his most trusted companion and teammate, Barnabas. Only years later did Paul realize his perceptual blindness and encourage others to receive Mark as a valuable companion, who he himself benefited from (2 Timothy 4:11; Philemon 1:23; Colossians 4:10).

The good news is that Paul, famously perceptive as one of the primary writers of the New Testament, was not immune to this common myth and other cognitive biases, giving us hope that this myth can be overcome.

### How to Overcome This Myth:

1. **Be patient:** Give yourself time to fully understand situations. Don't rush to conclusions.
2. **Allow perception to unfold:** Accept that it may take time for you to perceive the full complexity of a situation or a relationship. Hastily made assumptions are often missing critical nuance and context.
3. **Stay open to change:** As you gather more information, be open to adjusting your initial perceptions based on new insights.

## OVERCOMING OBSTACLES TO PERCEPTION

Perception is a vital skill that helps us navigate life's complexities, but it's often blocked by common mistakes and limiting myths. Whether it's ignoring feedback, relying too much on first impressions, or overlooking subtle cues, these obstacles can prevent us from seeing situations and people clearly. Additionally, myths about perception—such as the belief that it's an inborn talent or something that happens instantly—can hold us back from developing this crucial skill. By recognizing and overcoming these roadblocks, we can enhance our awareness, improve our decision-making, and deepen our relationships. Whether in personal life, leadership, or family dynamics, sharpening our perception allows us to connect more fully with the world and achieve EPIC status.

# 10

# HOW TO SHARPEN YOUR PERCEPTION

Perception is a skill that allows us to navigate our relationships, careers, and personal experiences with greater clarity. It helps us understand not just what is happening around us, but why it's happening, how it affects others, and how we can respond effectively. But perception isn't something that automatically happens. It's not something you are simply born being able to do. It's a skill that can be sharpened and honed through intentional practice.

In this chapter, we will explore various techniques for sharpening your perception. These include cultivating mindfulness, developing awareness through meditation, practicing presence, honing active listening skills, and challenging your own biases. The goal is to become more aware, more attentive, and more thoughtful in how you engage with the world.

## HOW TO CULTIVATE MINDFULNESS IN EVERYDAY LIFE

Mindfulness is an effective way to sharpen your perception. It's about being fully present in the moment, aware of your surroundings, thoughts, and feelings without becoming overly reactive or overwhelmed. Cultivating mindfulness helps you pay attention to the details you might otherwise miss, allowing for insights into the situations and people around you. I believe that mindfulness is about keeping still and knowing you are in the presence of the "other" whether that other is divine or just an acquaintance. Silencing the noise is necessary to be able to perceive what is happening. What often gets in the way is a noisy or uneasy soul.

I am convinced that when we learn how to actively manage our emotions by being alert to how our own souls—our mind, will, and emotions—are being influenced, life springs forth from that awareness. An EPIC life can flow out of us like a natural spring if we learn to guard our hearts.

### How to Incorporate Guarding Your Heart into Your Daily Routine

1. **Mindful morning practice:** Start your day with a few minutes of selfless thinking where you focus on God. Whether through meditation, deep breathing, or simply sitting quietly with a cup of coffee, use the time to become aware of your surroundings, how your body feels, and what God may be trying to tell you.
2. **Mindfulness during daily activities:** You can practice mindfulness while doing routine activities like washing dishes, walking, or commuting. Instead of letting your

mind wander, focus on the sensations, sounds, and actions of the moment. Try to notice something about what you are doing that you've never noticed before.

3. **Pause and breathe throughout the day:** Whenever you feel overwhelmed or stressed, take a minute and pause. Close your eyes, take deep breaths, and refocus on the present. This helps you avoid reactive responses and sharpens your perception of what's really happening around you.

By weaving this type of awareness into your everyday life, you become more attuned to subtle changes in your environment, emotions, and the behavior of others. This heightened capacity to discern is the first step in sharpening your perception.

## DEVELOPING AWARENESS THROUGH MEDITATION AND PRAYER

Meditation is another powerful tool for improving perception. It's not just about relaxation; it's about training your mind to observe without self-condemnation, helping you develop a deeper awareness of your surroundings.

### How Meditation Enhances Perception

1. **Increased focus and clarity:** Meditation strengthens your ability to focus on the present moment, reducing distractions and noise. With practice, this focus carries over into everyday situations, allowing you to perceive details more clearly and make better decisions.

2. **Greater emotional awareness:** Meditation helps you become more aware of your emotions and feelings and how they influence what you perceive. When you understand your emotional responses, you can better separate your feelings from reality and see situations more objectively.
3. **Enhanced self-reflection:** Regular meditation leads to greater self-reflection, allowing you to understand your own biases and assumptions. This self-awareness helps you avoid letting those biases cloud your judgment, which sharpens your perception of others.

I meditate and pray just about every day and have for thirty or more years. If you're not accustomed to it, just start with five minutes a day. Focus on gently bringing your attention to sensory inputs, the feel of the pants on your legs, the texture of the chair fabric you are sitting on, the subtle noise of birds chirping behind the hectic noise of road traffic. It is natural to have your mind wander. Don't worry about it; every time your mind wanders just bring it back to the present. After I've settled, I like to ask God how He is doing today and express my appreciation for how He accepts and loves me despite my flaws. Over time, extend your meditation practice to ten or fifteen minutes, and you'll notice an increase in both your perceptive capacity and clarity.

### PRACTICING PRESENCE: BEING IN THE MOMENT

Being present is about giving your full attention to the moment, whether you're engaged in a conversation, working on a task, or simply experiencing your surroundings. When you're truly present, your perception sharpens naturally because you're not distracted by worries, plans, or external noise. Attention to the moment becomes a gateway to clarity and deeper connection. It is where distractions dissolve and you engage fully with what matters most, fostering insight, creativity, and meaningful progress. By anchoring yourself in the present, you create space for intentionality, allowing focus to flow more effortlessly and transforming ordinary experiences into opportunities for growth and fulfillment.

### How to Practice Presence:

1. **Focus on one task at a time:** Multitasking dilutes your attention and weakens your perception—it fosters the inattentional blindness discussed in Chapter 9. Whether you're listening to a friend or working on a project, focus on one thing at a time, giving it your full attention.
2. **Engage with your senses:** Use all your senses to experience the present moment. Whether it's noticing the warmth or coolness of the air, the sounds of your environment, or the smell of your coffee, engaging your senses enhances your ability to fully perceive what's happening around you.
3. **Let go of the future and past:** Thoughts about the future or past can pull you out of the present moment. If you catch yourself drifting into these thoughts, gently bring yourself back. Practicing presence sharpens your awareness and improves your ability to recognize and respond to what's in front of you.

## THE ART OF INTENTIONAL LISTENING

Active listening has been part of professional education programs and training for decades. I almost hesitate to mention it because it is so familiar, we tend to assume we know what it is and how to do it. But is that really true? One of the most valuable ways to sharpen your perception and interactions with others is through intentional listening. Listening is more than just hearing words, repeating what you heard someone say, or asking clarifying questions—it's about understanding the message behind them, reading between the lines, and picking up on nonverbal cues.

### Learning to Listen Without Interrupting

Interrupting while someone is speaking disrupts the flow of conversation and signals that you're more focused on what you want to say than on truly understanding the other person. When you interrupt, you miss valuable information and risk misinterpreting what's being communicated. Interruption is more than just inserting yourself before the other person has finished speaking. A much more heinous form of interruption is disengaging with what is being said so you can think of a response, counterpoint, or rebuttal. It doesn't feel as rude, but it is very damaging. To sharpen your perception, practice employing the following ideas:

1. **Wait for a natural pause:** Resist the urge to jump in with your thoughts or responses before the other person has finished. Allow them to complete their point, and then respond thoughtfully.
2. **Use body language to show you're engaged:** Nod or provide verbal affirmations like "I see" or "go on" to

show that you're actively listening and processing what the speaker is saying.

3. **Clarify if necessary:** If something isn't clear, ask questions rather than interrupting with assumptions. This helps ensure that you fully understand before responding.
4. **Stay engaged:** Do not disengage to think of a rebuttal or response to what is being said.

## PAYING ATTENTION TO NONVERBAL CUES AND BODY LANGUAGE

In his book, *What Every Body Is Saying*, author Joe Navarro describes nonverbal communication as conveying information through facial expressions; gestures; haptics, which is physical touch; physical movements; posture; body adornment (e.g., clothes, jewelry, hairstyle, tattoos); and even the tone, timbre, and volume of an individual's voice. So much so that these things are often considered to be more important than the spoken words themselves. We have all had the experience of feeling that what someone said was not what they meant. Likewise, we all have had the experience of people acting or responding to something we said but did not mean. Accurately reading and interpreting body language and nonverbal cues are critical to perception.

William Shakespeare said, "All the world's a stage." In other words, people are always communicating, even if they are not talking! Learning to watch the actors on the stage of life is important for learning how to be more perceptive.

**How to Improve Your Perception of Nonverbal Cues:**

1. **Observe body language:** Notice the other person's posture, gestures, and facial expressions. Are they relaxed or tense? Open or closed off? These cues can give you deeper insight into their emotional state or level of engagement. Don't just assume someone is bored or being rude. Give them the benefit of the doubt. Be open to the possibility that, right now, you're not being all that engaging, or that you haven't stopped to take a breath in a long time. Many times, people's body language is a silent cue to you to stop whatever it is you're doing, which might mean it's time to stop talking.
2. **Listen to tone of voice:** The way something is said can be just as important as the words themselves. Is the speaker's tone calm, excited, frustrated, or hesitant? Paying attention to tone helps you understand the emotions behind the words.
3. **Watch for incongruity:** Sometimes, nonverbal cues don't align with what someone is saying. If a person says they're "fine" but their body language is closed off or tense, it may indicate that they're not fully expressing their true feelings. Picking up on these incongruities allows you to probe deeper, ask better questions and gain more accurate insights. Keep in mind that it's not possible to notice everything, so don't try; you can overdo it. But you can improve.

## CHALLENGING YOUR OWN BIASES

We all have and exhibit biases—assumptions that influence how we perceive the world. These biases can cloud our judgment, leading us to misinterpret situations or people. To sharpen your perception, it's essential to recognize and challenge your own biases.

### Recognizing Your Biases and Learning to Overcome Them

Biases often operate unconsciously, they are a set of assumptions (or heuristics, rules of thumb) we form over time about the world and the people in it. Biases influence our worldview. James W. Sire's book, *The Universe Next Door: A Basic Worldview Catalog*, is a foundational text on the concept of worldviews. In it, Sire explores how different worldviews shape the way people perceive reality, make decisions, and interpret their experiences. Sire describes a worldview as a framework through which individuals perceive the world and answer fundamental questions about existence, knowledge, morality, and purpose. He provides a detailed examination of various major worldviews, including theism, naturalism, existentialism, and postmodernism, among others. Sire breaks down the core beliefs and assumptions of each worldview, explaining how they influence a person's perception of truth, human nature, and the universe. Sire encourages his readers to reflect on their own beliefs and understand the perspectives of others, fostering greater awareness of the diverse "universes" of thought that exist alongside their own. To bring clarity to your own worldview ask yourself questions like:

- What assumptions am I making about this person or situation?

- Why do I believe this?
- Is what I believe about this based on facts or preconceived notions?
- Is what I believe about this based on a single incident?
- How might my personal experiences or beliefs be influencing my perception?

By becoming aware of your biases, you can consciously work to counteract them, if needed, leading to clearer, more objective perceptions.

## SEEKING DIFFERENT PERSPECTIVES TO SEE THE FULL PICTURE

One of the best ways to overcome biases and sharpen your perception is to seek different perspectives. In my work with contextual intelligence, I refer to this as *cognitive diversity*, or embracing others' ideas. Talking to people from diverse backgrounds with varying viewpoints broadens your understanding of situations and challenges your assumptions. Do this by engaging with people who think differently. Whether in personal or professional settings, have conversations with people who have different viewpoints, logic patterns, experiences, or backgrounds. This exposes you to new ways of seeing the world and prevents you from falling into the trap of narrow-minded thinking. Read widely. Don't just read more but read different genres too. Books, articles, and other media from diverse sources can provide new insights and help you perceive issues from different angles.

### The Power of Sharpened Perception

Sharpening your perception isn't a one-time effort—it's an ongoing practice. By cultivating mindful spirituality, developing awareness through meditation and prayer, honing your listening skills, and challenging your own biases, you can train yourself to see the world more clearly. The benefits of sharpened perception extend far beyond personal insight. They lead to better decision-making, stronger relationships, and a more thoughtful approach to life.

Ultimately, perception is about more than just what you see or hear. It's about how you interpret and respond to the world around you, and it's a skill that, with practice, can be refined to help you live with greater awareness and intention, which are fundamental to becoming EPIC.

# 11

# APPLYING PERCEPTION IN EVERYDAY LIFE

Perception is more than just an abstract skill. It's a practical ability you can use to make better decisions. Whether in personal interactions, high-stress environments, or crucial decision-making processes, perception helps you see beyond what appears on the surface.

In this last chapter of Part 2, we will explore how to apply perception in daily life, focusing on four key areas: reading people and understanding their motives, becoming more perceptive in high-stress situations, improving decision-making, and developing contextual intelligence.

## PEOPLE LITERACY

Reading people accurately and understanding their motives is one of the most valuable applications of perception. Author and expert jury consultant Dr. Jo-Ellan Dimitrius asserts in her classic book, *Reading People: How to Understand People and Predict Their*

*Behavior—Anytime, Anyplace*, that body language is one of the most potent forms of communication. According to Dimitrius, body language provides more insights about a person's real feelings, thoughts, and intentions than the words they choose to express themselves. Whether in a business meeting, social interaction, or personal relationship, knowing why someone behaves the way they do helps you respond in ways that are thoughtful and effective. Body language can help give away some of the *why* of behavior. Perception goes beyond hearing what people say—it's about picking up on unspoken signals, interpreting their emotional state, and understanding the deeper reasons behind their actions.

### Observe Body Language and Nonverbal Cues

As we've noted, people often communicate more through their body language than their words. If, for example, someone crosses their arms during a conversation, they may be feeling defensive or uncomfortable. On the other hand, open posture and relaxed facial expressions indicate that a person feels more at ease. If someone avoids eye contact, it could signal discomfort, dishonesty, or anxiety, while steady eye contact suggests engagement and confidence.

### Listen for Emotional Tone

The tone of someone's voice can reveal their underlying emotional state. Even if someone says they're "fine," a hesitant or shaky tone may indicate that they are anything but fine. Pay attention to changes in pitch, volume, and speed of speech, which can provide clues about how someone is feeling beneath the surface. When a colleague is giving you feedback in a fast and elevated tone, it may indicate that they are stressed or anxious. It can also mean that they need to be somewhere else and may be subconsciously signaling you to "let them go." By recognizing this, you can respond in a way that diffuses tension, perhaps by acknowledging their concerns and offering reassurance. This also helps you establish trust, making it easier to interact in the future.

### Ask Questions to Clarify Motives

Sometimes it's difficult to read people's motives solely based on observation and body language. In these situations, asking open-ended questions can help you understand their intentions more clearly. Instead of making assumptions, show curiosity and encourage the other person to explain their thought process. For example, if someone seems frustrated but isn't vocalizing their concerns, asking, "Can you tell me more about what you're thinking?" can open the door to understanding their motivations and help you address any underlying issues.

## BECOMING MORE PERCEPTIVE IN HIGH-STRESS SITUATIONS

High-stress situations can easily cloud our judgment and impede clear perception. When emotions run high, it's easy to misinterpret people's intentions or make snap judgments that lead to poor decisions. Becoming more perceptive in these situations requires maintaining clarity, staying calm, and stepping back to gain a broader understanding of the dynamics at play. Slowing down, refocusing, and attunement are three ways to maintain clear perception during high-stress situations.

### Slow Down Your Reactions

In high-stress situations, the pressure to act quickly can lead to reactive decision-making. Sharpening your perception in these moments means taking a step back and slowing down your reactions. It means engaging in what Daniel Kahneman calls system 2 thinking. By pausing, you give yourself the opportunity to assess the situation more accurately and avoid rash decisions.

If a tense disagreement arises in a team meeting, instead of immediately reacting out of frustration, take a moment to breathe, observe the emotions of those involved—including your own—and assess the broader context and the possible triggers of the tension. This will help you respond in a way that deescalates the situation and leads to a more productive resolution.

### Stay Focused on the Bigger Picture

High-stress situations can cause you to fixate on small details or personal grievances, losing sight of the bigger picture. Reminding yourself to remain aware of the overarching goals helps you stay objective and perceptive in these moments. In a heated negotiation, it's easy to become overly focused on winning each small point. However, by keeping the larger goal in mind and being willing to concede some minor things, you can navigate your behavior and responses more thoughtfully. Losing sight of the big picture is dangerous. Consider the following business scenario.

James, the CEO of a mid-sized start-up tech company, was deep in negotiations with a potential partner, a large software firm interested in acquiring a stake in James's start-up. The partnership promised major benefits: access to a broader customer base, additional resources for product development, increased brand visibility, and a big payday for James. But as the negotiations dragged on, James, not wanting to lose "his baby," became increasingly fixated on smaller details, like the exact percentages of equity and control over minor product features.

Despite the significant potential of the partnership, James couldn't let go of these minor points. He spent hours in meetings arguing about them, and the discussions grew more tense. His focus on control over a few small operational decisions clouded his judgment of the bigger picture and what this partnership could mean for the future of his company. He didn't take the time to step back and realize that the concessions on those small issues were insignificant compared to the growth opportunity this deal would provide.

Eventually, frustrated by the prolonged discussions, the larger firm decided to walk away. They felt that James was too difficult to work with, and they began seeking more flexible partners. James was left with his start-up still under his control, but without the partnership that could have propelled his business to the next level. By fixating on the little picture, James lost sight of the bigger picture. His inability to zoom out and see the overall value of the deal ultimately cost him the opportunity.

### Stay Attuned to Others' Emotional States

During high-stress situations, everyone involved may be experiencing heightened emotions, which can obscure communication and intentions. Being perceptive means recognizing these emotional states and adjusting your approach accordingly. By understanding how stress affects others, you can respond with greater empathy and effectiveness. When a colleague becomes agitated due to a tight deadline, recognizing that their frustration may stem from stress or outside expectations rather than a personal issue helps you manage the situation with patience and understanding.

I can't imagine how often other people made inaccurate assessments of our interaction simply because I was distracted by external trauma. Even more significant is how many cues I missed because I was internally focused on what I was dealing with in my personal health. Sometimes our perceptions about people are completely wrong for no other reason than that we are distracted by what is happening in our own lives. I have gone on record with my sons, telling them for years that "everyone has a story." We can never know everything that people are going through, but if we stay attuned to their emotional cues, we might be able to perceive something that triggers us to ask a more meaningful and thoughtful question that ultimately ends up helping them move forward.

## HOW PERCEPTION CAN IMPROVE DECISION-MAKING

Accurate perception is a key determinate in making better decisions. By understanding the nuances of a situation, considering multiple perspectives, and interpreting hidden dynamics, you can make more informed and thoughtful choices that lead to better outcomes. Here are a few recommendations on how developing your perceptive capacity can help your decision-making.

### Gather Information from Multiple Sources

Relying on one perspective or piece of information can lead to biased or incomplete decisions. Sharpening your perception involves gathering input from diverse sources, which helps you see a fuller picture. Here is a story that could have happened in any of our family lives.

Sam was considering transferring his job to a new city. His boss offered him a promotion and better pay if he'd help launch their product in this new market. The offer sounded promising—better pay, new career opportunities, and a bigger house. Naturally, Sam was excited and ready to jump on the opportunity, but something made him pause. Instead of making a quick decision, he decided to gather information from multiple sources before committing. First, he asked his wife, Sarah, for her input. She expressed concerns about the school system and how their two kids, Emily and Jack, might adjust.

Next, Sam called a few coworkers who had lived in the potential new city. They shared insights on the opportunity but also warned that the traffic was notoriously bad, and the cost of living was higher than expected. He even connected with a local realtor to get a better sense of the housing market and checked online reviews from local families to understand the community vibe. Finally, he talked to Emily and Jack, asking them how they felt about the idea of moving. Emily, a high school senior, was nervous about leaving her friends and school during such a critical year. Jack, younger and more adaptable, was excited about a bigger house.

Armed with this new information, Sam realized that while the job offer was great, the timing wasn't right for the family. Emily's upcoming graduation, the high cost of living, and the impact on their family life outweighed the job's immediate benefits. Instead of moving, Sam decided to negotiate with his company for a remote work arrangement, allowing him to advance his career while keeping the family in their current home.

This simple illustration depicts how important it is to seek external input, even if the people with diverse perspective are from your own family. Diverse perspectives are everywhere. It is not always necessary to go through great lengths to find external stakeholders with diverse cultural or ethnic backgrounds to give you a different perspective.

### Read Between the Lines

Perception sharpens decision-making by helping you interpret information that isn't immediately obvious. When faced with a decision, look beyond the surface data and ask yourself what might be influencing the situation or what factors have not been openly discussed. Remember, everyone has a story. If a business partner seems hesitant about moving forward on a project that requires hosting a new acquaintance but is cautious about opening their home to new people, consider that there may be unspoken concerns at play. By reading between the lines—such as noting their hesitation, tone, or body language—you may discover deeper reasons for their reluctance or ask better questions leading to a more informed and collaborative decision.

### Anticipate Potential Outcomes

Perceptive individuals anticipate potential outcomes based on their understanding of current dynamics. This foresight allows you to weigh the consequences of each decision and choose a path that leads to the most favorable outcome.

Foresight is dramatically different from fantasy. Perceptive people can use foresight to anticipate outcomes and describe where they are going, the actions and attitudes needed, and the obstacles that can get in the way. On the other hand, without much perception, foresight is lost, and fantasy steps in. Without perception, the future is merely a fantasy and little more than a dream that something good might eventually happen. By using foresight to anticipate outcomes, there is a much better chance of ending up in a desirable situation.

One of the best-known examples of foresight saving the day is what we covered in chapter 3: Netflix's shift to streaming. In the early 2000s, Netflix was primarily a DVD rental service, thriving in the era of physical media. However, CEO Reed Hastings had the foresight to recognize the potential of the internet and saw that streaming video would be the future of home entertainment.

In 2007, despite Netflix still making significant profits from DVDs, Hastings took a bold step and introduced the streaming service. This decision came before broadband internet was widespread and long before competitors like Blockbuster saw the threat. By the time streaming became the dominant way people consumed content, Netflix was already positioned as a leader in the market.

Hastings's anticipation of potential outcomes is legendary. Having the foresight to see the decline of physical media and the rise of digital content allowed Netflix to thrive and stay ahead of its competitors. This ultimately transformed it into the global entertainment giant it is today.

## DEVELOPING PERCEPTION THROUGH CONTEXTUAL INTELLIGENCE

Perception is not only understanding what's in front of you; it's about grasping the bigger picture and seeing how various elements in a situation interact, influence one another, and shape the outcome. This is where contextual intelligence factors in. Contextual intelligence allows you to understand the specific context in which a situation occurs, enabling you to apply your perception more effectively. By combining perception with contextual intelligence, you can see deeper layers of meaning, anticipate the impact of decisions, and make more informed choices.

Contextual intelligence involves understanding the social, cultural, political, emotional, and practical contexts. This is the contextual ethos, the setting where events unfold in real time. By developing your contextual intelligence, you sharpen your ability to perceive not just the immediate details but also the broader environment in which those details exist, including historical significance (hindsight), present day realities (insight), and anticipated outcomes (foresight). Insight, hindsight, and foresight converge to create 3D thinking.

One of the most critical elements of perception is recognizing how context shapes meaning. Context is everything. In *Hard Times: Leadership in America*, acclaimed author Barbara Kellerman explores how context plays a crucial role in shaping leadership. Kellerman argues that leadership is not solely defined by the leader's traits, behaviors, abilities, or decisions but is mostly influenced by the context. She emphasizes that broader social, economic, political, and technological forces—context—shape and constrain leadership more than their will or personality.

Kellerman asserts that it's context that influences not only what leaders can do but also how they are perceived and how followers respond to them. She calls for greater attention to understanding the context in which leadership unfolds, arguing that ignoring context can lead to a limited view of leadership.

Failing to recognize the influence of context in how you perceive is conceding to be irrelevant or perhaps mediocre at best.

### Identify the Underlying Dynamics of Situations

Contextual intelligence sharpens your perception by helping you recognize the underlying dynamics of a situation. It invites you to assess not just what is happening but why certain things may be happening. It helps you recognize the relationships, power structures, and emotional states at play. Having contextual intelligence means paying attention to the larger forces that influence individual behavior, including your own.

For example, if a team member is resistant to a new initiative, the surface issue may seem like laziness or stubbornness. However, with contextual intelligence, you might recognize that the underlying dynamic is concern about job security. By perceiving this deeper issue, you can address the real concerns instead of treating the resistance as defiance.

### Anticipate Consequences Based on Context

Contextual intelligence helps you sharpen your perception by allowing you to anticipate the consequences of actions. When you understand how different factors interact in each context, you can better predict how a situation might evolve and what the outcomes of your decisions might be. This foresight is enhanced by accurate hindsight and improves your ability to make informed decisions in the present.

Before implementing a major change at work, a perceptive leader with good contextual intelligence will consider how this change will impact different departments, employees' morale, stakeholders, and the organization's overall culture. Even before that though, the leader makes herself aware of past decisions and how they were made, and how they impacted morale and company culture. Armed with this hindsight, this allows her to anticipate challenges and address them proactively, leading to smoother transitions and better results.

**Learn to Adapt Your Perception Based on Context**

Perception is not a one-size-fits-all skill. Perception is fluid. It must be adapted to different situations; using contextual intelligence helps you adjust your perception based on those situations. Realizing that the metrics that determine success are always shifting allows you to constantly be mindful of how and what you perceive. By developing this ability, you can approach each situation with the most appropriate mindset and strategy, leading to clearer insights and better decision-making.

In a family, a perceptive parent may recognize that their teenager's withdrawal is not just about typical adolescent behavior but is influenced by the unique stress of a new school, new peer groups, and their growing uncertainty about their place in the world. This level of contextual intelligence equips the parents to stay engaged and possibly help their child navigate their new context. Understanding the context helps the parent approach the issue with more compassion and support, rather than frustration or misunderstanding.

Perhaps there is no greater example of contextual intelligence helping navigate uncertainty than the story of how the tribe of Issachar helped transition the nation of Israel to a new king and new government. The story is told in the Old Testament in 1 Chronicles 12:32. The tribe of Issachar are described as those "who understood the times and knew what Israel should do." This brief mention highlights their ability to perceive the broader context of their era and provide wise counsel in response to it. During a period of great political transition and uncertainty, the Issacharians were able to read the situation clearly and offer explicit action steps toward success.

### Understanding the Times

The tribe of Issachar recognized the shifting political and social dynamics in Israel. Saul's leadership was faltering, and a new leader was emerging. Instead of clinging to the old regime, they saw the need for change and aligned themselves with David, offering their support when many were still undecided, worried, or wavering. The Issacharians had the capacity to discern what was best for Israel in that critical moment. However, discerning what is happening is not enough. This is only step one—and the easier step—of a two-part process. Once you determine the climate is changing, you need to be able to know what to do about it.

### Knowing What to Do

Issachar's contextual intelligence didn't just lie in understanding the broader situation; it also translated into decisive action. Perception must ultimately end in action! A decision needs to be made on what to do and where to go. By interpreting the political landscape, having a keen awareness of history, and reading the mood of the people, they knew Israel needed new leadership. Their decision to support David helped solidify his claim to the throne and contributed to unifying the nation under his rule, and they continued to counsel David and the nation on other matters of state.

### How Their Skills Demonstrate Contextual Intelligence:

1. **Foresight:** The tribe of Issachar anticipated the future and aligned themselves with the inevitable rather than

misremembering the past and holding on to what was familiar.

2. **Understanding complex dynamics:** The Issacharians had insight into the complexity of Israel's political situation, considering both God's will and the practical realities of power and loyalty.
3. **Strategic action:** Rather than acting impulsively, the tribe of Issachar made a calculated decision, backed by historical knowledge (hindsight) of how God moved and supported David when the time was right.

The Tribe of Issachar's ability to "understand the times" and "know what Israel should do" serves as an example of how contextual intelligence enhances perception. Their perceptiveness and strategic alignment with the emerging leadership of David helped bring stability to Israel, showcasing their wisdom and ability to navigate complex and shifting circumstances.

## WHERE DOES PERCEPTION COME FROM?

Perception is shaped by both internal and external influences—a combination of experience, belief, and awareness. King Solomon noted the value of wisdom and understanding, teaching that perception begins with seeking knowledge and insight. He said, "The beginning of wisdom is this: Get wisdom. Though it cost all you have, get understanding." This reflects the idea that perception grows through intentional reflection and openness to learning.

Jesus said, "But blessed are your eyes because they see, and your ears because they hear." This verse highlights that true perception comes not just from physical sight but from a heart attuned to understanding deeper truths. Perception grows as we develop spiritually, learning to discern beyond surface-level appearances.

Research shows that perception is shaped by a combination of cognitive biases, past experiences, emotional states, and mindset. Studies indicate that individuals with higher emotional intelligence, mindfulness, and cognitive flexibility tend to develop sharper perception, enabling them to interpret situations more accurately and empathize with others. By practicing contextual intelligence and empathy, people become better at reading social cues and navigating complex situations. Modern psychology consistently reinforces the idea that perception is not fixed but can be refined through self-awareness and intentional effort.

## APPLYING PERCEPTION IN EVERYDAY SITUATIONS

Perception isn't just a passive skill—it's a dynamic tool you must use to navigate everyday situations with greater clarity, understanding, and effectiveness. By reading people and understanding their motives, staying perceptive in high-stress situations, improving your decision-making process, and developing contextual intelligence, you can apply perception to enhance every area of your life.

Through practice and mindfulness, perception becomes a lens that helps you see beyond the obvious, grasp the complexities of life, and make decisions that are more thoughtful and well informed. Whether you're in a personal relationship, a professional setting, or simply navigating daily challenges, sharpening your perception gives you the edge in becoming EPIC.

PART 3

# ON INSPIRATION

# 12

# THE NATURE OF INSPIRATION

Becoming EPIC also means living inspired. Obviously, we all cannot be inspired all the time, but it can be the norm. Inspiration is a powerful force that fuels creativity, drives growth, and sustains a sense of purpose. It's what propels individuals beyond the ordinary, encouraging them to dream big, think outside the box, and pursue bold actions. But what exactly is inspiration? How does it differ from motivation or creativity, and why is it so essential for facilitating growth?

According to researcher Victoria Oleynick and her colleagues at the College of William and Mary, Mozart once described his creative process by explaining how he would hum ideas that pleased him, keeping them in his memory until he found ways to develop them further. He compared it to turning small morsels into a satisfying dish, igniting his passion along the way. This vivid description captures the essence of inspiration—recognizing exciting new possibilities, having ideas come to mind naturally, and feeling driven to bring them to life. Like Mozart, many artists and writers highlight inspiration as a vital part of their creative work. However, despite its significance, scientists have only recently begun to study inspiration and understand its role in creativity.

In this chapter, we'll explore the nature of inspiration, distinguish it from motivation, and examine how passion and purpose play a critical role in tapping into this transformative power. Understanding the essence of inspiration will help you cultivate it more effectively, sparking new ideas and opportunities for growth.

## INSPIRATION VS. MOTIVATION

While the terms "inspiration" and "motivation" are sometimes used interchangeably, they refer to different concepts. Both are crucial for success and progress, but understanding the distinction between them can help you better harness each in the right context.

### What Is Motivation?

Motivation is most often extrinsic—externally driven—and rooted in the desire to achieve specific goals or avoid negative outcomes. It is the practical force that compels us to act, typically fueled by a reward system or the fear of consequences. Motivation can come from a variety of sources: financial incentives, recognition, deadlines, or the need for security.

Frederick Herzberg, a psychologist and management theorist, explained what motivates employee satisfaction and performance. Herzberg proposed that job satisfaction and dissatisfaction are driven by two distinct factors: motivators and hygiene factors.

Motivators (like achievement or recognition) facilitate higher performance and long-term job satisfaction, while hygiene factors (such as salary, company policies, work conditions, and job security) prevent dissatisfaction. He found that even if hygiene factors are perfectly addressed, they don't necessarily lead to increased performance—they simply create stability.

Imagine you're being paid to take a course that develops a necessary new skill, but the materials are outdated, the instructor is unclear, the room is too hot or too cold, and the class schedule is disorganized. Even if you're excited about the content, these factors can be demotivating. Now imagine taking a course you're excited about, but at your expense. If the course is well structured, the materials are relevant, and the instructor is engaging, you'll feel more motivated and able to focus.

Consider a student who may be motivated to study hard for an upcoming exam because they want to get good grades or avoid failing. Similarly, an employee might feel motivated to meet a work deadline because they fear the repercussions of missing it.

In other words, motivation is about doing something because of an external pressure not an internal drive, often focusing on short-term accomplishments or material gains. While it is effective at getting things done, motivation tends to fade once the goal is achieved or the pressure is removed. As a result, motivation can be inconsistent and less sustainable over time.

### What Is Inspiration?

Inspiration is often intrinsic—it comes from within and is fueled by a sense of wonder, passion, or connection to something larger than oneself. It is less about achieving specific goals and more about being drawn toward a vision or idea that energizes you.

Tom Sawyer, Mark Twain's mischievous character in *The Adventures of Tom Sawyer*, was a master at inspiration. Remember the iconic scene where Aunt Polly asked Tom to whitewash the fence? Tom pretended to love the job to get the other boys to *really want* to do it for him. It was in this moment that Tom realized, "Work consists of whatever a body is obliged to do, and that play consists of whatever a body is not obliged to do." In other words, intrinsic motivation is far superior to extrinsic.

Take, for instance, our previous example of a student driven by the desire to avoid failing a class. While this motivation may keep them on track, any benefit is short lived. An inspired student, on the other hand, has an internal desire to learn something valuable—something they find meaningful and believe will benefit them in the future. Their goal, regardless of grade, is to learn what is presented. In my experience, inspired students are far more engaged and curious, and build more satisfying careers. Inspiration has a deeper, more lasting effect because it taps into your inner values, curiosity, and creativity.

An artist might feel inspired by nature, leading them to create a new painting; or an entrepreneur might be inspired by the desire to solve a global problem, pushing them to innovate in ways they never thought possible.

Inspiration is about being pulled toward something greater, often sparked by a sense of awe, possibility, or a meaningful connection to purpose. Unlike motivation, which can fluctuate, inspiration tends to be more enduring because it aligns with your core values and identity.

Of course, inspiration can fade over time, but that usually only happens when our actions fall out of alignment with our core values. I am convinced that if we engage life with our spirit and stay aware of how our soul is responding to external stimuli, we can sustain inspiration.

## WHY INSPIRATION IS ESSENTIAL FOR CREATIVITY AND GROWTH

Inspiration is often seen as the spark that ignites creativity and personal revival. It opens the door to new ideas, encourages exploration, and pushes individuals to pursue goals that align with their interests. While motivation might get you started, it's inspiration that sustains your efforts and drives long-term success.

### Inspiration Fuels Creativity

Creativity thrives on inspiration. When you're inspired, you're more likely to see the world with fresh eyes, approach problems from different angles, and generate ideas that are innovative and impactful. Inspiration allows your mind to break free from conventional patterns of thinking and venture into new territory, where solutions and possibilities are not yet defined. Inspiration encourages us to face the unknown.

Inspiration unlocks creative potential by tapping into your curiosity and imagination. Author Erwin Raphael McManus says in his book *Mind Shift* that "your imagination is not a toy, it is a tool" (p. 11). When used correctly it encourages you to think beyond the limits of what you know and explore new concepts, designs, or strategies. Whether you're an artist, entrepreneur, leader, or scientist, inspiration is the driving force behind groundbreaking work and your imagination is a huge part of that.

Steve Jobs, cofounder of Apple, often spoke about how he was inspired by the intersection of technology and the humanities. His inspiration led to the creation of innovative products, which not only revolutionized technology but also transformed how people interact with the world. He learned to listen to the spark of inspiration and it resulted in some iconic products.

Sun Tzu's famous work, *The Art of War*, offers profound insights on leadership, strategy, and the subtle art of inspiring others to achieve victory. While the book doesn't explicitly focus on inspiration as a standalone concept, its lessons about leadership, morale, and strategic influence are filled with guidance on how to inspire others toward success. Sun Tzu teaches that clear communication of goals and alignment of purpose are essential for inspiring people to move in the right direction. An army (or a team) that knows its mission and is fully aligned with its leader's vision is far more powerful than one that is uncertain or confused about its role.

Tzu states, "In all fighting, the direct method may be used for joining battle, but indirect methods will be needed in order to secure victory." Here, Sun Tzu underscores the need for flexibility in approach, or indirect methods. Unconventional interventions and a leader's creativity inspire troops to be adaptable and resourceful. Inspiration often comes from showing people a new way to approach old problems, which reignites their passion and curiosity.

### Inspiration Drives Personal Growth

Inspiration is also a critical component of personal development. When you're inspired, you're more likely to push yourself out of your comfort zone, take risks, and pursue goals that challenge you to evolve. Unlike motivation, which may push you toward immediate rewards, inspiration drives long-term development by encouraging you to explore your potential and grow as an individual.

Inspiration fosters flexibility because it's deeply tied to curiosity and sense of purpose. Even when challenges arise or setbacks occur, inspiration keeps you focused on the bigger picture, allowing you to persevere through difficulties with a sense of enthusiasm and optimism.

Malala Yousafzai was inspired by her passion for education and equality. Despite being shot by the Taliban for advocating girls' education, Malala's inspiration fueled her courage to continue her mission, leading her to become a global symbol for education and human rights. Her journey demonstrates how inspiration can sustain personal growth even in the face of adversity.

Going back to *The Art of War*, Sun Tzu places great value on knowing and using the strengths of one's army or team effectively. By recognizing each person's unique abilities and inspiring them to utilize their full potential, a leader can guide them toward success. Tzu states, "If you know the enemy and know yourself, you need not fear the result of a hundred battles." In this sense, inspiration comes from understanding not only the external challenges but also the internal strengths of your people. A leader who inspires confidence by demonstrating knowledge of their team's abilities empowers them to act boldly and strategically.

## INSPIRATION LEADS TO AUTHENTIC JOY

Inspiration leads to the kind of joy that is not just identified by external achievements but by personal fulfillment and alignment with your values. When you're inspired, your actions are motivated by a sense of purpose, making your accomplishments feel more meaningful and rewarding. Success achieved through inspiration often brings a deeper sense of joy because it aligns with who you are at your core. The problem seems to be that few people can articulate what they value. Ask someone who they are, and they are likely to say, "I am a man," or "I am a mom," or "I am a carpenter … or nurse." Others may say they are a manager, a leader, a father, a husband, a woman, a wife, or a friend. Those are what you do, not who you are. Inspiration may pass you by if you are not able to describe to others what it is that you get excited about and how those align with your values.

In contrast to motivation-driven success, inspiration-driven success is rooted in authenticity and passion. It's about pursuing goals that resonate with your *ontological self.* The ontological self refers to your core being or existence—who you fundamentally are at your deepest, most essential level. In philosophical terms, "ontology" is the study of being or existence, so when applied to our life, the ontological self deals with your identity that exists independent of external influences or experiences. Your ontological self is a way to understand your true identity beyond social labels, achievements, or the roles you play in society. Paul modeled this behavior to the Philippians when he wrote to them that he had learned to be content in all things. He noted that contentment and even joy were not contingent on what he had or didn't have.

A real-life example of inspiration-driven success rooted in the ontological self is the story of Mother Teresa, who founded the Missionaries of Charity. Her work was not motivated by external rewards or recognition, but by a deep sense of purpose and connection to her core being—her belief in the dignity of every human being and her commitment to serve "the poorest of the poor."

Mother Teresa's inspiration came from her faith and compassion, which aligned with her true identity as a servant of God. She chose to live among the poor and care for the sick, not for worldly success, but because it resonated with her ontological self. Her fulfillment came from living authentically, embodying her values of love and service. She famously said, "Not all of us can do great things. But we can do small things with great love," reflecting how her joy wasn't tied to grand achievements but to acts of kindness.

Her legacy continues to inspire, demonstrating that inspiration-driven success is about living in alignment with your deepest purpose. For Mother Teresa, success wasn't measured in external accolades, but in her commitment to her values, which brought her profound fulfillment and authentic joy.

## THE ROLE OF PASSION AND PURPOSE IN INSPIRATION

Inspired people do hard things! Passion, in its original sense, is rooted in pain and suffering—a deep emotional commitment that often involves sacrifice and hardship. This concept is most powerfully illustrated in the phrase "Passion of the Christ." Jesus chose to do the hard thing. In this light, passion isn't only about excitement or enthusiasm; it's about embracing the pain that comes with a deep commitment to do the hard thing.

Passionate people do hard things because their purpose demands it. They make the hard choices, understanding that true passion requires suffering. This suffering becomes the fertile ground from which inspiration grows. They are willing to endure hardship because they see meaning in their struggle—whether it's an entrepreneur poring long hours into a vision, a parent enduring sleepless nights for their child's well-being, someone getting up before the sun when tired and unmotivated to work out for the benefit to their mental and physical health, or an activist standing firm against injustice.

Through their willingness to make hard choices, passionate individuals find inspiration. The momentary pain of their choice becomes a seedbed for an active imagination, antifragility, and new ideas. It fuels their resolve, pushes them beyond limits, and transforms obstacles into opportunities for growth. Passion, in its true form, invites us to face discomfort and suffering, knowing that it's through these trials that we discover our deepest sources of inspiration.

### The Fire That Ignites Inspiration

Passion is also the intense enthusiasm or excitement you feel about something. It's what makes you come alive and pursue goals with vigor and determination. Passion often acts as the initial spark of inspiration, drawing you toward activities, causes, or ideas that resonate with your heart.

In *The Element: How Finding Your Passion Changes Everything*, Sir Ken Robinson's groundbreaking book, he emphasizes the transformative power of passion in unlocking potential. He argues that finding "the Element"—the intersection of personal passion and natural talent—is essential for people to truly thrive. Without it there is no or little zest to life. For Robinson, passion is the key to living authentically and meaningfully, leading to personal fulfillment and innovation.

Passion is what makes inspiration feel effortless, although it never is. When you're passionate about something, you don't have to force yourself to engage with it—your excitement naturally draws you in, making the process enjoyable and fulfilling.

Elon Musk's passion for space exploration led him to found SpaceX. Despite facing numerous technical and financial challenges, Musk's passion has kept him focused on his goal of making space travel accessible. His passion—like yours—fuels inspiration, providing the fuel to drive toward innovation. For Musk, that passion fuels his creativity to innovate in the aerospace industry.

### Purpose: The Anchor That Grounds Inspiration

Purpose, on the other hand, is the sense of meaning or direction that guides your actions. While passion is the fire that gets you excited, purpose is the foundation that keeps you grounded. It provides a sense of clarity about why you're pursuing a particular goal and helps you stay focused on what truly matters, even when challenges arise.

Purpose is essential for sustaining inspiration. When your inspiration is connected to a larger purpose, it and you become antifragile, allowing you to push through and even grow from obstacles and stay committed to your goals over the long term.

Going back to Mother Teresa's example, her deep sense of purpose—her commitment to serving the poorest and most vulnerable—was the driving force behind her lifelong work. Her purpose gave her the strength to continue her mission in the face of enormous challenges, and her unwavering sense of direction inspired millions around the world.

## THE TRANSFORMATIVE POWER OF INSPIRATION

Inspiration is a powerful, transformative force that goes beyond mere motivation. EPIC living requires inspiration. The shepherd boy David was inspired by Goliath's taunts and derision because they violated his core belief system, which drove him to do the hard thing of facing Goliath in battle himself, even when no other professional soldier would. His inspired action ended in an epic struggle where he came out the victor and forever changed the trajectory of his life. Living inspired can be a life-altering, trajectory-changing reality.

While motivation pushes you to act, inspiration pulls your greater future self toward where you are now, igniting creativity, driving personal transformation, and fostering authentic joy. When fueled by passion and anchored by purpose, inspiration becomes a sustainable source of energy that allows you to do hard things in pursuit of your goals.

As we continue to explore the process of cultivating inspiration, the next chapters will provide practical strategies for fostering inspiration in your personal and professional life, allowing you to harness this incredible force and transform it into meaningful action.

# 13

# WHAT BLOCKS YOUR INSPIRATION

Inspiration can be a transformative force and source of endless energy. It drives creativity, fuels personal growth, and gives meaning to our actions. However, many people struggle with staying inspired or finding inspiration at all. Despite our best intentions, there are common mistakes, myths, and misconceptions that block our ability to tap into inspiration consistently.

In this chapter, we'll explore what blocks inspiration—from waiting for it to strike to over-relying on external sources—and challenge common myths that may be holding you back from living an inspired life. By identifying these barriers, you can take intentional steps to cultivate inspiration consistently and unlock your full creative potential.

My inspiration was severely threatened after my diagnosis. Much of what inspires me is based in foresight. I am a hopeless romantic who imagines that the future is better than the past or present. The kind of diagnosis I received threatened any future at all. This life-altering diagnosis forced me to reevaluate everything, including how I maintain inspiration and motivation in the face of uncertainty and physical challenges. I've faced these obstacles head-on, and the lessons I've learned along the way have shaped my approach to inspiration in my own life, and I hope it can inspire yours.

## COMMON MISTAKES PEOPLE MAKE

The road to inspiration can be blocked by several avoidable mistakes. These behaviors or habits might seem harmless, but over time they limit your ability to experience inspiration fully. Recognizing these pitfalls is the first step toward clearing the path to a more inspired life.

### Mistake #1: Waiting for Inspiration to Strike

One of the most common mistakes people make is waiting for inspiration to strike. Inspiration should be something you actively seek; and when you find it, take it. It's easy to believe that inspiration is something that will simply arrive in a flash of brilliance or a sudden moment of insight. As if it really does come from the mythical Greek goddesses, the Muses. Many people sit idly, hoping for that perfect idea or surge of inspiration to come, and in the meantime, they miss out and lose opportunities to create or act.

After my diagnosis, this was a lesson I had to learn the hard way. There were days when I felt utterly depleted, both mentally and physically, waiting for that magical burst of inspiration to keep moving forward. But it didn't always come on its own. What I found was that inspiration comes in the doing. The mundane iterative process is what most often produces inspiration. I had to push myself to act first, whether that meant writing a little every day, continuing to engage with my work, or simply finding new ways to contribute to my family and community. The act of moving forward, even in small ways, would eventually reignite my sense of purpose and creativity.

The reality is that inspiration often emerges in the process of doing, not in waiting. Rather than waiting, start moving toward your goal, even if it feels unclear at first. Action itself can spark inspiration. In Chapter 3, I mentioned Brené Brown's concept of the shitty first draft (SFD), it applies here as well. The SFD is often the first step toward greater inspiration.

Whether it's writing a few sentences, painting a small section of a canvas, or brainstorming new ideas, the simple act of beginning can lead to the flow of creativity and insight. Waiting for inspiration to magically appear can paralyze progress, whereas taking small steps forward creates momentum.

### Mistake #2: Relying Solely on External Sources for Inspiration

Another common mistake is relying solely on external sources for inspiration. While it's natural to look to others for motivation—whether through books, speakers, art, or leaders—depending too heavily on external stimuli can limit your ability to find inspiration within. I believe that within the spirit of humankind lies unlimited inspiration. The more you rely on outside influences, the greater the risk of disconnecting from your spirit, which is the source of inspiration fueled by your values, experiences, and creativity.

This became particularly true for me. During my treatments I would look outward, hoping that others' stories, medical advice, or external sources of inspiration would give me the fuel to keep going. However, I soon realized that true inspiration came from my spirit—from reflecting on my own journey, my core beliefs, and what I still wanted to accomplish in life. The frustration and uncertainty brought on by cancer didn't take away my ability to inspire myself, but I had to learn to dig deeper and draw from an internal spiritual well.

External sources can be helpful, but only as a spark; true inspiration often comes from within—rooted in your own experiences, desires, and purpose. When you look inward and connect with what personally drives you, the inspiration that follows tends to be deeper and more meaningful.

I recommend spending time reflecting on your own passions and interests. What excites or moves you? Regular spiritual disciplines, like the ones I described in Chapter 6, can help you tap into an internal wellspring of inspiration.

### Mistake #3: Chasing Too Many Ideas at Once

For some, the issue isn't a lack of inspiration but an overabundance of ideas, like with the dog in the Pixar movie *Up!* who was always distracted and chasing squirrels. While it might seem like a blessing to be flooded with creative thoughts and possibilities, chasing too many ideas at once can become overwhelming and counterproductive. The scattered energy leads to frustration and prevents you from finishing any one project.

This is a struggle I've faced firsthand. After receiving my diagnosis, I was flooded with ideas on how to live life more fully, how to channel my work into something meaningful, and how to advocate for others in similar situations. But with so many ideas spinning around in my head, I found myself paralyzed by indecision. It took time to realize that focusing on just one or two ideas was far more productive than trying to tackle everything at once. Honestly, it wasn't me who had that breakthrough; it was my wife, Angie, who helped me realize that. Together we learned that clarity and the sense of purpose that comes from narrowing one's focus allows you to make real progress, even in the face of extreme adversity.

Inspiration flourishes with focus. It's important to choose one idea and pursue it with commitment, rather than bouncing from one concept to another without making progress. Trying to tackle too many projects simultaneously can dilute your energy and prevent you from seeing any of them through to completion. Instead, prioritize your ideas. Choose one to focus on and commit to it fully. By homing in on a single project, you give it the time and energy it needs to grow and come to life.

## MYTHS ABOUT INSPIRATION

Beyond common mistakes, there are several myths about inspiration that can block your progress. These myths create unrealistic expectations and can lead to discouragement. Many people believe that inspiration strikes randomly or only during moments of extreme passion, but in reality, it can be cultivated through regular practice and openness. Others think inspiration fades quickly, when often it can grow stronger with action and momentum. By debunking these myths, you can remove barriers and open yourself to more consistent and authentic inspiration.

### Myth #1: Inspiration Only Comes from Big Moments

A common myth is that inspiration only comes from big, dramatic moments—those once-in-a-lifetime experiences or grand revelations that change everything. We've come to know it as the "Eureka Effect." People often imagine that inspiration only strikes during major life events, such as traveling the world, meeting a mentor, or experiencing a life-changing breakthrough.

John Kounios and Mark Beeman's book *The Eureka Factor: Aha Moments, Creative Insight, and the Brain* explores the science behind sudden moments of insight, commonly known as "eureka" or "aha" moments. Kounios and Beeman explain how insights often arise when the mind is relaxed and not actively focused on the problem at hand. They argue that these moments of inspiration don't come from continuous hard thinking or big moments, but from allowing the brain to make connections unconsciously. In fact, they describe how taking breaks, relaxing, or even sleeping can facilitate inspirational breakthroughs.

This directly exposes the myth that inspiration only comes from big moments. In fact, inspiration often emerges during ordinary, everyday activities—when your mind is wandering, while you're exercising, or even while you're daydreaming. These moments may feel small, but they lead to significant insights. Inspiration can strike in the most unassuming circumstances, discrediting the idea that only grand or dramatic events bring inspiration. Instead, it's the quiet, everyday moments that frequently serve as the backdrop for these flashes of insight. And by expecting inspiration only from big moments, you may overlook the rich opportunities for inspiration that are already present in your daily life.

I fell into the trap of this myth myself. After my diagnosis, I was waiting for some grand epiphany, something life-changing to set me back on the path of inspiration. But over time, I noticed inspiration found me in unremarkable moments—a walk with my wife, a quiet conversation with a friend, reorganizing my bookshelves, or private prayer. These small experiences slowly built up, giving me the energy and insight I needed to keep moving forward in meaningful ways.

A perfect example of inspiration striking in an ordinary moment comes from the life of Sir Isaac Newton. The famous story of Newton observing an apple fall from a tree is often romanticized as a grand, dramatic event that led to the discovery of gravity. However, Newton's insight was sparked by a simple occurrence—something as ordinary as watching apples fall, something he had likely seen countless times before.

Newton was not in a laboratory or delivering a lecture; he was in a garden, quietly reflecting. The falling apple was not a moment of sudden revelation but rather a small trigger that nudged his thoughts in a new direction. His relaxed state of mind allowed him to make connections between the falling apple and the forces that govern planetary motion. Newton's apple reminds us that by staying open to the small, seemingly insignificant experiences of daily life, we create space for some of the most transformative ideas to take root.

### Myth #2: If I'm Not Inspired, I'm on the Wrong Path

Another myth that blocks inspiration is the belief that if you're not constantly inspired, you must be on the wrong path. People often assume that inspiration should be a constant presence, and when they hit a lull, they question their choices or direction. This myth can lead to unnecessary self-doubt and cause people to give up too early on pursuits that require persistence.

In my own life there were long stretches where I felt uninspired, exhausted, and unsure. I questioned whether I was still doing what

I was meant to do, whether I was losing my way, and even if I was being punished. But through those darker periods, I learned that inspiration ebbs and flows. It doesn't always come in steady doses, and that's okay. The key is to continue walking the path, even during the uninspired days.

In fact, this book was inspired by the mundane habit of daily writing. When I started radiation, I committed to writing 1,000 words every morning before my treatment. I hoped to have a 37,000-plus word manuscript. I hoped it would be cathartic for me; it was. However, it wasn't easy, and words didn't always come, but I persisted. Somewhere in the midst of that writing, the inspiration for this book took place. In fact, it was during that writing period that I remembered shortly before my diagnosis I had run in a local 8K road race. That led me to search for the picture of me crossing the finish line of that race. I found instead a picture of me taken by a fellow runner, giving a thumbs up sign, and I noticed I was wearing one of my own T-shirt designs that said, "EPIC LIFE." (It's included in the inside dust jacket cover if you want to see it.) That triggered some emotions because at the time of that picture, I had an advanced case of prostate cancer but didn't know it yet. That got me thinking of a second writing project, this book. The mundane habit of getting up early to write, even when no words came, or the same words just kept coming, led to inspiration.

Like any other emotion, inspiration ebbs and flows. It's perfectly normal to experience periods of low energy or creative blockages, even when you're on the right path. But as Seth Godin says in his book *The Practice: Shipping Creative Work*, "Lost in all the noise around us is the proven truth about creativity: it's the result of desire—the desire to find a new truth, solve an old problem, or serve someone else. Creativity is a choice, it's not a bolt of lightning from somewhere else." Rather than assuming you need new scenery, consider that inspiration may simply need time to return, especially if you're dealing with stress, fatigue, or other life factors.

Instead of abandoning a project when inspiration fades, take a step back and recharge. Press on, keep iterating. Inspiration often returns after a brief step away followed by reengagement. Trust the process and give yourself permission to take breaks without abandoning your journey.

## HOW TO OVERCOME BLOCKS AND CULTIVATE INSPIRATION

Now that we've explored some of the common mistakes and myths that block inspiration, how can you overcome these obstacles and cultivate inspiration more consistently? Here are some strategies to help you stay connected to your sense of purpose and creativity:

1. **Embrace action:** Don't wait for inspiration to strike. Take action, even in small ways, and let the momentum build.
2. **Connect with your curiosity:** Regularly check in with yourself. What motivates you at a deeper level? Frequently ask yourself, what sparks my curiosity? By staying connected to what makes you curious, you'll find that inspiration comes more naturally.
3. **Learn to articulate your values:** Practice describing to others, verbally or in writing, what values drive your actions.

4. **Practice prayer:** Slow down and pay attention to your surroundings. Inspiration can be found in the present moment if you take time to acknowledge and focus on God.
5. **Celebrate progress:** Don't wait for the completion of a project to feel fulfilled. Celebrate small victories and milestones along the way, which will keep you inspired to keep going.

## INSPIRATION THROUGH EMBRACING COMPLEXITY

In her book, *The Creativity Leap: Unleash Curiosity, Improvisation, and Intuition at Work*, Natalie Nixon states that creativity is a competency. She explores how creativity is not just an artistic endeavor but a critical skill in every field. Nixon emphasizes that creativity is about crossing boundaries—whether between disciplines, industries, or ideas—and that true inspiration often arises from blending different perspectives and tapping into one's curiosity. Nixon highlights that creativity is about more than mere problem-solving; it's about transforming how we approach challenges by drawing on intuition, improvisation, and curiosity to foster innovation and growth.

One of the key distinctions she makes is between complexity and complication—something I have done in detail in my book on Contextual Intelligence (remember the LEGO vs. Play-Doh analogy in Chapter 8). She asserts that complicated problems are linear, technical, and often have clear solutions. Complex problems, on the other hand, involve multiple, interconnected factors and require more adaptive and creative approaches. Nixon argues that creativity thrives in complexity because it calls for boundary-crossing and innovative thinking. To be inspired in the face of complexity, we must let go of rigid frameworks and embrace ambiguity, allowing curiosity and improvisation to lead the way.

This idea directly connects to becoming EPIC. Just as inspiration fuels our ability to dream beyond current limitations, Nixon's insights remind us that creativity is about stepping outside our comfort zones and allowing our ideas to evolve by interacting with unfamiliar challenges. Boundary-crossing—whether intellectual, cultural, or practical—enhances our capacity for creative leaps.

## FUELING INSPIRATION

Nixon highlights three core elements—curiosity, improvisation, and intuition—as essential tools for unlocking creativity and inspiring new ways of thinking. Curiosity sparks the desire to explore, to ask questions, and to pursue the unfamiliar. Improvisation teaches us to adapt on the fly, take risks, and find new solutions in the moment—to PIVOT. Intuition is the quiet, internal compass that guides us toward innovative choices even when we can't see the full path ahead; that's perception.

To nurture these qualities in our work and lives we need to deliberately engage in activities and conversations outside our usual domains. She emphasizes that by expanding our perspectives and embracing the unknown, we can better connect the dots between seemingly unrelated ideas, leading to inspired insights.

## RECOMMENDATIONS FOR NURTURING CREATIVITY AND INSPIRATION

Nixon makes several recommendations that can help us harness the power of creativity in our journey toward becoming EPIC:

1. **Engage in interdisciplinary learning:** Regularly expose yourself to fields outside your expertise. Whether through reading, attending conferences, or collaborating with people from different industries, you can spark new ideas and see connections you wouldn't otherwise notice.
2. **Embrace ambiguity:** Recognize that complex challenges often require creative solutions that evolve over time. Don't shy away from complexity—lean into it, and allow your curiosity to guide you.
3. **Practice improvisation:** In your personal and professional life, make space for experimentation and improvisation. Try new methods, be flexible, and adapt as new information emerges.
4. **Reflect on hindsight:** Take time to look back on past experiences to identify the patterns that were invisible in the moment. Use this reflection as a source of inspiration for future endeavors.

Incorporating these principles into our journey means fostering curiosity, embracing improvisation, and trusting our intuition. Inspiration is sparked by crossing boundaries and engaging with the complex, not the complicated. As we move toward becoming EPIC, we must lean into the unknown, trusting that the leaps we take will lead to inspiration.

## REMOVING THE BLOCKS TO INSPIRATION

Inspiration isn't a rare, fleeting experience reserved for a lucky few—it's a powerful force that anyone can access by overcoming the common blocks that stand in its way. Whether it's waiting for inspiration to strike, relying too much on external sources, or chasing too many ideas at once, these obstacles can be addressed with mindful action, focus, and self-awareness. Additionally, breaking free from myths about inspiration—such as the belief that it only comes from big moments or that you're on the wrong path if inspiration fades—will allow you to stay grounded in your journey.

Overcoming these blocks was not just a theoretical exercise for me but a lived reality. I had to fight through fatigue, self-doubt, and the constant temptation to wait for some external inspiration to give me direction. Instead, I learned to find inspiration in small moments and internal values, to act before I felt ready, and to trust that inspiration would return in time.

By understanding what blocks inspiration and taking intentional steps to overcome these challenges, you can cultivate a deeper, more lasting connection to your creativity and purpose. Inspiration will flow more freely, and you'll find yourself more aligned with the goals that truly matter to you, leading to a more fulfilling and EPIC life.

# 14

# HOW TO CULTIVATE INSPIRATION

Inspiration isn't something that arrives by chance or in rare flashes of brilliance—it's a state of mind that can be cultivated daily. By building consistent habits, staying open to new experiences, and learning to appreciate the beauty in everyday moments, we can cultivate inspiration more regularly and use it to fuel our lives and be a model for others.

To cultivate something implies intentional action and care, much like tending to a garden. It involves creating the right conditions, consistently investing time and effort, and patiently allowing growth to unfold. Just as a garden thrives with attention and care, inspiration flourishes when we actively seek it and remain attuned to the possibilities hidden in our daily lives.

In this chapter, we'll explore a few practical ideas for making inspiration a part of your everyday life. From creating routines that spark creativity to finding inspiration in small moments, we'll cover how to design a life that invites inspiration. You'll also learn how to sustain that inspiration over time, ensuring that your creativity and sense of purpose remain strong and vibrant.

## CREATING ROUTINES THAT SPARK INSPIRATION

Inspiration doesn't have to be fleeting or unpredictable. By establishing daily routines that encourage creativity and self-reflection, you can set the stage for inspiration to strike regularly. Seth Godin says, "If you are willing to do something that might not work, you are closer to being an artist." Risk taking is a key ingredient of inspiration. Do not be the person who doesn't create because they are afraid to fail. Engaging in a routine mitigates fear and creates a structure that allows you to tap into your imagination, clear your mind, and make space for new ideas to emerge.

### How to Build a Morning Routine Focused on Creativity

One of the best ways to cultivate inspiration is to start your day with intention. For me that usually involves a long walk or writing. A morning routine that prioritizes creativity and gratitude can set the tone for an inspired and productive day. The key is to engage in activities that quiet your soul; it will tend to rage against you if you don't keep it still. Several times in the Psalms, David asks, "Why are you cast down, O my soul? And why are you disquieted within me?" If you don't create opportunity for inspiration, your soul will take over your spirit. Don't allow that. When David noticed this was happening, he redirected his soul (i.e., mind, will, and emotions) and told it what to do and where to focus. David's full declaration reads, "Why are you cast down, O my soul? And why are you disquieted within me? Hope in God, for I shall yet praise Him for the help of His countenance." David was acutely attuned to the state of his soul, and when it was agitated or wasn't serving him, he commanded his soul to refocus and get back to hoping.

Putting your soul in its place is a good practice to do every morning. Try training inspiration to outrun the soul's desire to focus on thoughts of stress and the day's demands. Be intentional about letting inspiration cross the finish line first in the race for prominence in your mind. Here are my recommendations for how to create a morning routine that fosters inspiration:

1. **Engage in mindful meditation or prayer:** Begin your day by focusing on God. Spend 5–10 minutes in mindful meditation or prayer to refocus your mind on the divine. This practice helps reduce mental clutter, making it easier to access creative thoughts.
2. **Journal:** Spend time each morning writing in a journal. Freewriting, in particular, is an excellent way to unlock your creativity and let your thoughts flow without judgment. You can write about your dreams, ideas for projects, or anything that comes to mind. This process helps clear mental blocks and stimulates new ideas.
3. **Do creative tasks:** Dedicate the first part of your morning to a creative task or exercise. Whether it's sketching, writing, a brisk walk, weightlifting, brainstorming, or even planning your day with creativity in mind, engaging in something creative first thing helps build momentum for the rest of the day.

By starting your day with intention, reflection, and creative exercises, you prime your mind to stay open and receptive to inspiration throughout the day.

## JOURNALING, VISION BOARDS, AND REFLECTION PRACTICES

Journaling, vision boards, and other reflective practices are powerful tools for cultivating daily inspiration. They help you articulate your desired outcomes, visualize your aspirations, and reflect on your progress, which keeps your mind focused and engaged in the pursuit of creativity and growth. For example, in my home office there is a large whiteboard directly in front of my desk. Instead of looking out the window, I look at the whiteboard, which is full of ideas, opportunities, and inspirational pictures that rouse me to keep creating.

### Journaling for Inspiration

Daily journaling provides a space to record your thoughts, ideas, and experiences. This practice can help you identify patterns in your thinking, process emotions, and discover new insights. Regular journaling also encourages self-reflection, helping you stay connected to your inner values and purpose, which are critical sources of inspiration.

For me, journaling became a lifeline after my diagnosis. I was dealing with a whirlwind of emotions—fear, uncertainty, and even anger. In those early days, it felt like the ground had been pulled out from beneath me, and I struggled to find clarity and meaning. It wasn't just about surviving the disease; it was about finding ways to still live a life filled with purpose, despite the circumstances.

When I first started journaling. I just needed to get my thoughts out, uncensored. As I wrote, I began to recognize patterns in my thinking—some that were holding me back, like fear of the unknown or doubts about my ability to contribute to my family and community while undergoing treatment. Over time, journaling helped me shift my mindset. I began to focus less on the things I couldn't control and more on the actions I could take to stay connected to my purpose.

One of the most profound effects of journaling for me was the ability to see how inspiration could still thrive, even in the midst of adversity. Writing about my small victories—whether it was managing a particularly hard treatment day, spending quality time with my family, or finding new ways to work on my projects—reminded me that life, and inspiration, were still very much within my grasp.

### Vision Boards and Concept Maps

A vision board is a collage of images, quotes, and ideas that represent your dreams and goals. It's like a concept or mind map, but with only pictures. It's a visual reminder of what inspires you and what you're working toward. Creating a vision board helps you clarify your aspirations and keeps your mind focused on your larger purpose. Place it somewhere you can see it daily, so it continually serves as a source of inspiration. For example, I love the space in my son's apartment where he keeps his desk. Yes, it's a little messier than it should be, but I am encouraged to see that on the corkboard in front of his desk are several of his detailed sketches from an imaginary fantasy world he and his brother created as young boys. Those sketches are not only pretty good, but they serve as a reminder to be and stay creative.

A concept map is a visual diagram that shows how ideas or words relate to each other. Concept maps are made up of words that are connected by lines or arrows, called cross-links. The lines are often labeled with words or phrases that explain the connections between concepts.

When I was first diagnosed, I struggled to see beyond the daily battles. The long treatments, the fatigue, and the emotional toll clouded my ability to imagine a future that wasn't dominated by cancer. But creating a mental concept map changed that. I started with the word "battle," which was a symbol of hope and purpose. The word evolved into an acronym for Be brave, Armor up, Trust your team, Triumph over fear, Lean into your faith, and Engage in life (see the epilogue for more details). This mnemonic helped me personally, and it eventually inspired several others. It also evolved into a T-shirt and prostate cancer awareness walk, Battle for the Bulge (www.battleforthebulge.com), which helped bring healing and connection to my local community.

### Reflection Practices

Taking time for daily reflection allows you to pause and assess how your actions align with your goals and values. Set aside time in the evening to reflect on your day and ask yourself the following questions:

- What went well today?
- What surprised me today?
- What inspired me?
- What challenges did I face?
- How did I handle those challenges?
- What assumptions did I rely on to get through the day?

These reflection practices help you stay grounded, mindful, and consistently connected to your sources of inspiration.

Reflection became an essential part of my journey. Each evening, I would spend time thinking about what I had accomplished that day, no matter how small. Some days, the victories were modest—getting through a treatment without being incontinent, having a meaningful conversation, or simply getting outside for a walk. But these reflections allowed me to see that I was still moving forward, still making progress toward my goals, even in the face of major challenges.

Reflection also helped me reframe setbacks. On difficult days, I would reflect on the challenges I had faced and ask myself how I could approach them differently in the future. This process kept me from becoming discouraged, reminding me that each day was an opportunity to learn and grow, even when things didn't go as planned.

## FINDING INSPIRATION IN THE SMALL MOMENTS

One of the biggest misconceptions about inspiration that I mentioned in Chapter 13 is that it only comes from big, dramatic events. In reality, inspiration is all around us—it's just a matter of training yourself to see it. By becoming more aware of the small, beautiful moments in everyday life, you can draw on these experiences as sources of creativity and meaning. Here are a few ways to find inspiration in the small moments:

1. **Pause and observe:** Throughout your day, take short breaks to observe your environment. Whether it's watching sunlight filter through the trees, noticing the rhythm of people walking on a busy street, or simply

appreciating a quiet moment of reflection, these small observations can provide new perspectives and insights. You may not need to sweat the small stuff, but you should definitely try to notice the small stuff.

2. **Cultivate gratitude:** Practicing gratitude helps shift your focus from what's missing to what is there. By acknowledging the good things in your life, even the seemingly mundane, you open yourself to the flow of inspiration. There are many things that you can be thankful for, even during great struggle, such as:
    a. **Health** – The ability to move, breathe, and experience life at all.
    b. **Loved ones** – Family, friends, and relationships that provide support and joy.
    c. **Opportunities for growth** – The chance to learn, evolve, and face challenges that help you become stronger.
    d. **Nature** – The beauty of the world around us, from the sky to the oceans, and everything in between.
    e. **Life's simple pleasures** – A good meal, a restful night's sleep, or a peaceful moment of silence.
3. **Mindful engagement:** Engage with your tasks mindfully, whether it's cooking, walking, or working. Being fully present in what you're doing can reveal new details or ideas that might otherwise go unnoticed.

For example, my wife and I are avid neighborhood walkers. Most days, we walk several miles, following a few favorite routes that have become familiar over the years. Despite the routine, we are often surprised by how frequently one of us says, "I've never noticed that before." A small detail—a unique pattern on a house, a particular flower blooming in someone's yard, the color of a door, or the way the light filters through the trees at a certain time of day—suddenly stands out, even though we've passed by it countless times.

Some days, we intentionally make the entire purpose of our walk to notice things we've overlooked. We challenge ourselves to slow down and look more closely, searching for those hidden details that normally blend into the background. This simple shift in mindset transforms an ordinary walk into a mindful experience, reminding us how much beauty and intrigue can be found in the familiar when we pay attention.

## HOW NATURE, ART, AND MOVEMENT CAN INSPIRE YOU

Nature, art, and movement are powerful sources of inspiration. They can break you out of mental ruts, provide fresh perspectives, and help you reconnect with your creative energy.

### Nature as a Source of Inspiration

I learned to be inspired by nature from my dad. He was not an outdoorsman in the sense of being a rugged hunter or camper, but he did love to walk in the woods and fish. When my siblings and I were young, he insisted we take family vacations every year, even if it wasn't a financially sound decision to do so. He insisted on making memories. Many of those memories were trips to national or state parks. I remember being inspired by how awed he was by the scenery of a lake or mountain range.

He loved to make up fictional stories about who or what lived in the deep forest or mountain ranges to entertain us kids. But most of all, I remember him coming back from walks in the woods or a park freshly inspired by a conversation he had with God. This impacted me greatly and fostered in me a love for walking in the woods to pray.

Spending time in nature can clear your mind and restore your sense of wonder. I love walking in the woods and around water. Whether it's a hike in the mountains, a walk in the park, or even just sitting quietly in your garden, nature provides a space for reflection, inspiration, and creative thinking. I try and make time each week to be in nature, whether by taking a long walk, kayaking, hiking, or simply sitting outside and observing my surroundings. Nature's rhythms and beauty can reignite your creativity and provide a sense of calm.

It's obviously a family thing. Both of my boys have embraced the family's secret source of inspiration—their grandfather, who they never met, would be proud. My wife and I have albums full of photos capturing moments where our sons are gazing out into the beauty of the natural world, their imaginations ignited by the wonders around them. From the waterfalls of Rwanda to the bush and beaches of Australia, they've chased adventure through the rainforests of Uganda, marveled at the Great Barrier Reef, and stood in awe at Yosemite and the Grand Canyon. Together, we've hiked Angel's Landing at Zion, backpacked some of the Appalachian Trail, explored Acadia National Park, rafted the New and Gauley Rivers in West Virginia, and trekked through the stunning landscapes of New Zealand. Whether near or far, nature has a timeless ability to inspire. It's no wonder my boys are so creative. That same creativity can be awakened in you—just get outside!

### Art as a Catalyst for Creativity

Exposure to art—whether through paintings, music, literature, or film—can spark new ideas and ways of thinking. It's not my favorite, but with the wise influence of my wife, I am exposed to things that inspire me that I normally would not seek. Art and classical music challenge your perceptions, evoke emotions, and can serve as a catalyst for your own creative work. Visit a museum, listen to a new genre of music, or watch a thought-provoking film. Reflect on how art makes you feel and what ideas it stirs within you. Use these reflections as fuel for your own creative projects.

Creating art, even if you are not an artist, can also foster inspiration. According to art educator, Mallory Shotwell, creating art is a deeply fulfilling experience that offers a range of psychological and physical benefits. It can instill a sense of purpose, accomplishment, and joy, while also serving as a powerful tool for reducing stress and boosting self-confidence. Through the creative process, individuals often develop stronger problem-solving skills and gain a greater sense of personal growth.

Art provides a meaningful outlet for expressing emotions and processing difficult experiences, helping individuals better understand and navigate their feelings. Engaging in artistic activities can alleviate anxiety, improve mental well-being, and foster a more positive self-image. Beyond its emotional benefits, the practice of creating art stimulates creative thinking, encouraging innovation and enhancing problem-solving abilities across various aspects of life. Ultimately, art opens the door to greater self-awareness and inspiration.

**Movement as a Path to Inspiration**

Physical movement, like exercise, dance, stretching, or even a simple walk, can inspire you by helping you shake off mental cobwebs and release pent-up energy. Movement encourages mental clarity and often leads to unexpected moments of insight. I believe it is imperative that you incorporate movement into your daily routine. Physical activity can help reset your mind and encourage inspiration to flow.

The American College of Sports Medicine promotes a global initiative called Exercise Is Medicine. Exercise and movement have a profound impact on brain function, enhancing both mental clarity and overall cognitive health. When you exercise, the brain increases its production of neurotrophic factors, such as brain-derived neurotrophic factor (BDNF), which promotes the growth and survival of neurons. This improves memory, learning, and adaptability, or neuroplasticity.

Exercise also increases blood flow to the brain, delivering more oxygen and nutrients, which enhances mental sharpness and focus. Additionally, physical activity helps regulate mood by balancing neurotransmitters like dopamine and serotonin, reducing symptoms of anxiety and depression, and promoting a sense of well-being.

Regular exercise has been shown to stimulate the hippocampus, the brain region responsible for memory and learning, which can help protect against cognitive decline as we age. In short, movement refreshes the brain by improving neuronal health, increasing cognitive function, and enhancing mood, leading to clearer thinking and better emotional regulation, all of which are critical components to inspired thinking.

## SUSTAINING INSPIRATION OVER THE LONG TERM

Finding inspiration daily is important but sustaining it over the long term requires consistent effort and commitment. By setting personal milestones, reflecting on your progress, and building momentum through action, you can keep inspiration alive for the long haul.

### Setting Personal Milestones to Keep You Focused

One way to sustain inspiration is by setting personal milestones. These are small, achievable goals that keep you moving forward and give you something to celebrate along the way. When you set milestones, you break down larger goals into manageable steps, which keeps you focused and inspired. Try identifying a larger goal you're working toward and break it into smaller, actionable steps. In fact, you can reframe your larger goal as a desired outcome. Now, ask yourself what needs to happen for that outcome to become a reality? Repeat the process with the "what needs to happen" list, and eventually you have small, manageable action steps that move you closer to breakthrough.

### Building Momentum Through Action and Reflection

Inspiration thrives on action. By taking consistent, small steps toward your goals, you build momentum that keeps your creativity and energy flowing. Reflecting on your actions allows you to adjust course or PIVOT (Persevere, Improvise, Visualize, Overcome, and Transform) when necessary and stay connected to your purpose. Regularly reflect on the progress you've made. What actions helped move you forward? What adjustments can you make to stay aligned with your goals? What behaviors did you need to overcome? Use this reflection to guide your actions for the coming weeks.

### Cultivating Inspiration Daily

Inspiration doesn't have to be rare or fleeting. By creating routines that encourage creativity, reflecting on your progress, and finding inspiration in the small moments, you can make inspiration a part of your everyday life. Nature, art, and exercise can also serve as powerful sources of inspiration, helping you stay inspired. Finally, by setting personal milestones and building momentum and good habits through action, you can sustain inspiration over the long term, keeping your creativity alive and your sense of purpose strong.

Incorporating these practices into your daily life will help you tap into a consistent well of inspiration, fueling your personal and creative growth and helping you achieve your most meaningful goals on your way to becoming EPIC.

# 15

# USING INSPIRATION TO DRIVE GROWTH

Inspiration is more than just a fleeting feeling; it is a catalyst for change. When harnessed effectively, inspiration can spark your initiative, sustain you through difficult times, trigger creative and innovative ideas, and give hope to others. But to make inspiration a tool for growth, it must be nurtured and balanced with practical action.

In this chapter, we'll explore how to stay inspired during challenging times, how to use inspiration to advance your career and creativity, how your journey can inspire others, and how to strike a balance between inspiration and practicality for long-term success.

## HOW TO STAY INSPIRED IN CHALLENGING TIMES

One of the biggest challenges in life is maintaining inspiration during difficult periods. Whether you're facing personal setbacks, professional roadblocks, or health issues, it can feel like the light of inspiration dims when life becomes overwhelming. However, inspiration doesn't have to disappear during tough times—it can become a source of resilience, helping you push through and find meaning in adversity.

This lesson is personal to me. The news of cancer was life-altering, and for a while, I found myself in a fog of fear, uncertainty, and frustration. I had been someone who drew inspiration from growth, from contributing to my profession and my faith community, and from leading an intentionally purposeful life. But in those early days after the diagnosis, my inspiration seemed to vanish. I was left with questions I'd never faced before, like how could I continue to contribute meaningfully when my future was now clouded by such uncertainty? How could I stay inspired when everything I thought I had control over felt upended? What did I do to deserve this; and what didn't I do to prevent this? The answer was nothing. In the words of my genetic therapist, I was just "unlucky."

It wasn't an easy process, but I learned to draw inspiration from small wins. When the bigger picture seemed too daunting to confront, I focused on the little victories—the times when I managed to work despite the frustrating uncertainty; the days when I had the energy to spend time with my wife, kids, and granddaughter; or even the moments when I could simply get outside and do some yard work. I remember the first time I mowed my lawn after my surgery—it felt so rewarding. These small achievements reminded me that, while my circumstances had changed, my ability to experience joy hadn't been taken away.

I also realized the importance of reconnecting with my deeper sense of purpose. My diagnosis didn't erase the core values that had always driven me—teaching, leadership, and service to others.

Those things were still within me, even if how I approached them had to evolve. By reconnecting with what truly mattered to me, I found a renewed sense of clarity. I could still contribute, inspire, and create impact, even in ways I hadn't anticipated before. This deeper connection to my purpose helped me push through the difficult days and gave me the strength to keep going. It brought a greater sense of clarity to the things I was doing. It reminded me of what was really important and helped me identify what I needed to spend my time and energy doing.

Finally, I learned to seek inspiration from others. Not just through support groups, clergy, counselors, or staying connected with my friends. But in relationships I didn't know could add value to me. I became aware of how many people had significant struggles and adversity and were still making it. Before this diagnosis, they were the "other"; they were who I needed to help dig out of their problems. Now I was one of the people who other people thought they needed to help. I didn't like it, not one bit. This realization was more than coming to see that I wasn't alone in my struggles. There were connections with people who I didn't think could help me. That was a surprising source of inspiration. It taught me a new dimension of humility. There were others who had fought their own battles, and their stories of perseverance fueled my resolve. It reminded me that even in the darkest times, there is always something—whether it's a story, a lesson, or an experience—that can reignite inspiration.

One powerful example of inspiration in the face of extreme adversity is the story of Joseph. Sold into slavery by his own brothers, falsely accused, and imprisoned for years, Joseph faced countless roadblocks that could have easily led him to despair. Yet, through it all, he remained faithful and allowed his circumstances to shape his character rather than break his spirit. Even in prison, Joseph used his gifts to interpret dreams, bringing hope to others and eventually paving the way for his rise to power. When he was finally elevated to a position of influence, he didn't allow bitterness to take root. Instead, he saw purpose, famously telling his brothers, "You intended to harm me, but God intended it for good." Joseph's story is a testament to the power of inspiration—how purpose-based foresight can transform even the most difficult seasons into opportunities for growth and redemption, a true demonstration of antifragility.

## DRAW INSPIRATION FROM SMALL WINS

In challenging times, finding small wins can help you regain momentum. These are the small, incremental steps that bring you closer to your goals, even when progress feels slow. Celebrating small achievements, no matter how minor, helps maintain a sense of progress and purpose.

A great example of drawing inspiration from small wins is seen in the film *The Pursuit of Happyness*, based on the real-life story of Chris Gardner, played by Will Smith. In the movie, Chris faces overwhelming professional and personal challenges—homelessness, financial ruin, and raising his son alone. Despite the daunting obstacles, he finds motivation in small victories. One such moment occurs when he finally secures a short phone conversation with a potential client after days of failed attempts. Though this conversation doesn't guarantee success, it's a minor breakthrough in his quest to land a high-stakes job in the finance industry. That small win—the ability to make progress, however modest—fuels his persistence and inspires him to continue pushing forward, even when the odds are against him. These incremental steps, rather than any monumental achievement, demonstrate how small wins build confidence and momentum over time.

If you are in a battle or just don't feel very inspired, make, and keep, a list of your smaller wins. That's what I do, and it works. Angie and I call it our "Lions and Bears List." Before David killed Goliath, he told Goliath that he was going to kill him just like the lions and bears he killed while defending his sheep. In that moment, David realized that those "smaller" wins where preparation for this giant. I recommend, at the end of each day, note your wins, no matter how small. This will help you stay focused on positive progress rather than setbacks.

Angie and I have many lion and bear stories, but one that stands out is the time no one could sell our home. It was 2008 and the Great Recession was in full swing. We had just moved from Texas to Ohio and had a beautiful home in Texas to sell. It was a new build, and we had only been in it for two years. We couldn't afford two mortgages, and needed the equity before we could purchase a new home, so we had to live in my mother-in-law's basement, with two young and very active boys. It was not ideal. We had gone through two realtors and a property management company.

It seemed that no one was buying homes; banks and underwriters were just not approving loans. Out of desperation, we tried renting it, and the first tenants trashed the place. They were hoarders and let rats in the house who ate through the duct work in the walls. It was a mess and the property management company we hired saw fit to absolve themselves from any negligence. Adding to our stress was the cost of those repairs.

Our realtors literally gave up on us. We must have had eight or nine legitimate offers that underwriters denied, several times only days before the scheduled closing. It was a very stressful time. We were desperate, and as amazing as my mother-in-law was, we needed our own space.

Without the help of realtors and powered only by prayer, we took on the task of selling the house ourselves from thousands of miles away—it was no small feat. It was terrifying and we were hemorrhaging money. But then, as if out of the blue, we had a potential buyer who had seen one of our ads. He was perfect—a family man with a solid income, and his wife was a nurse with a great job too. He and his family were moving to Texas from Wisconsin. They loved our place and wanted it badly. It was their "this-is-it" place. After taking care of some legal logistics and a short period of renting, because the underwriters denied them too the first time, we pulled off what the real estate industry could not. We sold the home without the aid of realtors, during the 2008 financial crisis. That seemed huge.

That's the thing about fighting lions and bears, they're pretty formidable, and when you're fighting them, they seem like the giant. It's only when you're facing the next giant do you realize that the last trial was only a lion or a bear. Those lions and bears add up, and eventually, you realize that, with God's help, you can beat any giant. The giant in front of you—cancer, divorce, financial ruin, unexpected tragedy—all will be just like those others and fall. Keeping a list of small wins can be a huge source of inspiration for you when facing the adversity that life brings you.

### CONNECT WITH YOUR PURPOSE

During difficult times, reconnecting with your deeper sense of purpose can reignite your inspiration. Ask yourself: Why did I begin this journey in the first place? What core values or long-term visions are driving me? When you can tie your current struggles to your larger purpose, it becomes easier to stay motivated and inspired, even when the road gets tough. In my case, one of my larger purposes is to bring value to people and help them navigate life well. I thought that was through leadership research and coaching. Well, life threw me a curveball and now I can leverage my disease to fulfill the same purpose in ways that never occurred to me before now.

Take time to reflect on your core values and your overall life mission. Whether through journaling, meditation, or talking with a mentor, reconnecting with the bigger "why" behind your actions can help you stay grounded in difficult times. In Simon Sinek's book, *Start with Why: How Great Leaders Inspire Everyone to Take Action*, he explores how great leaders and successful organizations inspire action by focusing on their core purpose—their "why." Sinek argues that while most people and companies know *what* they do and *how* they do it, only the most influential ones understand and communicate *why* they do it. This *why* represents their core belief, purpose, or cause that drives them beyond profits.

Knowing your why acts as a powerful source of inspiration. When you are clear about the deeper purpose behind your actions, you draw inspiration from that purpose, which fuels perseverance, creativity, and passion—even during difficult times. Understanding your why gives meaning to challenges and helps you stay aligned with your goals, making it easier to inspire yourself and others.

Sometimes your *why* needs a *where*. A good friend of mine, Professor Jeff Konin, has a keynote address about knowing your *where*. His point is in addition to knowing your why, you must also know your where. Without a where you have no idea how to prepare or plan. He asks us to imagine packing for a trip when we don't know where we are going. Do I pack cold weather clothes or a swimsuit? Should I take sandals or boots? Without knowing where you want to be it is impossible to know how to prepare correctly. His talk reminds me of Seneca the Roman philosopher's famous lines, "If a man knows not the harbor he seeks, any wind is the right wind." To live inspired you must also have an idea of where you want to go. Things may change as you go, but you'll likely never go if you don't believe you have a place to be.

## SEEK INSPIRATION

I believe that true inspiration comes from within and is internalized. Despite that, there are times when you believe your personal reservoir of inspiration is completely empty. If there is nothing within you to draw from, it may be helpful to look outward. Drawing inspiration from the experiences of others—whether through books, conversations, or personal connections—can remind you that you are not alone in your struggles. Other people's stories of perseverance and success can fuel your own resolve.

One of my all-time favorite book series is *The Lord of the Rings* by J.R.R. Tolkien. The books are rife with encouragement for any person who feels empty of inspiration. A powerful example of relationships that give inspiration is the story of Samwise Gamgee. Sam is not a warrior, king, or wizard—he's a humble gardener from the Shire. Yet, his unwavering loyalty and belief in the mission to destroy the One Ring become the backbone of the entire quest. While others are driven by duty or glory, Sam is inspired by love, friendship, and the hope for a better world.

As the journey grows darker and Frodo begins to succumb to the Ring's corrupting influence, Sam's inner fire keeps burning. In moments of despair, it's Sam's unshakable hope and ability to see beyond the present hardship that rekindles Frodo's resolve. One of the most inspirational moments comes when Sam says, "There's some good in this world, Mr. Frodo, and it's worth fighting for." This belief—simple yet profound—inspires them through their greatest trials.

Sam's story reminds us that inspiration often comes not from grand acts, but from ordinary people who allow hope and commitment to guide them through impossible circumstances.

## USING INSPIRATION TO FUEL YOUR CAREER AND CREATIVITY

Inspiration plays a critical role in both career advancement and creative work. It provides the energy to explore new ideas, innovate, and push through obstacles. To harness inspiration for your professional life, it's important to align your career with the things that make you curious, maintain a growth mindset, and embrace creative risk-taking.

### Align Your Career with Your Passions

What makes you curious? Knowing what makes you curious is the prerequisite to finding your true passion. Too often we skip the curiosity step and jump right to passion. The problem is what most people think is their passion isn't. I believe that's because not enough time was spent experimenting with our curiosity. Arriving at a passion without having gone through the process of chasing the rabbit trails of what you have questions about or beginning interest in results in a shallow passion. When things get tough you realize very quickly you have a false passion and lose motivation and inspiration. Before you can align your career with your passion, take the time to chase the things that make you curious. But be warned: that often takes years to become fruitful.

The more your career aligns with your authentic passions, the easier it becomes to stay inspired and engaged over the long term. When your work is connected to something you genuinely care about, you'll find yourself more motivated to put in the effort, overcome challenges, and pursue long-term growth.

Ask yourself whether your current career path aligns with what truly excites you. If there's a disconnect, before considering a career shift determine the last time you pursued something you were curious about. Then, pursue it. If you're not sure where your passions lie, reflect on what activities or topics consistently excite you. Are there ways to bring these questions into your work life?

## THE TED LASSO EFFECT

I am a Ted Lasso fan. There is a scene in season 1, episode 8 where Ted needs three miraculous dart throws to win a bet with his rival, Rupert, and save his boss from embarrassment and humiliation.

The dart match was down to the last few throws. In the crowded hum of the pub, tension thickened around the dartboard. Rupert leaned back with his usual air of superiority, sure of his victory. Ted Lasso stood calmly, holding a dart between his fingers, his easygoing demeanor unwavering.

"What do I need to win?" Ted asked.

Mae, watching from behind the bar, replied without hesitation, "Two triple twenties and a bullseye."

Rupert smirked. "Yeah, good luck."

Ted nodded, eyes still on the board. "Ya know, Rupert," he began, spinning the dart slowly, "guys have underestimated me my entire life. For years I never understood why. Used to really bother me."

He squared his shoulders, lining up his first throw. "Then one day, I was driving my little boy to school. I saw this quote by Walt Whitman, right there on the wall. It said, 'Be curious, not judgmental.'"

Boom. The dart flew through the air and struck dead center in the triple 20. The pub went quiet, eyes widening in disbelief.

Ted smiled, soaking in the moment. "I liked that."

He shifted slightly, readying his next shot. "So, I get back in my car, driving to work, and all of a sudden it hits me. All them fellas who used to belittle me—not a single one of them was curious. They thought they had everything all figured out. So they judged everything, and they judged everyone."

Ted paused, spinning the next dart. "And I realized ... their underestimating me had nothing to do with who I was."

He let that settle, glancing Rupert's way. "Cuz if they were curious, they would've asked questions. Yeah, questions like—'Have you played a lot of darts, Ted?'"

With precision, Ted flicked the second dart. It hit the second triple 20, and the crowd stirred louder, leaning in.

"To which I would have answered, 'Yes, sir. Every Sunday afternoon at a sports bar with my father from age ten till I was sixteen ... when he passed away.'"

Ted held the final dart for just a moment longer, the weight of his words filling the room. Then, without a hint of doubt, he said,

"Barbeque Sauce" and confidently threw his dart. Bullseye. The pub erupted, and Ted was the winner of the match and bet.

Many lessons ripple through that iconic dart scene, but one stands out—the power of curiosity.

In a world that often rushes to judgment, curiosity becomes a rare and invaluable skill. Ted's story is a reminder that, too often, people operate under the assumption that they already know the answers. They see someone different, someone who doesn't fit their mold, and their first instinct is to judge—to categorize and dismiss without a second thought. But judgment is a door that locks from the inside, keeping growth and connection on the other side.

Curiosity, on the other hand, gently knocks on that door and asks to be let in. It opens possibilities where judgment builds walls. In that moment at the dartboard, Ted didn't just teach Rupert a lesson about darts; he revealed the deeper flaw in his opponent's approach to life. Rupert assumed Ted was unskilled, simply because he didn't know otherwise. A single question—"Have you played much darts?"—could have changed the entire course of their interaction. But Rupert, like so many others, didn't think to ask.

That's where the magic of curiosity lives. When we stop assuming and start wondering, life unfolds in ways we never expected. Curiosity isn't just about acquiring knowledge; it's about developing empathy, sharpening our skills, and uncovering hidden strengths—both in ourselves and in others. It is then that we discover our true passion!

Think about how this plays out in real life. When we judge a situation or person, we cut off the chance to learn. But curiosity draws us closer. Instead of writing off a difficult project as impossible, curiosity encourages us to ask, "What if there's another way?"

Instead of assuming someone's perspective is wrong, curiosity whispers, "I wonder why they see it that way?"

That single shift in mindset can lead to remarkable discoveries. It's often the curious ones—the question-askers and possibility-seekers—who find their passions. They try new things, stumble across hidden talents, and pursue paths that others never even noticed.

Curiosity turns the ordinary into the extraordinary. It pushes us to master skills, to stay hungry for knowledge, and to show up fully engaged in our own lives. So, the next time you feel the tug to assume rather than ask, remember that dartboard moment. Go ahead and ask the question. Abandon your assumptions and be curious. Because the answers you uncover might just reveal your true passion.

## FOSTER A GROWTH MINDSET

A growth mindset is key to using inspiration to fuel both career and creativity. People with a growth mindset believe that skills and intelligence can be developed through dedication and hard work. This perspective allows you to see challenges as opportunities rather than as setbacks. Staying open to learning and improvement, you'll be more willing to take risks, experiment with new ideas, and push your creative boundaries. When inspiration comes, a growth mindset helps you turn those ideas into reality by staying focused on progress rather than perfection.

A great example of someone with a growth mindset is the fictional character Rocky Balboa from the *Rocky* film series. Rocky starts as an untalented underdog boxer with poor skills and few opportunities, but he refuses to believe he won't improve with the right training. He continually embraces challenges, learns from his defeats, and believes he can improve with hard work and persistence. Despite numerous setbacks—losing fights, facing tougher opponents, and enduring personal hardships—Rocky demonstrates that hard work and work ethic combined with a willingness to learn from failures can lead to success.

Growth mindset drives Rocky to keep training, adapt his techniques, and never give up. He sees challenges as opportunities for growth rather than as roadblocks, which ultimately leads him to becoming a champion. Rocky's journey is a classic illustration of how a growth mindset can lead to success and self-improvement. When facing a professional challenge or creative block, remind yourself that setbacks are a natural part of the learning process. Look for lessons in failures and use them to fuel future success.

## EMBRACE CREATIVE RISK-TAKING

Living inspired is risky business. Innovation and creativity require taking risks. Inspiration can guide you toward ideas that may initially seem unconventional or uncertain, but these are often the ideas that lead to the most significant breakthroughs. When you're inspired, you're more willing to step outside of your comfort zone and explore new possibilities.

Albert Einstein's theory of general relativity is a masterclass in risk taking. Early in his career, Einstein faced significant rejection and skepticism. After proposing his groundbreaking special theory of relativity in 1905, he worked on expanding his original ideas to include gravity. This was extremely risky, even dangerously close to committing career suicide, because it challenged the long-standing Newtonian model of gravity. The scientific community was resistant to his new theory because it contradicted conventional wisdom and required a radical rethink of fundamental concepts in physics.

In 1915, after a decade of meticulous work and multiple rejections, Einstein published his theory of general relativity, which proposed that gravity is the warping of space-time by mass. It largely fell on deaf ears and was met with hostility. That was until May 29, 1919, after four years of ridicule, when an expedition led by Sir Arthur Eddington was able to capture on film the sequence of a solar eclipse, confirming that light bent around the sun as Einstein had predicted. This discovery revolutionized the field of physics, transforming our understanding of space, time, and gravity.

Einstein's willingness to embrace risk, iterate, play the long game, and face the rejection of his ideas ultimately led to one of the most significant breakthroughs in the history of science. Whether it's introducing a bold new idea at work, experimenting with a new creative technique, or taking a calculated risk in your business, leaning into your inspiration can help you push past fear and embrace new opportunities.

I recommend practicing small acts of risk-taking to spark inspiration. Start with low-stakes experiments, then gradually increase the scope of your creative risks as you grow more comfortable.

## INSPIRING OTHERS THROUGH YOUR OWN JOURNEY

As you pursue living an inspired life, you have the opportunity to inspire others along the way. Sharing your journey—both the successes and the struggles—can motivate those around you, whether in your personal life, workplace, or community. Authenticity, vulnerability, and perseverance are key to inspiring others, as people are drawn to those who remain true to themselves while navigating life's challenges.

### Be Authentic and Vulnerable

People are inspired by authenticity and influenced by vulnerability. When you openly share both your victories and your challenges, it allows others to see that inspiration isn't about always having it together—it's about pushing through difficulties with determination and grace. Being vulnerable about your struggles makes your success even more relatable and inspiring to those around you. For example, after my diagnosis, I learned the power of sharing my story authentically. It wasn't easy to be vulnerable about my fears, uncertainties, and challenges, but in doing so, I found that others felt encouraged and inspired.

Brené Brown is a social science researcher whose work focuses on the power of vulnerability and how embracing it can lead to personal growth, stronger connections, and true courage. In her bestselling books *Daring Greatly*, *The Gifts of Imperfection*, and *Braving the Wilderness*, Brown argues that vulnerability—often seen as a weakness—is actually the foundation of courage, creativity, and meaningful relationships.

In *Daring Greatly*, she explains that vulnerability involves risk, uncertainty, and emotional exposure, but it's essential for authentic living and leadership. Brown emphasizes that by opening ourselves up to vulnerability, we foster deeper connections with others, build resilience, and move beyond shame. Brown asserts that embracing vulnerability leads to a fuller, more engaged life, allowing us to overcome fear and other things that steal our inspiration. Ultimately, Brown's work highlights that vulnerability is not a sign of weakness, but a path to courage, strength, and connection.

Embrace vulnerability by refusing to be afraid to share the parts of your journey that feel imperfect. Put a face to it, don't hide behind the anonymity of social media. Whether in personal conversations, public forums, or professional settings, authenticity is what connects and inspires you to others.

### Lead by Example

Inspiration doesn't always have to come from words—it often comes from doing. When others see you persevering in the face of obstacles, pursuing your passions, and staying committed to your goals, they are inspired to do the same. Actions speak louder than words, and when you model resilience and determination, it creates a ripple effect of inspiration.

James Kouzes and Barry Posner's concept of *modeling the way* is one of the five key practices of exemplary leadership, as outlined in their seminal book *The Leadership Challenge: How to Make Extraordinary Things Happen in Organizations.* This practice emphasizes that leaders must set a clear example by aligning their actions with their stated values. Kouzes and Posner argue that leaders who model the way do so by clarifying their own values and beliefs, then consistently demonstrating those principles through their behavior.

They assert that one way to do this is by setting an example in your daily actions, thereby earning credibility. Kouzes and Posner stress that small actions—such as following through on commitments, showing integrity in decision-making, and practicing what you preach—are vital in shaping a culture of trust and accountability.

By modeling the way, leaders create a strong foundation for inspiring and guiding their teams toward shared goals.

## BALANCING INSPIRATION WITH PRACTICALITY

Inspiration is a powerful force for growth, but it must be balanced with practicality. Inspiration alone won't get you where you want to go—you also need a plan, discipline, and actionable steps to turn your ideas into reality. Don't be so heavenly minded that you are no earthly good. The purpose of inspiration is to make a literal difference, not to just be inspired. Inspiration must lead to action, otherwise it will consume your mind and make you mad.

St. Augustine of Hippo is noted for saying, "Pray as though everything depends on God. Work as though everything depends on you." Inspiration is no good without work, and hard work at that. Inspiration without action is the same as having faith without works, something the epistle of James says is "dead."

### Set Clear Goals and Take Action

Inspiration provides the vision, but it's your work that brings that vision to life. Once inspiration strikes, the next step is to work toward your desired outcome. There are myriads of ways to bring vision to life. Here are a few recommendations:

1. **Visualize the outcome:** Create a vivid mental image of what success looks like. Immerse yourself in the details of your vision regularly—through journaling, creating vision boards, or meditating. This keeps the vision clear and emotionally resonant, motivating you to stay on course.

2. **Build a support network:** Surround yourself with mentors, peers, or a community who share or support your vision. Engaging with others who can provide guidance, accountability, and encouragement will help sustain momentum and inspire new ideas or approaches.
3. **Embrace flexibility:** Be open to adjusting your methods as new challenges or opportunities arise. A personal vision is rarely achieved through a rigid plan—stay adaptable and willing to change your approach without losing sight of the end goal.
4. **Develop consistent habits:** Focus on creating habits that align with your vision. For example, if your vision involves writing a book, commit to writing regularly, even if it's not a structured schedule. Building habits connected to your vision helps maintain progress.
5. **Leverage resources and tools:** Identify and utilize the tools, technology, or resources that can help you realize your vision. Whether it's taking advantage of new software, learning platforms, or other technologies, leveraging these can make your journey more efficient and effective.

### Don't Wait for Perfection

One of the biggest obstacles to turning inspiration into growth is the belief that everything has to be perfect before you can move forward. I discussed this a lot in the earlier chapters on excellence. Suffice it for now to remember: waiting for perfect conditions or flawless execution can lead to stagnation. Instead, embrace progress over perfection—start with what you have, and refine your approach as you go.

### Balance Creativity with Realistic Expectations

While it's important to dream big, it's equally important to balance your creative ideas with realistic expectations. Inspiration can lead to ambitious visions, but making those visions a reality requires careful planning, resource management, and time. Staying grounded in what's achievable ensures that you make steady progress without becoming overwhelmed or discouraged.

It is a good idea to review your goals periodically to ensure they're both inspiring and realistic. That can be a tricky balance. Adjust timelines or expectations if necessary to keep moving forward at a sustainable pace. I am a big fan of the TV show *Parks and Recreation*. An excellent example of setting and pursuing realistic goals is Leslie Knope. A passionate government employee, Leslie has grand ambitions to make her town of Pawnee a better place. While she dreams big, she often pursues her goals in realistic, actionable ways.

There is an episode where Leslie dreams of turning an abandoned lot into a community park. She starts with the small manageable step of forming a committee to gather support. She builds on this by securing funding, rallying community involvement, and navigating political hurdles one at a time. Her story demonstrates that while her long-term goal is grand, she grounds it in realistic actions by working within her resources, enlisting help, and focusing on immediate, tangible steps. Through perseverance and practical planning, Leslie shows that even lofty dreams can be realized with a focus on attainable goals.

## USING INSPIRATION TO DRIVE GROWTH

Inspiration requires consistent nurturing, practical action, and balance. By learning how to stay inspired during challenging times, using inspiration to fuel your career and creativity, and leading by example to inspire others, you can turn your ideas into something meaningful. Remember to balance your inspiration with practicality—set clear goals, take consistent action, and embrace progress over perfection.

When you learn to harness inspiration, you'll find that it becomes a positive force that propels you toward growth, fulfillment, and long-lasting success.

This became especially true for me when I had to dig deep to stay inspired, especially on the tough days when energy was low and the path forward felt uncertain. But by reconnecting with my purpose, celebrating small wins, and sharing my journey, I was able to use inspiration as a tool not only to keep myself moving forward but others as well. Remember, inspiration is not a one-time spark—it is a resource you can tap into again and again, even when life throws its biggest challenges at you.

Whether you're inspired by Samwise Gamgee, Rocky Balboa, or Leslie Knope, inspiration often comes from the courage to keep going, the belief in something greater than yourself, and the unwavering commitment to those you care about—even when the odds seem insurmountable. This kind of inspiration fuels the journey toward becoming EPIC.

PART 4

# ON COMPASSION

# 16

# THE POWER OF COMPASSION

To be honest, I am not known to be overly compassionate. I am working in it. Compassion is more than a fleeting feeling of sympathy or a reaction to someone's suffering—it's an active, intentional choice to care deeply for others, share in their experiences, and respond with kindness and support.

In this chapter, we will explore the essence of true compassion, how it differs from pity, and why compassion is crucial not only for personal fulfillment but also for fostering meaningful connections with others. Being compassionate is the final aspect of becoming EPIC.

## WHAT IS COMPASSION?

Brené Brown says, "When we're looking for compassion, we need someone who is deeply rooted, is able to bend and, most of all, embraces us for our strengths and struggles." At its core, compassion means "to suffer with." It involves recognizing the struggles, pain, or hardships of others and feeling moved to take action to alleviate that suffering. Compassion isn't passive; it requires engagement and a willingness to step into someone else's shoes, even if it means experiencing discomfort or hardship yourself.

Compassion is the convergence of empathy and personal connection. It's not simply feeling sorry for someone from a distance; it's about understanding their pain, being present in their suffering, and offering a sense of shared humanity. It transcends judgment and goes beyond offering mere solutions or fixes. Compassion doesn't seek to solve someone's problems for them but to walk beside them as they find their way through their adversity.

For me, learning the true depths of compassion came in a very unexpected way. Before my diagnosis, I thought I understood compassion. As a teacher, mentor, and leader, I believed I was empathetic and compassionate toward others. But after my diagnosis, I realized that the type of compassion I was familiar with was different from the deeper, more humbling compassion I would soon need to embrace.

I started by learning how to receive compassion from others. That was a challenge. I was used to being the one giving support and care, not the one needing it. But as the emotional toll of cancer began to weigh on me, I learned to accept the compassion of family, friends, and even strangers. This experience reshaped how I understood compassion. It wasn't just about offering comfort or words of encouragement—it was about showing up for someone.

True compassion is transformative for both the giver and the receiver. When you extend compassion, you open yourself up to understanding someone's experiences deeply, which in turn helps you grow as a person. Compassion connects us to the broader human experience, making us aware of the shared struggles and joys that unite all people.

A compelling example of transformative compassion is Father Gregory Boyle and Homeboy Industries, the world's largest gang intervention and rehabilitation program in Los Angeles. Father Boyle saw beyond the gang members' criminal behavior, understanding their actions were shaped by trauma, poverty, and a lack of opportunity. Instead of rejecting them, he extended deep compassion, offering jobs, therapy, and a community where they could heal.

This compassion had a profound impact on both the givers and the receivers. Father Boyle and his staff, through their work with people society often discarded, learned valuable lessons about forgiveness, humility, and the power of human connection. Engaging with these individuals forced them to confront their own judgments and grow in empathy and patience.

For the former gang members, receiving compassion was transformative. Many had never experienced kindness or belief in their potential. At Homeboy Industries, they found dignity, purpose, and the chance to rebuild their lives. This compassion helped them break free from the cycle of violence, heal from their trauma, and envision a future where they could contribute positively to society. Compassion became a powerful, two-way street. By extending compassion, the givers grew in their understanding of humanity, while the receivers gained the tools to change their lives. True compassion—understanding and connecting with someone's experience—leads to mutual transformation, fostering an EPIC life for all involved.

## THE DIFFERENCE BETWEEN COMPASSION AND PITY

Compassion and pity are often confused, but they are fundamentally different in how they view and respond to suffering. Compassion is about seeing others as equals, sharing in their experience, and being willing to accompany them through their pain. When you are compassionate, you approach others with humility and a desire to connect. You aren't offering help from a place of superiority or out of obligation—you are reaching out because you understand that, as human beings, we all face hardships and are responsible for lifting one another up.

During my treatment, I often felt a sense of isolation, as if no one truly understood what I was going through. Yet, it was during these moments that compassion from others made the most significant impact. It wasn't the sympathy or pity that helped; it was the people who showed up—those who sat with me, listened without judgment, sent me cards, prayed with me and for me, and stayed present. This taught me that true compassion is about connection. It's about standing with someone in their pain, not because you have the answers, but because you care enough to be there.

### Pity Creates Distance

Pity, on the other hand, tends to create distance between you and the person suffering. It often involves feeling sorry for them without truly understanding their situation. Pity comes from a place of superiority, where you view the other person as weaker or helpless. While pity may lead to charitable actions, it lacks the depth of emotional connection.

An example of the difference can be seen in how we respond to homelessness. Feeling pity for a homeless person might result in giving them money or offering a passing gesture of kindness, but the underlying attitude may be one of judgment or detachment. Compassion, however, looks beyond the surface and seeks to understand the individual's story, struggles, and humanity. A compassionate response might involve not only offering help but also acknowledging the person's dignity and trying to treat them with respect and empathy.

Compassion empowers the other person by reinforcing their worth and validating their experience. Pity, conversely, can make the person feel less capable or worthy, and it often focuses more on the emotions of the person offering help than on the needs of the one suffering.

Next time you encounter someone in need, ask yourself, "Am I approaching this person with a desire to connect and offer understanding, or am I simply feeling sorry for them from a distance?" Compassion seeks connection, while pity builds walls.

## WHY COMPASSION IS KEY TO FULFILLMENT AND CONNECTION

A powerful example of compassion leading to personal fulfillment and connection is the "Parable of the Good Samaritan." This story illustrates how showing compassion to others, regardless of background or differences, is central to living a fulfilling and connected life.

A Jewish man is attacked by robbers and left beaten and half-dead on the side of the road. Several people, including a priest and a Levite, pass by him without offering help. However, a Samaritan—a member of a group typically despised by Jews—stops, tends to the man's wounds, and takes him to an inn to recover, covering all expenses for his care.

The Samaritan's compassion is transformative. By stepping out of his comfort zone to help someone who, culturally, was his enemy, he demonstrates true love and empathy. His actions create a deep connection with the wounded man, showing that compassion transcends societal divides. Through his selfless act, the Samaritan experiences the personal fulfillment that comes from living out the commandment to "love your neighbor as yourself."

This parable teaches us that compassion is a path to true fulfillment and connection with others, emphasizing that loving and helping those in need—regardless of their identity—leads to a richer, more meaningful life. Compassion becomes the bridge that connects us to others, fostering personal growth and spiritual fulfillment as we live in alignment with the command to love.

### Compassion Deepens Relationships

When you demonstrate compassion in your relationships, it strengthens the bonds between you and others. Whether it's with friends, family, colleagues, or even strangers, showing compassion allows you to relate to others on a deeper level. Instead of maintaining surface-level connections, compassion encourages you to build meaningful, supportive relationships based on trust, vulnerability, and understanding.

In close relationships, compassion means being present for others during their hardest moments. When a loved one is struggling with mental health, facing financial hardships, or grieving a loss, your compassion—your willingness to listen, care, and provide support—helps them feel valued and understood. This, in turn, creates a reciprocal dynamic where both parties can lean on one another in times of need, building a relationship based on mutual empathy and care.

Experiencing compassion from others during my cancer journey deepened my relationships in ways I never anticipated. People who once felt distant became closer as they reached out in genuine ways—offering a listening ear, offering meals, or just sitting with me on tough days (thanks, Patchett!). I also found that as I became more open to receiving compassion, I became more compassionate in return. I developed a deeper understanding of the struggles others face, whether related to illness or life in general, and I felt a stronger desire to be present for them in their difficult moments. Compassion has a way of binding people together, creating bonds that are deeper and more meaningful than before.

**Compassion Enhances Personal Fulfillment and Healing**

On a personal level, compassion brings a deep sense of fulfillment and purpose. When you are compassionate, you are living in alignment with a spiritual virtue—caring for others, contributing positively to the world, and finding meaning in your relationships. Compassion allows you to step outside of yourself, broadening your perspective and increasing your sense of purpose.

By regularly practicing compassion, you become more attuned to the needs of others and more connected to your community. This sense of connection can give you greater emotional resilience, as you're not navigating life's challenges alone, but with the understanding that you are part of a broader human experience. Compassionate acts, no matter how small, create ripples, enhancing not only your life but the lives of those around you.

Compassion also has the power to heal. When someone is suffering, what they often need most is not a solution or a fix, but the knowledge that someone truly sees and cares for them. Compassion brings comfort, not because it helps reduce some of the suffering, but because it provides a sense of connection and shared humanity.

Compassion became a critical part of my healing journey. As I accepted the compassion of others and began offering it in return,

I found that it not only helped me cope with the physical aspects of my illness but also gave me emotional strength. Knowing that people were there for me, and being able to be there for others, became a source of healing in itself. Compassion helped me recognize that suffering is part of the human experience, but it's through connection with others that we find hope and resilience.

## THE IMPACT OF COMPASSION ON LEADERSHIP AND PROFESSIONAL GROWTH

Compassion is not only critical for personal relationships and fulfillment—it is also a powerful force in leadership and professional growth. Compassionate leaders foster environments of trust, collaboration, and innovation. When leaders demonstrate compassion, they inspire loyalty, commitment, and a sense of purpose among their teams.

In the workplace, showing compassion as a leader means listening to your employees' needs, understanding their challenges, and offering support when they face personal or professional difficulties. Compassionate leadership doesn't mean avoiding tough decisions or coddling employees; it means creating an environment where people feel valued, heard, and empowered to contribute their best work.

Hamdi Ulukaya, an immigrant from Turkey, is the founder and CEO of Chobani. Ulukaya built Chobani into one of the most successful yogurt brands in the United States. And his leadership is defined not just by business success but by his deep care for his employees and community. In 2016, Ulukaya made the rare decision to give 10 percent of the company's shares to his employees, instantly turning many into millionaires.

Beyond financial generosity, Ulukaya is known for his commitment to hiring refugees, providing job opportunities to those often overlooked by society. He believes that businesses have a responsibility to uplift communities and address inequalities. This compassionate leadership has fostered immense loyalty and dedication within Chobani's workforce while also earning the company widespread respect and admiration. Ulukaya's commitment to compassionate leadership can transform lives, create stronger communities, and fuel sustainable growth.

## THE POWER OF COMPASSION

Compassion is an essential force in personal and professional life. True compassion goes beyond sympathy or pity—it is about connecting with others, sharing in their experiences, and responding with care, empathy, and action. By cultivating compassion, you can deepen your relationships, find greater personal fulfillment, and make a positive impact on those around you.

As we demonstrate compassion in our daily lives, we not only uplift others, but we also create a sense of purpose and connection for ourselves. Compassion reminds us that we are all part of a larger human family, and through caring for one another, we enrich our own lives and contribute to a more empathetic, united world. Compassion is not a weakness—it is a strength that drives both personal growth and collective well-being. It is a powerful tool for navigating life's challenges and for creating lasting, meaningful connections that go beyond superficial interactions. Most importantly, it teaches us how not to be selfish.

As I've learned through my own adversity, compassion isn't just about helping others—it's also about learning how to receive care when you're the one in need. It's about letting down the walls of independence and realizing that compassion is a two-way street. When we allow ourselves to be vulnerable enough to accept the compassion of others, we are reminded of our shared humanity. We see that life's struggles don't have to be borne alone and that compassion from others can fuel our strength in ways we didn't know were possible.

# 17

# THE OTHER SIDE OF COMPASSION

Compassion is most often viewed through the lens of gentleness, kindness, and empathy. It's easy to think of compassion as a soft, nurturing quality—one that involves providing comfort and support to others in times of need. However, there's another side to compassion that we must not ignore, one that is equally important but less frequently discussed.

It's the side that requires us to make hard choices. It is the side of compassion that requires us to hold ourselves and others accountable. Compassion mandates we choose to make the hard choice and do the difficult work of growth and transformation.

This chapter explores the deeper, more challenging side of compassion—the kind that pushes us to face difficult truths, take hard actions, and extend compassion not only to others but to ourselves.

## THE ORIGINS AND MEANING OF PASSION

To understand the full depth of compassion, we first need to revisit the word "passion." The word itself comes from the Latin root *pati*, meaning "to suffer." Most people associate passion with intense enthusiasm or love for something, but its original meaning is much deeper. Passion, in its true sense, is about enduring suffering, hardship, and struggle for the sake of something greater.

As noted in Chapter 12, the Passion of the Christ refers to Jesus's suffering and crucifixion. This profound act of enduring pain and sacrifice for the love and redemption of others is one of the clearest examples of how passion and compassion are intertwined. Compassion is not just about being gentle and nurturing; it's also about making hard choices and sacrificing for the sake of others—or for the sake of your future self.

When we realize that passion and compassion are two sides of the same coin, we see that true compassion is not passive—it is a courageous, active force.

## WHY DOING THE HARD THING IS COMPASSIONATE

There is great power in the act of doing what is hard, uncomfortable, or even painful. True compassion requires us to look beyond immediate comfort and convenience to do what is truly in the best interest of our future selves and those who depend on that person. This means taking action in tough situations and making choices that may feel uncomfortable in the moment but lead to growth in the long-term.

Some great examples of this are getting up at some god-awful hour of the early morning to exercise, disciplining yourself to eat nutritiously, or forgoing social media or screen time to read. These are incredible acts of compassion for your future self. Often, these acts of self-compassion are perceived to come at great expense and cost. These are, in fact, hard choices that lead to a better future for yourself and the ones who love you.

### COMPASSION MEANS HOLDING BOUNDARIES

Doing the hard thing might mean setting boundaries in a relationship or holding someone accountable when they're engaging in harmful behavior. It might involve saying "no" to someone when "yes" would be easier but ultimately harmful. These difficult acts are acts of compassion because they are protective. It's not compassionate to enable harmful behavior or to let someone continue on a destructive path. True compassion may involve hard conversations, firm boundaries, and tough love.

### COMPASSION REQUIRES TOUGH CONVERSATIONS

Similarly, compassion can also involve having difficult conversations with others. Whether it's providing constructive feedback, discussing uncomfortable truths, or addressing conflict, doing the hard thing means you care enough about someone to confront what's difficult, rather than avoiding it.

When someone is in pain, it can be tempting to simply offer comfort and leave it at that. But true compassion might mean encouraging them to face their pain, to seek help, or to make changes in their life that are necessary for healing. While these conversations may be tough, they are grounded in the belief that the person can grow, heal, or improve through that discomfort.

## DAILY PRACTICES FOR DOING THE HARD THING

Doing the hard thing doesn't happen in one grand gesture. It's the daily practice of making intentional choices, facing discomfort, and embracing growth. I have always believed that challenges are opportunities for growth. Maintaining a humble attitude despite these challenges is crucial for achieving greatness. In his book, *Chop Wood Carry Water: How to Fall in Love with the Process of Becoming Great*, author Joshua Medcalf tells the story of a young man who dreams of becoming a samurai. Medcalf describes the valuable life lessons associated with doing the hard things each and every day. Metcalf's message is that mastery and success require unshakable commitment to focused effort and believing that the journey itself is the reward, not the outcome. He says, "Everyone wants to be great, until it's time to do what greatness requires." He goes on to say that it is important to "Dream big. Start small [and be] ridiculously faithful." These sentiments capture the essence of what it means to do hard things.

Even Jesus taught that you must first prove yourself faithful with the small things before you can be trusted with the "big things." The truth is the little things *are* the big things! We've often had it backward, but it's in mastering the small, everyday acts of compassion that the foundation for being EPIC is built.

Making the difficult choice to get up early, make your bed, sacrifice your plans for your spouse, put your best foot forward, eat right, or exercise daily are all examples of little things that add up. Even going the extra mile at work, especially for a boss that doesn't appreciate you or recognize your potential and ability, can make a difference. If she asks you to do some ridiculous task, do it and then volunteer to do it again next time! Here are some daily practices that can help you build the muscles needed for doing the hard things, even when it's uncomfortable.

### Reflect

Take time to reflect on the challenges you face and how you plan to approach them with both courage and compassion. Take a few minutes to consider what might feel difficult today—whether it's a conversation you've been avoiding, a task you've been putting off, an emotion you haven't fully processed, or doing the exercise you know you need.

At the end of the day, do another reflection. It needn't be long. Just a few moments. But be intentional to reflect on what went well, what went wrong, and how you responded to both. Then make a commitment to improve on those observations.

Tell yourself that it is an act of compassion toward your future self. Spend time reflecting on your intentions. If there's a difficult task or situation you're facing, write down how you'll handle it with compassion. Keep the focus on growth, not perfection.

### Practice Radical Honesty

True compassion doesn't shy away from telling the truth. Radical honesty involves declaring truth with kindness and integrity, even when it's difficult. This doesn't mean we need to be harsh or critical with ourselves—it means being authentic and respectful in expressing our inner thoughts and feelings, especially in situations where it would be easier to lie to ourselves. I love Brené Brown's insight from her book *Rising Strong.* She practices using the statement, "The story I am telling myself is …" Brown says the most powerful stories are the ones we are telling ourselves, but to beware because they are usually fiction.

Honesty requires integrity and isn't cynical. I have been caught telling myself red herring lies. Those are lies that mask the real lie. For example, if I planned to work out but haven't yet, I'll say, "I'm too busy to work out today," or "I have way more important things to do." Those are red herring lies, because the truth I am avoiding is I don't want to make the hard choice, or I don't value my future self enough.

Once a day, commit to having at least one honest deep-thinking reflection that you've been avoiding. Approach the self-talk with kindness, but don't shy away from the truth. Whether it's setting a boundary or expressing a concern, embrace honesty with your thoughts and behaviors as a form of compassion.

### Embrace Discomfort

We all love being comfortable. I often tell myself I've earned it. I hate being uncomfortable. But comfort kills. Not just physically, but emotionally too. Discomfort is a natural part of doing the hard thing, and it requires incredible compassion in the sense of aligning with or coming alongside suffering. Whether it's physical discomfort (like getting up early to exercise) or emotional discomfort (like facing a difficult truth), learn to sit with it rather than avoid it. Compassion means acknowledging the discomfort without letting it dictate your actions.

You can try reflecting on one moment when you chose to face discomfort. It could be a small act, like tackling a task you didn't want to do, or something larger, like addressing a difficult issue in your personal life. Celebrate the fact that you chose growth over comfort and then, choose it again.

### Learning to Forgive Yourself

Forgiveness keeps you alive longer! Not forgiving can literally take you to an early death. In 2011, Loren Toussaint and fellow researchers published a paper in the *Journal of Behavioral Medicine* on forgiveness where they studied 1,232 older adults and found that forgiveness had a significant impact on longevity and health. Specifically, conditional forgiveness negatively impacted mortality. You were more likely to die early or have poor health if your forgiveness had conditions to it, like "I'll forgive if you promise to never do it again, or if you apologize first."

Putting conditions on forgiveness is uncompassionate and just mean. When you forgive, just do it. And that includes beating yourself up for failure. Don't offer forgiveness to others—or yourself—with conditions attached.

What does it sound like in your head to put conditions on forgiving yourself? I am glad you asked. We think things like:

- I'll forgive myself if I succeed at this next task.
- I'll forgive myself once I've suffered enough for this mistake.
- I'll forgive myself when I've proven I can be better.
- I'll forgive myself if I vow to never make this mistake again.
- If they don't think I deserve forgiveness, neither should I.

By putting conditions on your own forgiveness, you create barriers that often prevent you from healing and moving forward.

One of the hardest acts of compassion is learning to forgive yourself. We often hold ourselves to impossibly high standards or ridiculously low ones. We are creatures of extremes; when we fail, we often become our own harshest critics. But compassion is a critical part of moving forward in life and sometimes the hardest thing to do is stop punishing yourself for old mistakes. It's about recognizing that we're all imperfect, that we all make mistakes, and that those mistakes don't define us. In Toussaint's study, they reported that people who accepted God's unconditional forgiveness for themselves had the lowest mortality—they lived the longest!

### Self-Compassion in the Face of Failure

Failure is part of life, but how you respond to it is what matters most. Compassion allows you to acknowledge your mistakes without being consumed by them. Instead of beating yourself up, ask yourself: What can I learn from this? How can I grow from this experience? Then, when you have an answer to those questions, act on them!

In my battle with prostate cancer, I am learning the art of compassion for others and myself. For myself, because I am constantly wondering what I did to deserve this. A thought I have learned to take captive. If I let it go on too long, I end up in a dark place that isn't healthy for anyone. There were days when I felt like I wasn't doing enough—days when I felt like I wasn't strong enough, productive enough, or positive enough. But over time, I realized that this constant self-criticism wasn't helping me heal. In fact, it was making things worse. I had to learn to extend the same compassion to myself as I would give to others.

### Letting Go of Perfection

Perfectionism is one of the biggest difficulties in showing compassion. It's a problem all around with becoming EPIC. It's an obstacle to excellence and a barrier to compassion. When we expect ourselves (and others) to be perfect, we set ourselves up for failure, because perfection is impossible. True compassion means embracing your imperfections and allowing yourself to make mistakes, knowing that you can learn and grow from them.

Each day, take a moment to reflect. Acknowledge any mistakes or missteps, but instead of dwelling on them or beating yourself up, ask yourself what you learned and how you can move forward. Write down one positive thing you did that day, no matter how small.

## MOVING FORWARD WITH COMPASSION

Forgiving yourself allows you to move forward with a renewed sense of purpose. Compassion allows you to see mistakes as opportunities for growth, a chance to do the hard thing, rather than as sources of shame or guilt. When you practice self-compassion, you become more resilient and may actually stave off early death or even live longer. You're better equipped to face challenges, because you know that no matter what happens, you will be kind and understanding to yourself too. This allows you to take more risks, try new things, and pursue your goals with courage.

## THE OTHER SIDE OF COMPASSION

True compassion is complex. It requires us to do the hard things, to face discomfort, to be radically honest, and to forgive ourselves when we fall short. This other side of compassion is about growth, resilience, antifragility, and transformation.

Compassion isn't always easy—it requires courage, strength, and vulnerability. But when we embrace the full spectrum of compassion, we not only care for others more deeply, we also care for ourselves in ways that allow us to heal, grow, and move forward. True compassion, both for ourselves and others, is what makes the hard things in life bearable, and it's what ultimately allows us to become EPIC.

# 18

# DEMONSTRATING COMPASSION FOR OTHERS

Demonstrating compassion requires not only an open heart but also practical skills in communication, presence, and self-care. To show compassion, we must balance our desire to help with the understanding that we can't pour from an empty cup.

This chapter will explore the many ways we can demonstrate compassion for others, including listening well, being present without feeling the need to solve problems, setting boundaries, and showing empathy to even the most difficult people.

## LISTENING WELL

One of the most powerful ways to demonstrate compassion is by closely listening to others. Often, when people are in pain or going through challenges, what they need most is to be heard. Listening well involves not only hearing the words being said but also understanding the emotions behind those words.

When we practice active listening, we go beyond waiting for our turn to speak. Instead, we focus entirely on what the other person is saying, without judgment or interruption. Active listening means being fully present, mentally and emotionally, and trying to truly understand the message the person is trying to convey.

This form of listening involves paying attention to both verbal and nonverbal cues. The words someone uses are important, but so are their tone of voice, facial expressions, and body language. These subtle cues can reveal a deeper layer of emotions, often showing what the person might not be saying directly.

A hallmark of listening well involves asking clarifying questions and sometimes even repeating what you've understood the person to mean to ensure you've understood correctly. Don't make assumptions about what they are thinking. This is where your experience gets you in trouble. Don't inadvertently cut them off by saying, "Yeah, yeah, yeah" or "Yeah, right" before they've finished talking. Waiting to agree or reinforce shows the other person that you value their experience and are willing to take the time to truly understand their perspective.

Try this, next time someone shares something with you, focus on listening without thinking about how you will respond. Give them the gift of your full attention and let them guide the conversation. This simple act of presence can be one of the most compassionate things you can offer. The better we listen, the stronger the bridges we build.

## HOW TO BE PRESENT WITHOUT OFFERING SOLUTIONS

Many of us fall into the trap of thinking that compassion means solving other people's problems. While well-intentioned, this approach can sometimes make the other person feel unheard or minimized. Often, people don't need a solution—they simply need to know that someone is there for them, walking alongside them.

My wife is always reminding me not to try and solve her problems. She knows that when she comes to me with a concern, and I am offering solutions—which I know will work if she'd only listen to me—that I am not listening to her. I am actually scanning my memory banks while she is talking to find an experience close enough to the one she is describing so that I can save the day with a brilliant insight that will magically solve her problem. Don't do that. Just listen! Being that problem-solving husband or employee means you are likely NOT listening to what is being said and more likely are visiting your hindsight, which is always biased, because you place yourself as the central character in every memory that you have. I have news for you: you aren't the lead role in the memory at present. Someone else is. Regardless, when we do that, we often miss what is being said and assume we already know, so we check out of the conversation to explore our own memories of a similar or related issue.

### Being Present in Difficult Moments

Being present means offering your full attention and empathy without the need to fix the situation. It's about acknowledging the other person's pain and letting them know that they don't have to go through it alone. This can be difficult, especially if you're someone who naturally wants to help. But true compassion means allowing the other person the space to process their emotions, even if it's uncomfortable for you.

For example, if a friend is grieving the loss of a loved one, they may not want advice on how to move forward. They might just need you to sit with them, listen to their stories, or even just provide quiet companionship. In these moments, your presence is more valuable than any solution you could offer.

### The Importance of Silence

Sometimes, silence can be the most compassionate response. When someone is sharing their pain, they may not need immediate feedback. Offering moments of silence allows them to reflect on their own feelings and gives them space to continue sharing if they choose. Silence can also provide comfort, showing that you're there with them, and words aren't necessary.

Try this as a social experiment: The next time someone confides in you, resist the urge to jump in with solutions. Instead, offer your presence and be okay with silence. Simply being there can often provide more comfort than any advice you could give someone.

## BALANCING COMPASSION WITH BOUNDARIES

While compassion is essential for building deep, meaningful relationships, it's also important to recognize that showing compassion doesn't mean sacrificing your own well-being. To give compassion effectively, you need to maintain healthy boundaries.

### How to Give Without Burning Out

Compassion fatigue is a real phenomenon. If you constantly give to others without taking time to care for yourself, you can become emotionally and physically drained. This exhaustion can lead to feelings of resentment or burnout, making it difficult to show genuine compassion.

To avoid compassion fatigue, it's important to recognize your own limits and set boundaries where necessary. This doesn't mean you stop caring for others—it simply means recognizing when you need to recharge in order to continue being present and compassionate. Taking time for yourself is NOT selfish!

### Setting Healthy Limits While Staying Kind

Setting boundaries can be challenging, especially if you're someone who enjoys helping others. However, boundaries are a form of self-compassion that allow you to continue offering support without depleting yourself. Healthy boundaries also teach others that you value your own well-being, which can create more respectful, balanced relationships.

In their bestselling book, *Boundaries: When to Say YES, How to Say NO To Take Control of Your Life*, authors Drs. Henry Cloud and John Townsend discuss how important boundaries are. They debunk the myths that setting boundaries is selfish or detrimental to relationships and set out to demonstrate that they protect our emotional, mental, physical, and spiritual well-being. Cloud and Townsend explain that boundaries are invisible lines that define what is and isn't our responsibility. They help us distinguish between what we can control (ourselves) and what we cannot (other people's feelings, actions, or problems). Healthy boundaries allow us to take ownership of our lives without overextending ourselves or being manipulated by others.

Setting a boundary might look like saying no to something that doesn't align with your capacity, or letting someone know that you can listen to them but won't be able to provide a solution. It could also mean taking a break from caregiving responsibilities when you feel overwhelmed.

## COMPASSION IN DIFFICULT RELATIONSHIPS

One of the greatest challenges in demonstrating compassion is doing so in difficult or strained relationships. It's easy to be compassionate toward people we love and feel close to, but what about when the relationship is toxic or when someone is hurtful?

### Demonstrating Compassion to Toxic People

Compassion doesn't mean allowing others to mistreat you. However, it does mean recognizing that even difficult or toxic people are often acting out of their own pain, fear, or insecurity. While this doesn't excuse their behavior, it can help you approach them with empathy rather than frustration. Showing compassion in difficult relationships might involve maintaining a respectful distance while still wishing the person well. It could also mean trying to understand their perspective, even if you don't agree with it. Compassion for difficult people is about seeing their humanity, even when their behavior makes it hard to connect with them.

### Being Kind and Firm

Compassionate assertiveness is the ability to stand firm in your boundaries while still being kind. It involves expressing your needs, feelings, and limits in a way that is respectful and empathetic. In difficult relationships, compassionate assertiveness allows you to take care of yourself while still extending understanding to the other person.

For example, if someone is consistently crossing your boundaries, you might say, "I understand that you're upset, and I want to be here for you. But I also need to make sure I am being respected. Let's take a break and revisit this conversation when we're both calmer." Compassionate assertiveness shows that you care about the relationship, but you also value yourself enough to set clear expectations for how you wish to be treated.

Practice compassionate assertiveness by speaking truth with kindness. Use "I" statements to express your feelings without blaming the other person. For example, "I feel overwhelmed when we argue like this, and I need to take a step back." Two of my favorite authors are Drs. John and Julie Gottman, directors of the Gottman Institute, aka the "Love Lab." The Gottmans' research shows that how partners start conversations, especially during conflict, is a major predictor of relationship success. They emphasize the difference between "I" statements and "you" statements. "I" statements allow individuals to express their own feelings, thoughts, and needs without making the other person feel attacked, while "you" statements often come across as blaming or accusatory. Benefits of "I" statements include:

1. **Owning emotions:** Using "I" statements helps a person take responsibility for their own feelings. Instead of saying, "You never listen to me," a person might say, "I feel unheard when we talk."
2. **Reducing defensiveness:** "You" statements often provoke defensiveness and can escalate conflict. For example, saying "You always interrupt me" may cause the other person to react defensively. By contrast, "I" statements like, "I feel unheard" reduce the likelihood of defensiveness by focusing on personal experience.

3. **Encouraging problem-solving:** "I" statements create a more collaborative environment where both partners can work together to find a solution. Instead of pointing fingers, it opens the door for understanding and mutual support.
4. **Promoting empathy and understanding:** By framing communication around personal experience rather than blame, "I" statements encourage partners to listen more empathetically. This fosters a deeper understanding of each other's perspectives.

## HOW TO DEMONSTRATE COMPASSION FOR OTHERS

Compassion for others is one of the most meaningful gifts we can give. Whether it's through active listening, being present in difficult moments, balancing compassion with healthy boundaries, or using "I" statements, true compassion requires both empathy and strength. It's about being there for others while also taking care of yourself, and it's about seeing the humanity in even the most difficult people. Compassionate relationships are built on understanding, presence, and the willingness to listen without judgment or the need to fix. By practicing compassion in these ways, you can create deeper, more fulfilling connections with people as you become EPIC.

PART 5

# ON BECOMING

# 19

# OVERCOMING IMPOSTER SYNDROME

Imposter syndrome is a psychological pattern in which individuals doubt their skills, talents, or accomplishments and have a persistent fear of being exposed as a "fraud." It kills your journey to becoming EPIC. Even when external evidence of success is present, those experiencing imposter syndrome struggle to internalize their achievements and often attribute their success to luck, timing, or the belief that they have somehow deceived others into thinking they are more capable than they are. It is a real challenge. In Chapter 4 I introduced imposter syndrome as the second limiting belief to excellence.

In this chapter, I want to dive deeper into unpacking imposter syndrome. I will describe how to battle it and how it derails you from becoming EPIC. Learning how imposter syndrome manifests and how it sabotages Excellence, Perception, Inspiration, and Compassion can be a valuable takeaway.

My personal struggle includes an ongoing battle with imposter syndrome. In fact, a dead giveaway of my imposter syndrome is that after receiving a compliment, I often say, "I am just making it up as I go." Or that I was just lucky or at the right place at the right time.

Another real challenge in the imposter syndrome battle, for many, including me, is faith. It seems counterintuitive, but it's not. Exclusively giving credit to a divine power can do two things: lessen your effort—after all, it's not you doing it, so why try?—and encourage us to make excuses for failure. It didn't happen because God didn't want it to, so this must not be His will. The truth is that most of the time we fail because we don't try hard enough or long enough; we become passive about accomplishments.

It is typical for people of faith to give credit to God for anything good that happens (and to blame the devil for everything bad). So, when something good happens we say, "I am just blessed" or "the Lord did it for me." While I believe that is true, it is still a cop out. I mentioned earlier that St. Augustine said, "Pray like everything depends on God. Work like everything depends on you." That applies here!

Louis Pasteur said, "Chance favors the prepared mind," meaning that being knowledgeable and skilled increases the likelihood of taking advantage of opportunities. The fact is I work, damn hard. In fact, King Solomon says, "Do you see a man who excels in his work? He will stand before kings; He will not stand before unknown men." I love this proverb because it explicitly teaches that the quality of our work determines who notices us and ultimately what opportunities we have. Imposter syndrome tries to take that away.

For anyone striving to live an EPIC life—one grounded in Excellence, Perception, Inspiration, and Compassion—imposter syndrome can be a significant barrier. It sabotages growth by undermining your confidence and limiting your ability to fully embrace potential. But when conquered, closing down imposter syndrome opens the door to becoming EPIC.

## WHAT IS IMPOSTER SYNDROME?

Imposter syndrome is the experience of feeling like a phony despite evidence of success. It was first identified by psychologists Pauline Clance and Suzanne Imes in the 1970s. They found that many high-achieving women believed their success was undeserved and feared being exposed as frauds. However, imposter syndrome affects people of all genders and backgrounds, particularly those who set high standards for themselves. Imposter syndrome manifests in several ways, including:

1. **Self-doubt:** Constantly second-guessing your abilities or knowledge, even when others recognize your competence.
2. **Perfectionism:** Feeling like anything less than perfection will expose you as inadequate or unqualified.
3. **Fear of failure:** An overwhelming fear that making even the smallest mistake will lead others to discover that you're not as capable as they thought.
4. **Attributing success to external factors:** Believing that your success is due to luck, timing, favors from colleagues, or other external factors rather than your own talent or hard work.
5. **Overworking:** Trying to compensate for perceived inadequacy by working excessively hard, believing that effort will make up for a lack of true ability.

Imposter syndrome is not just a fleeting feeling of insecurity or doubt. It can be a deeply ingrained belief system that holds you back from fully engaging with your potential, and it can prevent you from feeling capable of achieving excellence, becoming more perceptive, staying inspired, and being compassionate.

## WHY IMPOSTER SYNDROME IS SO INSIDIOUS

Imposter syndrome is insidious because it operates in the shadows of your mind, often going unnoticed until it has already done significant damage. It works quietly, feeding on your insecurities and magnifying your self-doubts to the point where you may not even attempt new opportunities or embrace your successes when they occur.

### It Undermines Excellence

Imposter syndrome sabotages excellence by convincing you that you're never good enough. When you constantly feel like a fraud, you're less likely to take the risks necessary for personal and professional growth. You may set impossibly high standards for yourself, become overly critical of your performance, and avoid opportunities that could advance your skills and success. Imposter syndrome makes you feel like you're not deserving of excellence, preventing you from living up to your true potential.

A well-known example of imposter syndrome negatively impacting excellence can be seen in Maya Angelou, the celebrated author and poet. Despite her numerous accolades, Angelou once admitted, "I have written eleven books, but each time I think, 'Uh-oh, they're going to find out now. I've run a game on everybody, and they're going to find me out.'" Her doubt could have easily hindered her from continuing her prolific career. Fortunately, Angelou persevered, but her case illustrates how imposter syndrome can create internal barriers even in the face of clear excellence.

### It Dulls Perception

Perception requires a level of self-awareness, openness to feedback, and confidence in interpreting the world around you. Imposter syndrome clouds your perception by making you hyper-focused on your flaws, rather than seeing the bigger picture of your abilities and contributions. It skews your perception of reality, making you believe that you're inadequate, even when evidence clearly shows otherwise. This distorted view makes it harder to develop insight into yourself and others, reducing your ability to perceive opportunities, growth, or success clearly.

Imposter syndrome distorts your perception of reality by fostering persistent self-doubt that hinders your ability to see your own achievements or makes you undervalue them. At the same time, it magnifies mistakes, causing you to fixate on even minor missteps and view them as evidence of incompetence. This creates a constant fear of being "found out," which shapes how you interpret others' perceptions of you, making genuine praise or recognition feel insincere. Over time, you may become hypercritical, judging yourself far more harshly than others would and dismissing your strengths, creating a significant gap between how you see yourself and how the world sees you.

Imposter syndrome also makes you dependent on external validation, distorting what you see. It impairs your decision-making, leading to hesitation or second-guessing, even in situations where you're experienced, and undermines your confidence. Finally, it blinds you to your own growth, making you forget that learning and improvement are natural processes. Instead, you remain trapped in a cycle of doubt, unable to perceive with clarity or feel any hope.

An example of imposter syndrome distorting perception can be seen in Howard Schultz, the former CEO of Starbucks. Despite his success in building a global coffee empire, Schultz has often spoken about his ongoing battle with imposter syndrome. He confessed in interviews that he sometimes felt like he didn't deserve his role or success, even after transforming Starbucks into a multibillion-dollar brand. His distorted perception of himself as someone not fully deserving of his achievements hindered his ability to fully internalize his accomplishments, affecting how he viewed his role as a leader and decision-maker.

### It Dims Inspiration

Imposter syndrome dims inspiration by creating a mental environment where fear dominates and destroys creativity, willingness to experiment, and innovation. When you're constantly worried about being exposed as a fraud, it's hard to feel inspired or motivated to push beyond your comfort zone. Instead of feeling empowered to pursue new ideas or paths, imposter syndrome keeps you playing small and focused on fear of failure or judgment from others. It saps the energy that should be fueling your dreams and passions, and eventually, it will make you feel disconnected from the things that once inspired you.

Albert Einstein, despite being one of the most celebrated physicists of all time, experienced imposter syndrome throughout his life. He often referred to himself as an "involuntary swindler" and doubted the merit of his accomplishments. This self-doubt likely made it harder for him to see his own genius for what it was. Einstein's case demonstrates how imposter syndrome can block even the most brilliant minds from fully embracing their creativity and innovation.

### It Sabotages Compassion

Compassion is often the first casualty of imposter syndrome. Doing hard things isn't an option with imposter syndrome. When you're constantly telling yourself that your success is undeserved, it's difficult to take risks. You become overly critical of your mistakes, and you may even start to believe that you're not worthy of kindness from others. Without self-compassion, it becomes harder to extend genuine compassion to others, as you're trapped in a cycle of self-criticism and inadequacy. Eventually, that carries over into how you show compassion to others. Often it manifests as criticism and harsh interactions.

A striking example of how imposter syndrome sabotages self-compassion can be found in Sheryl Sandberg, the former COO of Facebook and author of *Lean In: Women, Work, and the Will to Lead*. Despite her high-profile success, Sandberg has spoken openly about her struggles with imposter syndrome, particularly after her husband's unexpected death. Her self-doubt in her role as a leader and a widow contributed to an internal struggle where she found it hard to extend compassion to herself in the face of grief. Sandberg's experience highlights how imposter syndrome can block compassion, particularly when we're faced with personal or professional hardship. Imposters falsely believe they have to make up for the weakness or hardship by trying harder to prove they are worthy.

## HOW TO OVERCOME IMPOSTER SYNDROME

Overcoming imposter syndrome is not about eliminating self-doubt altogether—doubt is a normal part of the human experience. Rather, it's about learning to recognize imposter syndrome for what it is—a false narrative—and replacing it with a more balanced, realistic understanding of your abilities and achievements.

Imposter syndrome often thrives in silence, so one of the most effective ways to combat it is by speaking openly about your experiences. When you acknowledge your doubts and share them with trusted friends, mentors, or colleagues, you'll often find that others have felt the same way. This sense of shared experience can help dismantle the isolation imposter syndrome creates and remind you that feeling uncertain doesn't mean you are unqualified.

The following actions help you overcome imposter syndrome by shifting your focus from perfection to progress. Acknowledging and naming your imposter syndrome brings awareness to the false narratives that undermine your confidence. Reframing your thoughts allows you to challenge negative self-talk and view mistakes as opportunities for growth. Embracing your hard work reinforces the reality that your achievements are the result of effort and dedication, not luck. Seeking support and validation from others provides external perspective and reminds you that you're not alone in feeling this way. Finally, focusing on growth helps you cultivate resilience, turning imposter syndrome into a steppingstone rather than a stumbling block.

### Acknowledge and Name Your Imposter Syndrome

The first step in overcoming imposter syndrome is to acknowledge it. Naming it takes away some of its power. When you can identify those nagging thoughts as part of the imposter syndrome, you begin to create distance between your true self and the narrative of inadequacy that imposter syndrome feeds you. Simply recognizing "I'm feeling like an imposter right now" can help you see that these thoughts aren't an accurate reflection of reality.

### Reframe Your Thoughts

Once you recognize imposter syndrome at play, it's important to reframe your thoughts. Instead of attributing your success to luck or external factors, remind yourself of the hard work, skills, and dedication that contributed to your accomplishments. Challenge your negative self-talk by replacing it with evidence-based affirmations of your abilities.

For example, if you find yourself thinking, "I only got this promotion because they couldn't find anyone else," challenge that thought with, "I earned this promotion because of my hard work, leadership skills, and ability to meet challenges." You might tell yourself that "anyone could do this." Not true. Not everyone wants to and not everyone is capable. Own it. Own the fact you did it and someone else didn't.

### Embrace Your Hard Work

I used to believe—and have even been told to my face—that anyone could earn two PhDs, write seven books, and build an international speaking business. They say, if they wanted to, they could too. They've gone on to say, "You're not that smart; you just work hard." And they're right—I do. I'm a very hard worker. But here's the truth: not everyone is willing to put in that kind of effort, and few are prepared to work as hard as I have to achieve what I've done. At the same time, I know others have accomplished much more because they've been willing to make sacrifices I haven't. I'm not arrogant enough to claim I could do the same if I wanted to—I simply recognize that I've chosen a different path, and I'm at peace with that.

One of the most powerful ways to combat imposter syndrome is to fully embrace your effort. It's not an accident that you are where you are. This means not downplaying your achievements or attributing them to luck. Instead, take time to celebrate your accomplishments and recognize your role in achieving them. Keeping a "success journal" where you write down your achievements can help you internalize your successes and serve as a reminder during moments of doubt. Don't let people steal your hard work from you.

### Seek Support and Validation

Imposter syndrome thrives in isolation, it drives you to be alone and keep your thoughts to yourself. Reaching out for support is crucial. Sharing your feelings with a trusted mentor, colleague, or friend can provide you with the validation and perspective you need to see yourself more clearly. When being vulnerable about imposter syndrome, do not let yourself believe that they'll think you're fishing for compliments. You aren't, and they won't think that anyway. Often, others can see your abilities and successes more objectively than you can, and their reassurance can help quiet the voice of imposter syndrome.

### Focus on Growth

Perfectionism is a key component of imposter syndrome, but focusing on growth instead of perfection is one of the most effective ways to overcome it. When you shift your mindset from "I need to be perfect" to "I'm always learning and growing," you release the pressure to be flawless. This opens space for you to take risks, make mistakes, and see those mistakes as opportunities for growth rather than evidence of inadequacy.

When you overcome imposter syndrome, you unlock the door to becoming EPIC. Freeing yourself from the limitations of imposter syndrome allows you to embrace your full potential and step into your future self with confidence. Bringing the thoughts that imposter syndrome imposes on you into captivity ultimately enhances Excellence, Perception, Inspiration, and Compassion.

### EXCELLENCE BECOMES ATTAINABLE

When imposter syndrome no longer holds you back, you begin to believe in your ability to achieve excellence. Instead of viewing excellence as something unattainable or reserved for others who "really deserve it," you can pursue it wholeheartedly, knowing that your hard work and talent are enough. Overcoming imposter syndrome allows you to take risks, stretch your capabilities, and continue growing toward excellence without the fear of being "exposed."

### PERCEPTION SHARPENS

As imposter syndrome fades, your perception becomes clearer. You can view your accomplishments objectively, without the filter of self-doubt. This new clarity allows you to see yourself as others see you—a capable, talented individual who deserves their achievements. It also sharpens your perception, enabling you to offer more empathy, insight, and understanding without projecting your insecurities onto them.

## INSPIRATION FLOURISHES

Without the constant weight of self-doubt, you're free to be inspired again. Overcoming imposter syndrome reenergizes your creative spirit and reignites your sense of purpose. No longer shackled by fear, you can pursue your passions with renewed enthusiasm, knowing that you can achieve your dreams and that your ideas and contributions matter.

## COMPASSION DEEPENS

Overcoming imposter syndrome also deepens your compassion. As you let go of self-criticism and perfectionism, you learn to treat yourself with the same kindness and understanding that you extend to others. This self-compassion naturally leads to a more authentic, empathetic approach to those around you. Instead of judging yourself or others harshly, you recognize the shared human experience of growth, learning, and imperfection. Moving away from imposter syndrome also reduces a competitive and critical mindset. This frees you to be more compassionate to others.

## EMBRACING YOUR EPIC SELF

Imposter syndrome works hard to convince you that you're not enough, that you don't deserve success, that you're not truly capable, and that you'll eventually be exposed as a fraud. But these are just lies that hold you back. By recognizing, naming, and overcoming imposter syndrome, you open the door to becoming EPIC.

When you fight to be released from the grip of imposter syndrome, you'll find that you're capable of achieving far more than you ever thought possible. You'll step into your full potential with confidence, clarity, and a renewed sense of purpose. And as you continue your journey to becoming EPIC, you'll inspire others to do the same.

# 20

## NO ONE BECOMES EPIC ALONE

One of the most pervasive myths in personal development is the idea of the "self-made" person—the notion that individuals can rise to greatness entirely on their own. The truth is no one achieves greatness in isolation. Whether in science, business, art, or personal development, collaboration, support, and connection with others are essential. This is especially true when determined to become EPIC. Excellence, perception, inspiration, and compassion all require help and collaboration.

In this chapter, we will explore why no one can become EPIC alone, how scientific breakthroughs and innovations occur through collaboration, and how social bonds are crucial for growth. We will also examine the importance of building relationships that nurture our journey toward becoming EPIC.

Human beings are social creatures, wired for community and connection. From the dawn of civilization to modern society, breakthroughs and innovations have always occurred within a web of relationships, teamwork, and shared efforts. The phrase, "It is not good for man to be alone," echoes down to us from the dawn of time. This profound truth speaks not only to companionship but also to the necessity of collaboration and support in achieving our potential.

## THE SCIENCE OF HUMAN SOCIAL NEEDS

Human beings are biologically designed to connect with others. Our species has learned that our ancestors survived because they lived in tribes and social groups. Early humans faced threats from predators, environmental challenges, and scarce resources, but by working together, they increased their chances of survival. Cooperation, shared knowledge, and social bonds allowed our ancestors to not only survive but thrive.

Modern research supports the importance of social connection for mental, emotional, and even physical well-being. Psychologists such as Abraham Maslow identified "belongingness" as a fundamental human need in his hierarchy of needs. Similarly, studies in neuroscience show that social interaction stimulates the release of oxytocin, often called the "bonding hormone," which fosters trust and empathy. Social support systems have been shown to reduce stress, increase resilience, and improve overall well-being.

This innate need for connection isn't just about emotional fulfillment—it's essential for personal and collective progress. Throughout history, people have relied on each other to achieve remarkable feats, and this reliance is no less important when striving to become EPIC.

## NO BREAKTHROUGH HAPPENS IN ISOLATION

While we often celebrate individual inventors and scientists for their innovations, the reality is that no significant breakthrough in history has occurred without collaboration, shared knowledge, and teamwork.

Collaboration fosters excellence by allowing us to learn from others' strengths and insights, refining our own skills along the way. Perception grows when we actively seek diverse perspectives, broadening our understanding of complex challenges. Inspiration often comes from witnessing the determination, creativity, and resilience of those around us, motivating us to push further. And at the heart of it all is compassion—recognizing the value of collective success and lifting others as we climb.

Sir Isaac Newton's famous quote, "If I have seen further, it is by standing on the shoulders of giants," reflects this spirit, a powerful reminder that our greatest achievements are often the result of collaboration, teamwork, and the foundation laid by those who came before us. Even the most brilliant minds stood on the shoulders of others. Progress isn't made in isolation; it's built by drawing from the knowledge, experiences, and efforts of others. This ties directly into becoming EPIC—because true greatness is rarely the product of individual effort alone.

Newton's achievements were made possible by building on the discoveries of pioneers like Galileo and Kepler, demonstrating how breakthroughs are born through shared knowledge and teamwork across generations. As we strive to become EPIC, embracing collaboration not only accelerates our growth but also strengthens the communities we are part of. Recognizing the contributions of others doesn't diminish our success—it amplifies it.

Take, for example, Albert Einstein, often considered the quintessential "lone genius." While Einstein made groundbreaking contributions to physics, including his theory of relativity, he was deeply influenced by the work of scientists who came before him, such as Isaac Newton and James Clerk Maxwell. Additionally, Einstein collaborated with other physicists and mathematicians, discussing his theories and refining his ideas through dialogue and feedback. In his book, *When Einstein Walked with Gödel: Excursions to the Edge of Thought*, author Jim Holt meticulously describes the intellectual relationship between Einstein and Gödel. Despite being in different disciplines—Einstein, physics and Gödel, mathematics—they shared a unique relationship walking to and from work at Princeton every day. Their conversation sparked their imaginations and kept them active late into their iconic careers.

Similarly, Thomas Edison is often credited with inventing the light bulb, but the reality is far more complex. Edison's invention was the result of a team of researchers working at his Menlo Park laboratory. It was through collaboration, shared ideas, and the contributions of others that Edison's innovations took shape. Without his team and colleagues who pushed him, questioned him, and challenged him, many of Edison's inventions, including the light bulb, may have never occurred when they did.

### THE WRIGHT BROTHERS: POWERED BY PARTNERSHIP

A perfect example of how collaboration leads to greatness is the story of Orville and Wilbur Wright. The Wright brothers invented and built the world's first successful airplane, but their achievement would not have been possible if they had attempted the feat alone.

Orville and Wilbur worked in tandem, relying on each other's strengths and shared knowledge to develop their ideas. Wilbur was the meticulous planner, gifted with keen observation skills and an ability to learn from other pioneers in aviation, while Orville brought technical skill and mechanical expertise to the table. Together, they bounced ideas off each other, tested various models, and shared the workload as they experimented with gliders and flight controls. Often, their collaborations turned volatile. They were known to fight and scream at each other, often during intense and long days in their workshop as they challenged and pushed each other to do better and rethink.

Their success didn't just come from their partnership, though. The Wright brothers relied heavily on the knowledge of others—drawing inspiration from aviation pioneers like Otto Lilienthal and using scientific insights from engineers and physicists to improve their designs. The collaboration between these two brothers, their dedication to learning from others, and their willingness to share the work laid the foundation for their historic flight in 1903. This iconic partnership exemplifies the power of working together, proving that even world-changing breakthroughs, like human flight, cannot be achieved in isolation.

## EXCELLENCE: PUSHING BEYOND YOUR LIMITS WITH SUPPORT

To achieve excellence, we need others to push us beyond our perceived limits. Whether it's a mentor who challenges you to reach new heights or a colleague who offers a fresh perspective, striving for excellence is easier when you have people around you who encourage growth. In sports, for example, world-class athletes consistently speak of the importance of coaches, teammates, and rivals who push them to be their best. Excellence doesn't occur in a vacuum—it's fostered by the people who help us stretch our capabilities.

The value of others in our pursuit of excellence goes beyond simple encouragement; it often provides the honest feedback necessary for real growth. Left to our own devices, it's easy to settle into comfort zones, but having people who challenge and refine us can highlight blind spots we might otherwise miss. Constructive criticism, competition, and collaboration drive us to sharpen our skills and continuously improve. Just as iron sharpens iron, the influence of those around us polishes our strengths and helps us navigate weaknesses.

Surrounding ourselves with individuals who share our drive or possess strengths we lack creates an environment where excellence thrives. Their belief in our potential can reignite our motivation during difficult times and remind us of the bigger picture when obstacles arise. The simple truth is this: by surrounding ourselves with people who are better and more accomplished than us, we can and will grow.

## PERCEPTION: SEEING THROUGH THE EYES OF OTHERS

Perception is the ability to see clearly and understand the world around you. However, our perceptions are inherently limited by our individual experiences and biases. To develop true perception, we must rely on others to help us see beyond our own perspectives, biases, and blind spots. By engaging with people from diverse backgrounds and experiences, we expand our understanding of the world, challenge our assumptions, and gain deeper insights.

For example, in a leadership context, the wisest leaders often seek feedback from advisors or peers to avoid blind spots in their decision-making. A single viewpoint can only go so far, but when you surround yourself with people who offer new perspectives, you sharpen your perception, consider more options, and make better decisions.

In *The Empowered Manager: Positive Political Skills at Work*, author Peter Block introduced the Agreement-Trust Matrix. The matrix highlights how engaging with *opponents*—those we disagree with but trust—can significantly enhance our perception. Opponents challenge our assumptions and force us to consider alternative perspectives, sharpening our understanding and broadening our view of complex issues. Unlike adversaries, who lack trust, opponents provide honest feedback rooted in mutual respect, creating opportunities for growth rather than conflict. By valuing the insights of trusted opponents, we cultivate greater perception, allowing us to navigate challenges with more clarity and make more well-rounded, informed decisions.

## INSPIRATION: FINDING MOMENTUM THROUGH COLLECTIVE STRENGTH

Inspiration often comes from seeing the achievements, struggles, and successes of others. Whether it's a friend who overcame adversity or a colleague who pursued a creative idea against the odds, witnessing the journeys of others can fuel your own sense of inspiration.

Additionally, inspiration is not just about receiving; it's about giving as well. When you surround yourself with people who are working toward similar goals or striving for their own versions of excellence, you create a mutually inspiring environment. Inspiration thrives in community. Find people who uplift each other and encourage forward movement and connect with them.

Perhaps there is no greater example of inspired momentum than the Civil Rights Movement in the United States, particularly the leadership and collaboration between Dr. Martin Luther King Jr., Rosa Parks, John Lewis, and many others. While Dr. King is often seen as the face of the movement, the progress achieved was the result of a vast network of individuals and communities working together, drawing inspiration and strength from one another.

The Montgomery Bus Boycott, sparked by Rosa Parks's act of defiance, gained momentum through the collective action of the Black community in Montgomery, who united to organize carpools, walk miles to work, and refuse to patronize segregated buses. Their solidarity inspired similar actions across the country, demonstrating how individual courage, when supported by community effort, can inspire lasting social change. The strength and perseverance of countless unsung activists created the momentum necessary for legislative victories like the Civil Rights Act of 1964. This collective strength illustrates that inspiration is often amplified through shared purpose.

## COMPASSION: THE ULTIMATE EXPRESSION OF CONNECTION

Compassion is deeply rooted in our connections with others. To be truly compassionate, you must understand and empathize with the experiences, pain, and struggles of the people around you. Compassion cannot exist in isolation; it requires engagement with others.

When you practice compassion, you strengthen your relationships and create a supportive environment where everyone can thrive. Compassion helps you connect with others on a deep level, offering kindness, understanding, and empathy, nourishing your growth and the growth of those around you.

This was the hardest thing for me to do. When I was diagnosed it meant slowing down and doing less. I couldn't handle it. It was hard for me to let others help me or even to let them know I was in need. In fact, I can still hear my wife saying, "If you don't ask for help then I will." I couldn't even ask for help by myself. It is an ongoing battle—but we all must learn to embrace the reality that others are most often the important ingredient in our success!

## THE POWER OF TRIBES AND TEAMS: BUILDING YOUR SUPPORT NETWORK

Research consistently shows that humans thrive in tribes and teams. We are biologically wired to seek groups where we feel a sense of belonging and connection. Psychologists have found that social networks not only provide emotional support but also enhance motivation, creativity, and resilience. When you have a tribe of like-minded individuals around you, your goals become more achievable. The benefits of finding your tribe include:

1. **Increased accountability:** When you're part of a team or community, you're more likely to stay committed to your goals because others are holding you accountable. Whether it's a fitness group, a professional mastermind, or a circle of friends, having people who check in with you helps you stay on track.
2. **Emotional support:** Life's journey is full of challenges and having a support network provides emotional reinforcement during tough times. Knowing that others are there to offer encouragement, advice, or simply a listening ear makes it easier to persevere.

3. **Diverse perspectives:** Being part of a group exposes you to cognitive diversity, different ideas, backgrounds, and ways of thinking. This diversity of thought enhances your perception, sharpens your decision-making, and helps you navigate complex situations more effectively.

## BUILDING YOUR EPIC TRIBE

As you work toward becoming EPIC, it's essential to build a tribe of people who share your values and support your growth. These are the people who will challenge you, inspire you, and push you to be better. Surround yourself with those who are also striving for excellence, who seek to understand the world with clarity, who find inspiration in their journeys, and who show compassion in their relationships.

In his book *Tribes*, Seth Godin explores the idea that humans are wired to form tribes—communities bound together by shared values and a common cause. Godin argues that in today's world, anyone can lead a tribe by embracing their unique vision and inspiring others to follow. His message is simple yet profound: leadership is no longer about authority, but about connection and motivation. This idea is deeply relevant to the EPIC journey, as becoming a member of a tribe of like-minded individuals who share your values is crucial for growth. To truly embody Excellence, Perception, Inspiration, and Compassion, you need a tribe that supports, challenges, and inspires you. Godin asserts that tribes provide the needed structure for people to make meaningful change. The right tribe can help you stay aligned with the EPIC mindset, providing the feedback, resources, and encounters necessary to break through mediocrity and achieve more.

## THE JOURNEY TO BECOMING EPIC REQUIRES OTHERS

No one becomes EPIC alone. Whether in personal growth, professional success, or groundbreaking innovations, human beings need connection, support, and collaboration to reach their highest potential. Excellence, Perception, Inspiration, and Compassion are values that flourish in relationships, not in isolation.

We are designed for connection, and it is through our relationships that we grow, learn, and achieve greatness. Surround yourself with people who help you become the best version of yourself, and you will find that your journey to becoming EPIC is not only more achievable but also far more rewarding.

21

# LIVING A BALANCED LIFE

Living a life grounded in excellence, perception, inspiration, and compassion is not about aiming to be better than others but about striving for balance. Integrating these four maxims into your daily life leads to greater growth, fulfillment, and impact. It's a holistic approach that ensures you're not only pushing yourself toward achievement but also staying connected to your inner values, perceiving the world with clarity, staying inspired, and nurturing others through compassion.

In this chapter, we will explore how to integrate these maxims into your daily routine, practical tips for staying aligned with your growth, the importance of becoming your future self, and how to build a support system that fosters these values. We'll also look at how small, consistent actions can lead to lasting transformation, reinforcing the habits and mindset needed to sustain long-term progress.

## HOW TO INTEGRATE THESE MAXIMS INTO YOUR DAILY LIFE

Achieving balance among the EPIC maxims requires intentional action. It's about weaving these values into the fabric of your everyday life, so they become part of who you are and how you operate.

### Being Excellent

Excellence is about consistently showing up at your best. This doesn't mean being perfect, but it does mean committing to high standards in whatever you do, whether it's your career, personal life, or health. Striving for excellence is about growth and improvement. It requires knowing that your best is just that, your best. That means it fluctuates from time to time. Best is fluid. Don't beat yourself up if today's best doesn't outperform yesterday's best. Don't make that a habit, but don't think you're failing either. You're not. Here are a few action steps to integrate excellence:

1. **Begin with the end in mind:** Iconic counsel from Stephen Covey. Becoming excellent requires foresight to see and describe who your future self is and taking the steps today to become that person.
2. **Start small, aim big:** Choose one area in your life where you want to improve and focus on small, consistent actions that lead to growth. It could be your work, relationships, or personal fitness. The idea is to generate momentum by working toward doable outcomes that gradually become more and more ambitious.

3. **Daily reflection:** Take five minutes at the end of each day to reflect on how you showed up. Ask yourself, "Did I give my best effort today?" If the answer is no, identify what you can do differently tomorrow.
4. **Set stretch goals:** As your excellence grows, push yourself beyond your comfort zone with stretch goals that encourage you to develop your skills and knowledge. These should be challenging but realistic enough to keep you motivated.

## Being Perceptive

Perception is about sharpening your awareness—of yourself, others, and the world around you. It involves seeing situations and people with clarity, free from (or at least with awareness of your) assumptions or biases and understanding things from multiple perspectives. Here are a few action steps to integrate perception:

1. **Practice 3D Thinking:** Begin to make decisions with input from all three time orientations: hindsight, insight, and foresight.
2. **Practice prayer and meditation:** Engage in daily meditation to sharpen your self-awareness and perception of the present moment. This will help you stay grounded and avoid knee-jerk reactions to situations.
3. **Seek cognitive diversity:** Regularly ask for feedback from those around you—both personally and professionally—and believe whatever it is they tell you. Don't make excuses. This can give you a clearer

picture of how others perceive you and help you identify blind spots.

4. **Challenge your own assumptions:** Each day, challenge one assumption you've made about a situation or person. Ask yourself, "What rule of thumb am I using?" and "What other perspectives might be true here?"

### Being Inspired

Inspiration fuels creativity, innovation, and passion. It's the fire that keeps you motivated to pursue your goals, push through challenges, and embrace your unique potential. The troubles and turbulation of life would like nothing more than to steal your inspiration. Protect it. Make time for it. Nurture it. Here are a few action steps to integrate inspiration:

1. **Create a routine for inspiration:** Begin each day with practices that inspire you, such as journaling, reading, or listening to music or podcasts that uplift your spirit and creativity.
2. **Take breaks for creative exploration (not social media):** Throughout your day, take short breaks to explore something new—whether it's stepping outside, reading an article on a new topic, or engaging in a creative hobby.
3. **Surround yourself with inspirational people:** Keep your environment filled with things and people that inspire you, such as vision boards, meaningful quotes, or photos that remind you of your purpose.

4. **Reflect on past successes and milestones:** Take time to revisit moments when you overcame challenges, achieved goals, or felt deeply fulfilled. Reflecting on these experiences can reignite your confidence and remind you of your capabilities. Keeping a journal of wins—big or small—serves as a reservoir of inspiration when you need a boost.

### Being Compassionate

Compassion connects you with others. It's about understanding, kindness, and action in response to the suffering or needs of others, but it also involves self-compassion—treating yourself with the same understanding and kindness you would offer to someone else. Here are a few action steps to integrate compassion:

1. **Do hard things:** Don't let yourself off the hook. Do not allow mediocrity to become an acceptable standard.
2. **Practice self-compassion:** When you make mistakes or fall short, treat yourself with kindness rather than harsh self-criticism. Acknowledge that growth takes time and effort. But don't make excuses.
3. **Regularly perform one act of kindness:** Whether it's offering support to a colleague, helping a friend, or serving someone else, consciously choose to engage in one act of kindness each day.
4. **Listen with empathy:** When others share their experiences, practice deep, empathetic listening without

judgment or the need to offer solutions. Sometimes just being there is the most compassionate thing you can do.

## BECOMING YOUR FUTURE SELF

An integral part of living an EPIC life is bringing your future self into the present. This may sound backward. Most of us plan to be better sometime in the future, but the reality is our future self must come to us in the present. In other words, we bring our future self to us where we are today.

This is about envisioning the person you want to become and making intentional choices today to align with that vision. Your future self is not a distant goal but a guiding force that helps you make decisions, overcome challenges, and stay motivated along the journey. Benjamin Hardy, author of *Be Your Future Self Now: The Science of Intentional Transformation*, emphasizes that your decisions today shape your future. He suggests that by asking yourself, "What would my future self do?" you can make decisions that are more aligned with long-term goals rather than short-term comfort. Each decision, no matter how small, contributes to the person you are becoming.

Your past self is often what holds you back the most from being your future EPIC self. It is important to intentionally "forget" the things that happened in the past—not by ignoring the lessons from past mistakes, but by refusing to carry those failures with you. Instead, use foresight to focus on what lies ahead, reaching for future possibilities and bringing them into the present. To do that requires the integration of perception and inspiration. I have always believed you can't have what you can't see. Seeing your future self through a restored imagination is the key to realizing your future self.

Spend time regularly using your imagination to envision your future self. What does this version of you look like in terms of habits, mindset, and lifestyle? How do they act, think, and engage with others? The clearer you are about your future self, the easier it becomes to take actionable steps toward becoming that person. Try creating a "Future Self" vision board. Collect images, words, or symbols that represent the person you want to grow into. This could include aspects of your career, relationships, health, mindsets, personal achievements, and values.

Imagine you're deciding whether to invest time in learning a new skill or scrolling through social media. By asking, "What would my future self do?" as Hardy recommends, you might picture the version of yourself who is more knowledgeable, confident, and equipped with new opportunities. That future self would likely choose growth over momentary distraction. Writing down how dedicating even thirty minutes to microlearning contributes to your long-term goals creates a clearer path forward. Over time, these small, intentional decisions compound, gradually shaping you into the person you envision becoming. This simple shift in perspective transforms everyday choices into lasting personal growth.

### Act "As If"

Living as your future self doesn't mean waiting until you've achieved certain milestones to start behaving like that person. Instead, act "as if" you are already that version of yourself. If your future self is confident, compassionate, and disciplined, start embodying those traits now, even if they feel uncomfortable at first.

## PRACTICAL TIPS FOR STAYING ALIGNED WITH YOUR GROWTH

Consistency is key when integrating the EPIC maxims into your life. Here are some practical tips for staying aligned with your growth as you navigate the journey toward living an EPIC life:

1. **Track your progress:** Use tools like journaling, habit trackers, or digital apps to monitor your growth. Writing down your daily actions and reflections helps you stay aware of how you're living out excellence, perception, inspiration, and compassion.
2. **Recognize success:** Acknowledge and celebrate your progress, no matter how small. Recognizing your achievements keeps you motivated and reinforces that you're on the right path. Small celebrations can be as simple as sharing your success with someone close to you.
3. **PIVOT—Stay adaptable:** Living an EPIC life is a continuous journey of growth, which means you'll face new challenges and obstacles along the way. Stay adaptable and willing to pivot when necessary. Sometimes, your path will change, and that's okay. The important thing is to remain committed to your overall vision and values. Remember, PIVOT stands for Persevere, Improvise, Visualize, Overcome, and Transform.

## BUILDING A SUPPORT SYSTEM THAT ENCOURAGES THESE VALUES

You won't become EPIC without help! It's just not possible. Surrounding yourself with people who support your growth is essential. Building a community of like-minded individuals who share your values or support your growth helps you stay accountable, motivated, and inspired. Not everyone on your side should be a "yes-person." Include opponents on your support team. Opponents are people you trust and who you believe have your best interest in mind, but who are likely to disagree with you. Most people surround themselves with people they trust AND agree with. Those people are called allies and rarely challenge you or encourage you to be your future self. Opponents on the other hand, are more likely to get you to go outside of your comfort zone and move you toward your future self. The journey to living an EPIC life is not one you need to or should try and walk alone.

### Find Mentors and Role Models

Seek mentors or role models who embody the qualities you admire. These individuals can offer guidance, wisdom, and support as you navigate your own journey.

Find a group of peers or colleagues who are also committed to personal growth. Regularly check in with each other to share progress, challenges, and goals. Having accountability partners helps keep you on track and provides mutual encouragement during difficult times. One of my favorite examples of this is the Inklings.

The Inklings were an informal literary group that met in Oxford, England, during the 1930s and 1940s, composed of writers, academics, and friends who shared a love of storytelling, philosophy, and theology. The group is most famous for its core members, including C.S. Lewis, J.R.R. Tolkien, Owen Barfield, and Charles Williams.

The Inklings would gather regularly, often at Lewis's rooms in Magdalen College or at a local pub, The Eagle and Child, to read aloud and critique one another's work; discuss literature, philosophy, and theology; and exchange ideas about writing. Some of the most iconic works in modern literature, such as *The Lord of the Rings* by Tolkien and *The Chronicles of Narnia* by Lewis, were discussed and developed within this group. The Inklings were characterized by their shared interest in myth, allegory, and exploring deeper spiritual and moral questions through imaginative fiction. Like the Inklings, aligning yourself with other people who will challenge you and hold you to a higher standard is key to becoming EPIC.

## CULTIVATE A CULTURE OF GROWTH

Growth is a mindset. In your personal and professional relationships, encourage a culture of growth by sharing your commitment to these values. Creating a culture of growth requires that you see challenges as opportunities and commit to learning new things. Not doing old things in new venues, but literally committing to reinventing yourself. Seek constructive feedback and don't make excuses for or reject criticism. Be intentional to engage in meaningful conversations about how you and those around you can grow together and offer support to others as they work toward their own EPIC lives.

## BALANCING EXCELLENCE, PERCEPTION, INSPIRATION, AND COMPASSION

Living a balanced life is about integrating all four EPIC maxims into the fabric of your everyday existence. It's about striving for excellence in your actions, sharpening your perception of the world around you, staying inspired to pursue the things that make you curious, and showing compassion to both yourself and others.

By integrating these values into your daily routine, visualizing and acting as your future self, and building a strong support system, you'll find that living an EPIC life is not only possible but happening. It's a journey that requires dedication and intention, but the rewards—a life filled with purpose, growth, and meaningful connection—are well worth the effort.

22

# BECOMING THE BEST VERSION OF YOURSELF

The journey toward becoming EPIC is an ongoing, transformative process that never ends. To fully embody these principles, you must stay committed to your personal development, grow from challenges, and adopt the right habits that support your growth.

This chapter brings together much of what we have discussed so far, introduces the concept of quantum thinking, and provides actionable strategies to help you take the next steps toward becoming your EPIC future self.

## QUANTUM THINKING

Danah Zohar, in her book *The Quantum Leader: A Revolution in Business Thinking and Practice*, challenges traditional models of performance development and suggests quantum thinking as a necessary framework for thriving in today's complex, fast-changing world. Zohar draws on principles from quantum physics to highlight how we must think in dynamic, flexible, and interconnected ways—just as particles behave in the quantum world. For those striving to become EPIC, quantum thinking offers a powerful model for navigating the unpredictable, volatile, uncertain, complex, and ambiguous (VUCA) environment of the modern world.

Zohar explains that classical leadership models, based on control, hierarchy, and linear thinking, are no longer effective in today's business landscape. Instead, quantum leaders recognize the interconnectedness of systems and relationships, allowing them to think holistically and act with agility. This capacity for fluid, adaptive thinking is vital for leaders who want to not only excel but also inspire others to navigate complexity with creativity and compassion.

## QUANTUM THINKING AND THE EPIC MAXIMS

Zohar's quantum leadership framework aligns closely with the EPIC values, particularly in how leaders must use perception and inspiration to adapt in uncertain times. Quantum performers excel by perceiving the hidden patterns and relationships within their organizations and the wider environment. They do not view problems as isolated challenges but rather as interconnected parts of a larger system that must be understood holistically.

Quantum thinking, in this context, is not just about flexibility but also about anticipating change and embracing complexity—two traits essential for EPIC leaders. Instead of relying on rigid, top-down decision-making, quantum thinkers create environments that encourage innovation, collective intelligence, and shared purpose. This type of leadership is less about commanding control and more about fostering collaboration, intuition, and empowerment across teams.

## Navigating VUCA

The VUCA world demands leaders who can think and act beyond traditional frameworks. Quantum thinkers are those who thrive in uncertainty by using agility, vision, and perceptive awareness to see opportunities where others see chaos. This mindset is critical for anyone on the journey to becoming EPIC, as it encourages leaders to embrace the unpredictable nature of life, rather than resist it.

Quantum thinkers operate with the understanding that the future is not set in stone. In a VUCA environment, inspiration becomes even more critical as a guiding force. Inspired leaders can create shared visions that motivate teams to move forward with confidence, even when the path is unclear. They cultivate environments where creativity flourishes, enabling them to respond to change with compassion and excellence rather than fear or rigid thinking.

Zohar's vision of quantum thinking invites us to see the world through a lens of interconnectedness and possibility, where every challenge is an opportunity to innovate, adapt, and inspire those around us. To adopt quantum thinking and lead effectively in a VUCA world, Zohar recommends that we:

1. **Embrace interconnectedness:** Recognize that problems are part of larger systems. Develop the capacity to think holistically and identify patterns and relationships that can guide decision-making.
2. **Cultivate agility and flexibility:** Be prepared to adapt to change quickly and encourage your team to do the same. Let go of rigid structures and embrace creative solutions that emerge from uncertainty.

3. **Inspire through shared vision:** Lead with purpose, creating a shared vision that unites your team in a common goal. Use inspiration to help others see beyond immediate challenges and focus on long-term possibilities.
4. **Operate with compassion:** In the face of complexity and volatility, lead with compassion. Understand that people react to uncertainty in different ways, and providing support, empathy, and clarity can enhance team cohesion and resilience.

Integrating quantum thinking into the EPIC maxims can help us navigate the complexity of a VUCA world with agility, creativity, and empathy. Embracing the interconnectedness of systems, fostering shared visions, and empowering others through compassion will enable EPIC leaders to thrive in environments where flexibility and forward-thinking are paramount.

## BRINGING IT ALL TOGETHER

Becoming better requires more than just understanding each of the EPIC maxims individually. It's about weaving them together to create a life of intentionality, purpose, and balance. I am convinced that excellence drives your initiative, perception sharpens your awareness, inspiration fuels your passion, and compassion connects you to others. Together, these values form the foundation of a fulfilled and impactful life.

### Excellence: The Pursuit of Personal Growth

Throughout this book I've tried to clearly establish that excellence isn't about perfection; it's about striving toward being better and improving in all areas of your life. Whether in your career, relationships, education, personal skills, leadership, spiritual life, or health, the pursuit of excellence involves setting high standards for yourself and consistently working toward them.

High standards were the driver behind Marie Curie and her discovery of radioactivity that changed the world. Curie's relentless dedication to learning, curiosity, and personal growth propelled her to one of the most groundbreaking scientific achievements in history, despite facing overwhelming obstacles due to her gender and social status.

Born in Poland in 1867, Curie (born Maria Skłodowska) faced incredible barriers to accessing education because universities in Poland did not admit women. Instead of saying, "Well, I tried my best," she pivoted. Determined to pursue her education, she endured the stress and hardship of moving to France, where she enrolled at the University of Paris (Sorbonne) and studied physics, chemistry, and mathematics. Without a penny to her name, she had to support herself by working as a tutor and taking on other jobs.

Insistent on becoming better, Curie's commitment to personal growth did not end with her formal education—an incredible feat in itself. Even as she faced financial ruin and was an outsider in the male-dominated field of science, she continued to push the boundaries of scientific knowledge. In her research, she discovered that certain materials, like uranium, emitted rays that were more intense than could be explained by chemical reactions alone. Her insatiable curiosity led her to hypothesize that these rays were coming from the atomic structure itself, something that had never been suggested before.

Marie Curie, along with her husband Pierre Curie, worked tirelessly to isolate new radioactive elements. In 1898, they discovered polonium and radium, two elements that emitted radiation far more intensely than uranium. Curie's discovery of radioactivity fundamentally changed the field of physics and chemistry, leading to significant advancements in medical treatments, nuclear energy, and the understanding of atomic theory.

Curie's breakthrough came as a direct result of her personal commitment to excellence. She did not rest after achieving milestones or receiving recognition for her early work. Instead, she continued pushing her research, even after facing life-threatening health issues from exposure to radiation. She won two Nobel Prizes—the first in physics (1903, shared with Pierre Curie and Henri Becquerel), and the second in chemistry (1911)—making her the first person to win two Nobel Prizes in different fields.

Marie Curie's scientific achievements were not just the result of her brilliance but also her antifragility, discipline, and constant pursuit of excellence. Her dedication to her work and personal growth enabled her to overcome obstacles that many would have found insurmountable. She believed deeply in the power of education, often telling her daughters that "One must never stop learning." Curie's life demonstrates how the relentless pursuit of excellence can reshape entire fields of study.

To bring excellence into your daily life, commit to showing up fully in whatever you do. Don't ever give up or accept no as a final answer. Excellence is less about results and more about effort—it's about inviting the help of others to push yourself to be better, not for external validation, but because deep down inside you know you're capable of more. Excellence takes pride in a job well done, but it is not satisfied with the most recent achievement.

### Perception: Gaining Clarity and Insight

Perception allows you to see beyond surface-level realities, gain deeper understanding, and navigate life's complexities with clarity. It sharpens your ability to interpret situations, understand people, and see yourself more clearly. By honing your perception, developing 3D thinking, and learning to practice contextual intelligence you can make better decisions, foster healthier relationships, and approach life with a greater sense of awareness.

Henry Ford is a prime example of leveraging perception to gain clarity and insight. His development of the Model T and the assembly line in the early twentieth century were groundbreaking business breakthroughs. Ford's ability to perceive market needs, labor inefficiencies, and the changing landscape of industrial production led to one of the most transformative moments in business history.

Before Henry Ford revolutionized the automobile industry, cars were considered luxury items, available only to the wealthy. Most automobile manufacturers of the time focused on producing high-end, handcrafted vehicles that were expensive to make and purchase. However, Ford had a different perception of the future. He imagined that the average American could benefit from owning a car, and he believed that mass production could lower costs and make cars affordable for the general public. This was a key insight into a market that no one else was actively targeting at the time.

Ford's goal was to produce a car that was reliable, easy to drive, and affordable to the average person, truly a unique perception. This led to the creation of the Model T, which was introduced in 1908. The Model T was not only cheaper to buy, but its simplicity also made it easier to maintain and repair, which added to its appeal for the mass market. Ford's ability to perceive what the public needed—affordable, dependable transportation—was instrumental in his success.

Beyond recognizing the market potential, Ford also had a sharp perception of inefficiencies in the production process. At the time, cars were assembled slowly, with skilled craftsmen performing various tasks in sequence. Ford realized that this method was too slow and costly to produce cars at the volume and price point he envisioned.

Rumor has it that he gained a crucial insight into how to make manufacturing more efficient by observing the meatpacking industry's disassembly line approach, where animals were broken down into parts as they moved down a conveyor. Ford applied this insight in reverse to car manufacturing. He designed the world's first moving assembly line, which allowed workers to remain stationary while parts were moved along a conveyor system. This increased the speed of production dramatically and lowered costs, making the Model T even more affordable.

By 1914, Ford had refined the assembly line process so well that the time to build a single Model T dropped from 12.5 hours to 93 minutes, a 774 percent improvement. This breakthrough in production efficiency was directly tied to Ford's perception and insight into how industrial processes could be streamlined. The assembly line became a model for mass production in various industries, revolutionizing manufacturing worldwide.

Ford's clarity of vision—his ability to perceive a gap in the market and to innovate in the production process—led to immense corporate success. By making the Model T affordable and accessible, Ford was able to sell millions of cars. In 1914, Ford introduced the famous $5 workday, which was more than double the average wage at the time, and this initiative attracted better laborers, reducing employee turnover and further increasing productivity. His perception that workers should be paid well enough to afford the products they built contributed to both the company's success and the broader economy.

Rumor has it he said the Model T was available in any color, as long as it was black. Turns out, black paint was cheaper and more durable, which helped create a better product at a lower cost.

Ford Motor Company became the dominant automobile manufacturer in the world, and by the time production of the Model T ended in 1927, more than 15 million units had been sold. Ford's combination of business foresight, innovative production methods, and understanding of the needs of the middle class are examples of the power of perception.

To become more perceptive, begin to imagine how the existing norms and status quo can be changed. Ask questions about why things are the way they are. Who invoked this rule? What was this rule created to do or prevent? Talk to people about their experiences and ideas. Cultivate perception by asking people what they want and need and help them get it. Along the way you are likely to realize the true thing they need, and you may just change the world.

### Inspiration: Cultivating Creativity and Motivation

Inspiration is the driving force that keeps you motivated and engaged in your pursuits. It ignites your creativity and passion, helping you stay excited about the future and the possibilities that lie ahead. Inspiration isn't something that just happens; it's something you can cultivate through daily habits like journaling, reflection, and engaging in activities that align with your passions.

One of the most profound examples of how inspiration played a critical role in a creative breakthrough that impacted the world is the story of Alexander Fleming and his discovery of penicillin in 1928. Fleming, a Scottish bacteriologist, had been conducting research on staphylococci bacteria at St. Mary's Hospital in London. His primary focus was on discovering ways to treat bacterial infections, but the road to a breakthrough was not straightforward. In fact, the discovery of penicillin came about because of an accidental observation followed by an inspired realization of its potential significance.

Before leaving for a vacation, Fleming left several Petri dishes with staphylococcus cultures on his workbench. When he returned, he noticed something peculiar. One of the dishes had mold growing on it, which wasn't unusual; in fact, most people would have stopped there and cleaned up. What caught his attention was that the bacteria surrounding the mold were being killed off. Fleming realized that the mold, identified as Penicillium notatum, was releasing a substance that inhibited bacterial growth. This was an unusual observation, and many researchers might have dismissed it as mere contamination. However, Fleming's curiosity led him to investigate further, inspiring him to one of the most important discoveries in medical history.

Fleming's inspiration came from his ability to see something meaningful in what could have easily been ignored or discarded. He wasn't actively looking for an antibiotic, but his mind was open to unexpected findings, and he was inspired to pursue this observation further. This moment of creative insight came from a combination of scientific rigor and an openness to new possibilities—hallmarks of inspiration.

Rather than dismissing the mold as a lab error, Fleming's inspired thinking led him to extract the active substance from the mold and test it on various types of bacteria. His experiments showed that this "mold juice" was effective in killing a wide range of harmful bacteria, including those responsible for diseases like scarlet fever, pneumonia, meningitis, and diphtheria.

Inspiration is not the exclusive domain of artists, a common lie we tell ourselves. You do not have to write, paint, draw, or dance to be creative. Everyone can be inspired. Inspiration is the seedbed of creativity, but even if inspiration doesn't "strike" like you think it might, it can be developed through patience and iteration. Some of the most inspiring moments in the history of humanity came after great effort, trial and error, and keen observation.

### Compassion: Connecting with Others and Yourself

Compassion brings humanity to the process of becoming EPIC. It's about caring deeply for others, putting yourself in their shoes, and doing hard things. Compassion is essential for personal development, as it allows you to forgive more easily and embrace imperfections while moving forward on your journey.

Consider this common scenario where Sarah, an office worker, noticed that her colleague, Eric, was overwhelmed with his workload. It was a hectic time for everyone in the office, with multiple deadlines looming. Despite having her own work to finish, Sarah noticed that Eric was particularly stressed, trying to juggle several high-priority tasks. Instead of just focusing on her own work, Sarah made the choice to step in and offer help.

At first, Eric was hesitant, not wanting to burden anyone else. But Sarah reassured him, explaining that she had been in a similar situation and knew how difficult it could be to ask for help. Sarah offered to take on one of Eric's smaller tasks, something that wouldn't take much of her own time but would relieve some of the pressure Eric was feeling. By staying a little later that day, Sarah helped Eric meet his deadline.

What made this act of compassion significant wasn't just Eric's immediate gratitude—it was the longer-term impact. A few weeks later, when Sarah found herself in a tight spot with her own deadlines, Eric remembered Sarah's kindness. Without Sarah asking, Eric jumped in to assist with one of Sarah's tasks, returning the favor in a time of need.

This simple act of compassion had a ripple effect. By extending help to Eric, Sarah created a work environment where colleagues looked out for each other, fostering a sense of teamwork and mutual support. Small, compassionate actions can build trust and cooperation in the workplace, benefiting both the giver and the recipient. Compassion doesn't always have to involve grand gestures—sometimes it's the simple, everyday moments of kindness that make the biggest difference in how people relate to each other.

By integrating these four maxims into your life, you create a balanced foundation for personal and professional growth. Living an EPIC life means recognizing that growth doesn't happen in isolation—each maxim supports and enhances the others.

## STAYING COMMITTED TO YOUR DEVELOPMENT

Becoming EPIC requires commitment and consistency. Becoming the best version of yourself is a lifelong journey, one that does not have a destination. You can always be better. This means making a daily decision to invest in your development and embrace opportunities for learning and growth.

### Set Intentional Goals

Don't try and swallow the whole elephant at once; remember the wise old tale that the best way to eat an elephant is one bite at a time. One of the most effective ways to stay committed to your development is to set focused goals that align with your vision of your future self. Break those goals down into smaller, actionable steps that can be incorporated into your daily routine. Make sure the action steps are measurable. That way you stay focused, motivated, and accountable.

Take a moment right now to create a list of three to four goals that align with the EPIC maxims. Put them in columns and jot down two or three things that need to happen first before those goals can be achieved. Then repeat that and jot down two or three additional things that need to happen before those can be achieved. Now, integrate those third level actions into your daily routine. Review your progress regularly and adjust your goals as needed.

### Create Daily Habits for Growth

Habits are powerful tools for personal development because they create structure and consistency. Whether it's a morning reflection, an evening journaling session, or a weekly check-in with yourself, these small habits keep you grounded and connected to your personal growth journey. Several authors have offered recommendations on how to form habits. Here are a few; choose whichever technique sounds best to you and stick with it!

1. **Start small:** Research by BJ Fogg, creator of the Tiny Habits framework, shows that starting with small, easily achievable actions is crucial for habit formation. The idea is to make the habit so easy that it becomes almost automatic. For example, if your goal is to exercise regularly, start with just five minutes a day rather than committing to an hour. Small steps are more sustainable and build momentum.
2. **Use Cue-Routine-Reward (the habit loop):** According to Charles Duhigg's work in *The Power of Habit*, habits are built around a loop consisting of three parts:
    a. **Cue:** A trigger that initiates the habit.
    b. **Routine:** The action or behavior itself.
    c. **Reward:** The positive reinforcement that encourages the repetition of the behavior

    Identify the cue that will trigger your desired habit, engage in the routine, and then reward yourself for completing it. Over time, the loop becomes automatic. For example, if you want to start praying daily, use a cue like sitting down in a quiet space at the same time each day. The reward could be the sense of calm or accomplishment afterward.
3. **Make it easy and accessible (reduce friction):** Research from behavioral economists like Richard Thaler suggests that reducing barriers (friction) to the desired behavior makes it more likely to occur. To form a new habit, eliminate any obstacles that could prevent you from doing it. If your goal is to eat healthier, for

instance, prep nutritious meals in advance and keep healthy snacks visible and accessible.

4. **Stack new habits onto existing ones (habit stacking):** This method, advocated by James Clear in *Atomic Habits*, involves pairing a new habit with an established one. By anchoring the new behavior to something you already do regularly, you increase the chances of it sticking. For example, if you want to start journaling, tie it to something you already do daily, like drinking your morning coffee. After you brew your coffee, take five minutes to write in your journal.
5. **Set specific, actionable goals (implementation intentions):** Research by psychologist Peter Gollwitzer shows that implementation intentions—statements like "If X happens, then I will do Y"—significantly increase the likelihood of performing a desired behavior. Be specific about what you want to do and when you will do it. For example, instead of saying, "I want to exercise more," create a plan like, "I will go for a twenty-minute walk after lunch on weekdays."
6. **Track your progress:** Evidence suggests that tracking your habits can significantly increase your likelihood of success. Keeping a log or using a habit-tracking app can help you stay accountable and measure your progress over time. The act of checking off each completed habit provides a psychological reward and reinforces the behavior.

This is one I like to do. In fact, I have a template worksheet I call the 4x40 Challenge. I have a paper with forty boxes on it, each box represents one day. Inside each box are four things I have committed to do. I do four things for forty days, hence the 4x40 Challenge.

Last time I did it, I committed to not exceeding 2,000 calories every day for forty days. I committed to writing 1,000 words every day for forty days. I committed to running three miles every day for forty days. And I committed to pray for thirty minutes every day for forty days. After those forty days, I had lost twelve pounds, written a 40,000-word book called *42 Leadership Insights* and had many profound moments of spiritual insight. For those forty days, there are no excuses and no cheat days. If I falter, the forty days start over. I still do all four of those things habitually. I may not write 1,000 words every day, but I write almost every day. Same for everything else. While I can't run three miles every day since my diagnosis, I do try and exercise every day. Yes, habit tracking does work.

7. **Focus on identity-based habits:** James Clear's concept of identity-based habits suggests that people are more likely to stick with a habit if it aligns with their self-identity. Instead of focusing on the outcome (e.g., "I want to lose weight"), focus on the type of person you want to become (e.g., "I'm the type of person who exercises regularly"). This shift helps you internalize the behavior as part of who you are.
8. **Practice consistency and patience:** Research by psychologist Phillippa Lally found that, on average, it

takes about 66 days for a new behavior to become automatic. A far cry from the often reported 21 or 40 days. The exact time frame varies depending on the complexity of the habit, but the key is to stay consistent and be patient with yourself. Missing a day doesn't mean failure—just get back on track the next day.

9. **Leverage social accountability:** Studies have shown that involving others in your habit-forming process can increase success rates. Share your goals with a friend or join a community of like-minded individuals. Just ask anyone in the CrossFit community and they'll have you convinced in no time how well this habit formation system works. The Hawthorne effect—where individuals modify their behavior when they know they're being observed—plays a role here, as you're more likely to stick with habits when someone is watching. Just remember that when sharing your goals, the reason for sharing is for accountability and not congratulations.
10. **Make the habit enjoyable (immediate rewards):** Behavioral scientist BJ Fogg emphasizes the importance of making habits enjoyable. If a habit feels like a chore, you're less likely to maintain it. Find a way to make the process enjoyable or rewarding in the short term. For example, listen to your favorite podcast while exercising, or treat yourself to a small reward (like a healthy snack) after completing a task.

### Cultivate Discipline

While inspiration may come and go, discipline will keep you on track when motivation wanes. Cultivate discipline by committing to your goals even on days when you don't feel inspired. Discipline is what turns aspirations into achievements, and it's essential for staying the course.

Challenges and setbacks are inevitable on the journey to becoming EPIC. However, they don't have to derail your progress. In fact, the way you respond to them is one of the most significant factors in this process.

Instead of seeing setbacks as failures, view them as opportunities to learn and grow. Every challenge contains a lesson that can help you improve. Whether you've made a mistake at work, encountered a roadblock in your personal life, or faced unexpected difficulties, ask yourself, "What can I learn from this?" This mindset shift transforms setbacks into steppingstones.

### Build Antifragility

When setbacks occur, it's easy to be overly critical of yourself or discouraged. However, antifragility is built through focus and intention. Recognize that everyone faces challenges and that your setbacks don't define you. In fact, these setbacks are to your EPIC journey what weightlifting is to the body. It may hurt while you're doing it and cause muscle damage, but the recovery and repair process make the muscles stronger. So, too, does adversity and setbacks—they make you and your mental and emotional strength better!

After a setback, take time to recover in the same way you would after an intense workout. I recommend taking time to reflect on what happened. Write down what went wrong, what you've learned, and how you'll move forward. This process helps you turn challenges into opportunities for growth.

### Persevere Through Hardship

Perseverance is key to overcoming setbacks and becoming antifragile. When things get difficult, remind yourself of your commitment to becoming EPIC. Lean on your support system, rely on your daily habits, and trust the process. With each challenge you face, you grow stronger and more equipped to handle future obstacles.

You can read in Genesis the amazing story of Joseph, renowned for his "technicolor dream coat." Behind that story is one of pure perseverance. Joseph's journey from being sold into slavery to becoming the second most powerful man in Egypt showcases how perseverance through adversity can lead to significant personal growth and development.

Joseph was the favored son of Jacob, and his father's special treatment led to jealousy and hatred by his brothers. Out of envy, Joseph's brothers sold him into slavery when he was just a teenager, sending him to Egypt. Despite being betrayed by his own family, Joseph did not give up hope or let bitterness consume him. Instead, he persevered through the challenges he faced.

In Egypt, Joseph was sold to Potiphar, an officer of Pharaoh. He worked hard and earned Potiphar's trust, eventually becoming the overseer of his household. However, Joseph faced another trial when Potiphar's wife falsely accused him of attempted assault after he refused her sexual advances. As a result, Joseph was imprisoned, even though he had done nothing wrong.

During his time in prison, Joseph again showed remarkable perseverance. Instead of losing hope or giving in to despair, he continued to work diligently and gained the trust of the prison warden, who put him in charge of the other prisoners. Even in such dire circumstances, Joseph's perseverance remained steadfast.

Joseph's skill at interpreting dreams eventually became the turning point in his life. While in prison, he interpreted the dreams of two of Pharaoh's servants, which later led to him being called upon to interpret Pharaoh's troubling dreams. Impressed by Joseph's wisdom and insight, Pharaoh appointed him as his second-in-command, giving him authority over all of Egypt. Joseph's perseverance, even in the face of seventeen or more years of extreme adversity, positioned him for this remarkable role. His personal growth—spiritually, emotionally, and in leadership—was evident through his wise and compassionate actions during the famine.

During the famine, Joseph's brothers came to Egypt seeking food, not knowing that the powerful governor they were speaking to was their brother. Rather than seeking revenge, Joseph showed incredible compassion, choosing to forgive his brothers for their betrayal. His perseverance through years of hardship had shaped him into a compassionate and wise leader.

Joseph's perseverance led to his personal growth and development, and it also resulted in the reconciliation of his family. He famously told his brothers, "You intended to harm me, but God intended it for good to accomplish what is now being done, the saving of many lives." That is antifragility in action. Through perseverance, Joseph saw that his struggles had a greater purpose, and his personal growth had a positive impact on those around him.

## YOUR NEXT STEPS: ACTIONABLE GOALS TO START TODAY

To start living a more EPIC life today, focus on small, actionable goals that move you closer to becoming your future self. These goals should be practical and aligned with your values, making it easier to stay committed to them over time.

1. **Excellence: Focus on one area for improvement.** Identify one area of your life where you'd like to see improvement—whether it's your career, personal health, or a relationship. Set a specific goal for how you'll improve in this area and commit to taking consistent actions to reach that goal.

   **Example:** If you want to improve your emotional resilience, commit to developing a growth mindset. Track your progress by making a list of things you do not think you have the capacity or ability to learn. Pick one and begin to learn it. Start small and do not expect large strides. But make the strides nonetheless and assess your progress after ninety or more days!

2. **Perception: Practice prayer.** Mindfulness is a powerful tool for sharpening your perception. Commit to spending five minutes each day practicing prayer or meditation. This practice will help you stay present, reduce stress, and increase your awareness of yourself and others.

**Example:** Use a guided meditation or preset reading plan to help you stay consistent with your practice.

3. **Inspiration: Create a vision board.** Spend time visualizing your future self and the life you want to create. Then, put together a vision board that represents your goals, aspirations, and values. Place it somewhere visible and use it as a daily reminder of the life you're working toward.

   **Example:** Include images, quotes, or symbols that inspire you, and take time each day to reflect on how you can move closer to that vision.

4. **Compassion: Perform one act of kindness.** Compassion is most powerful when it's practiced daily. Make it a goal to perform one act of kindness each day—whether it's offering a compliment, helping a colleague, or simply being present for someone in need.

   **Example:** At the end of each day, reflect on the acts of kindness you've engaged in and how they've impacted both you and the recipient.

## THE POWER OF REFLECTION AND CONTINUOUS LEARNING

Reflection is a key component to becoming EPIC. Regularly reflecting on and discussing your actions, decisions, and progress helps you stay connected to your goals and values. It also allows you to course correct when necessary, ensuring that you remain aligned with your long-term vision.

### Weekly Reflection Practice

At the end of each week, take time to reflect on what went well, what challenges you faced, and how you can improve. Write down your thoughts in a journal, and use this reflection to adjust your goals or actions for the following week. Use reflection prompts like "What did I learn this week?" or "How did I show up as my future self?" to guide your journaling process.

### Lifelong Learning

Becoming the best version of yourself means embracing continuous learning. Whether through books, courses, or life experiences, seek opportunities to grow and expand your knowledge. The more you learn, the better equipped you are to navigate life's challenges and make informed decisions that align with your vision. Make a habit of reading for fifteen to thirty minutes each day on topics that inspire you or help you grow in your personal or professional life.

## FINAL TAKEAWAYS ON BECOMING EPIC

Living an EPIC life is about integrating Excellence, Perception, Inspiration, and Compassion into your daily routine. Here are the key takeaways to guide you on your journey:

1. **Excellence** is about consistently showing up as your best self, lifelong learning, and striving for personal growth, not perfection.

2. **Perception** sharpens your awareness of yourself, others, and the world around you, helping you make better decisions.
3. **Inspiration** fuels your creativity and passion, keeping you motivated to pursue your goals.
4. **Compassion** connects you to others and yourself, fostering kindness, empathy, and deeper relationships.

Becoming the best version of yourself is a lifelong journey that requires intention, action, and reflection. By integrating the EPIC maxims into your daily life, you build a foundation for continuous growth and fulfillment. As you move forward, stay committed to your development, embrace challenges, and surround yourself with a support system that encourages your progress.

Remember, the journey to becoming EPIC is about progress. Take small, consistent steps each day, and celebrate the wins—both big and small—along the way. As you do, you'll inspire others to do the same, and together, we can create a world that is EPIC.

# Epilogue

## MY PERSONAL BATTLE TO BECOME EPIC

In the fall of 2023, life took an unexpected turn when I was diagnosed with prostate cancer. Initially, the diagnosis seemed manageable—what doctors sometimes call "the easy kind"—with a promising 99 percent cure rate. Confident that we could handle it quietly, my wife, Angie, and I chose to keep the news private. But three months later, everything changed. The results of a biopsy revealed an aggressive form of cancer with a daunting Gleason Score of 8 (4+4). The cancer had metastasized to my bones and lymph nodes, transforming our initial hope into an overwhelming sense of uncertainty and fear.

In the face of this unforeseen battle, I had a choice: either surrender to the fear or rise to meet the challenge. To persevere, Angie and I developed a personal framework for this journey, which we call BATTLE:

- **Be Brave**
- **Armor Up**
- **Trust Your Team**
- **Triumph Over Fear**
- **Lean into God**
- **Engage in Life**

This framework not only guides me through the hardest days but also redoubled my commitment to live a life rooted in Excellence, Perception, Inspiration, and Compassion—the EPIC Leadership Loop™ (Figure 1, page xxvii), which I developed years before my diagnosis made it take on new meaning. The principles that shaped my journey long before the diagnosis would now have to motivate me to press on.

## BE BRAVE

As the reality of the aggressive cancer diagnosis sank in, fear became an unwelcome companion. It wasn't just the fear of pain or uncertainty, but the fear of losing the life I had envisioned. I had to make a conscious decision every day to choose courage over fear. It wasn't about dismissing the fear but about acknowledging it and choosing to move forward anyway. Bravery became a crucial cornerstone, not just for me but for those who were supporting me—my family, my friends, and the medical professionals working tirelessly to help me fight this disease.

## ARMOR UP

Preparing for this battle meant fortifying myself mentally and spiritually. I had to actively protect my mind from the onslaught of unwelcome thoughts and emotions. The treatment regimen—radical prostatectomy, androgen deprivation therapy (ADT), and eight weeks of radiation—took an enormous physical toll. But arming up meant more than medical interventions; it meant committing to routines and practices that built my resilience. It meant setting goals, even small ones, to keep myself moving forward.

Armor also comes in the form of mental readiness. When the side effects felt like they would break me, I reminded myself that resilience is not about avoiding adversity but finding a way to grow stronger through it. To Be Brave and Armor Up are two sides of the same coin—one is the decision to face the storm, and the other is the preparation to withstand it.

## TRUST YOUR TEAM

One of the most profound lessons I learned was that I could not navigate this journey alone. Trusting my team—the doctors, my family, and my friends—was essential. There were days when I had to let go of my desire for control and place my trust in the expertise of my medical team. They were on this battlefield with me, armed with knowledge and skill that I didn't have, working tirelessly to help me fight.

My team extended beyond healthcare professionals. Angie, my boys, and close friends provided unwavering support that kept me grounded. Their encouragement, prayers, and presence gave me the strength I needed on days when fear threatened to take over. I learned that leaning on others is not a sign of weakness but a source of immense strength.

## TRIUMPH OVER FEAR

Fear can be paralyzing, especially when facing something as life-altering as advanced cancer. Triumphing over fear didn't mean that it disappeared—it meant finding the courage to confront it daily. Even as the uncertainty loomed, I held onto the belief that fear could not dictate my actions or steal my hope.

One day at a time, one challenge at a time, I worked to triumph over the shadows of doubt. This wasn't a solitary effort; the prayers, love, and encouragement of those around me became a lifeline. Together, we fought fear by staying focused on what we could control and placing our trust in Jehovah Rapha, my healer. Fear has never completely gone away. It still raises its ugly head, but my goal isn't to irradicate it, just to beat it—one day at a time.

## LEAN INTO GOD

In this journey, faith has been my anchor. Leaning into God meant seeking purpose amid frustration and trusting that this battle was part of a greater plan. In moments of weakness, I turned to prayer, scripture, and the promises that God has laid out in His Word. Faith gave me the courage to believe in brighter days, even when the road ahead seemed filled with uncertainty.

This experience deepened my relationship with God, reminding me that true strength comes not from self-reliance but from surrendering. Leaning into God allowed me to tap into a well of hope that transcended the physical challenges I was facing.

## ENGAGE IN LIFE

Finally, I chose to Engage in Life. The temptation in such battles is to withdraw, to let the weight of the fight keep you from embracing each day. But engaging in life meant making the choice to be present, to find joy, and to hold on to hope even in the face of hardship. It meant finding small victories, celebrating meaningful moments, and embracing the opportunity to live excellently, despite the side effects and uncertainty.

## AN EPIC JOURNEY

None of this is easy. I may make it sound easy, but it is not! The fact is, I am dying. But then again, so are you. We are all dying. The question we must ask is, how will we die? I choose to die while becoming EPIC. I plan to be here for a few more decades, and until the day I meet my Maker, I intend to make the most of the life He has given me!

My battle with advanced metastatic prostate cancer has redoubled my effort to be EPIC. Each day, this journey reinforces my commitment to Excellence, as I strive to show up as my best self even in moments of weakness. It sharpens my Perception, reminding me to be present, listen, and find clarity amid the noise and fear. It fuels my Inspiration, as I draw strength from my God and the courage of those around me. I can find purpose in sharing this journey with others. And it deepens my Compassion, as I learn to extend grace to myself and others, knowing that we are all fighting battles no one else can fully see.

## A NEW PERSPECTIVE ON ANTIFRAGILITY

This journey has been about more than resilience—it's been about becoming antifragile. Resilience means bouncing back, but antifragility is about using adversity to grow stronger. I don't want to just survive this battle; I want to come out on the other side having gained something more—having become someone better. And I want this for everyone who faces their own struggles, big or small.

## AN INVITATION TO THE JOURNEY

The American Cancer Society's projections in 2024 include over 299,000 new cases of prostate cancer in the United States and approximately 35,000 deaths. One in eight men will be diagnosed with prostate cancer in their lifetime, and one in forty-four will die from it. These numbers are sobering, but they are not the end of the story.

I invite you to join me on this journey to becoming EPIC. Life is fragile, and adversity is inevitable. But together, we can strive for Excellence, sharpen our Perception, find Inspiration in each other's courage, and extend Compassion to those around us. We can be antifragile in the face of life's storms, growing stronger not despite them but because of them.

In this battle, and in yours, remember to BATTLE fiercely—**Be Brave, Armor Up, Trust Your Team, Triumph Over Fear, Lean into God**, and **Engage in Life.** The journey is not easy, but it is worth every step. And remember, no one becomes EPIC alone. We're in this journey together.

# RECOMMENDED READING (WORKS CITED)

Here is a list of the books I referred to throughout *Becoming EPIC* in alphabetical order by author. I list them here as recommended reading for you on your journey to becoming EPIC.

Ahmed, W. (2019). *The polymath: Unlocking the power of human versatility*. Wiley.

Brown, B. (2012). *Daring greatly: How the courage to be vulnerable transforms the way we live, love, parent, and lead*. Avery.

Brown, B. (2015). *Rising strong: How the ability to reset transforms the way we live, love, parent, and lead*. Random House.

Clear, J. (2018). *Atomic habits: An easy & proven way to build good habits & break bad ones*. Avery.

Cloud, H., & Townsend, J. (1992). *Boundaries: When to say yes, how to say no to take control of your life*. Zondervan.

Covey, S. R. (1989). *The 7 habits of highly effective people: Powerful lessons in personal change*. Simon & Schuster.

Dimitrius, J., & Mazzarella, W. P. (1998). *Reading people: How to understand people and predict their behavior anytime, anyplace*. Ballantine Books.

Duhigg, C. (2012). *The power of habit: Why we do what we do in life and business*. Random House.

Dweck, C. S. (2006). *Mindset: The new psychology of success*. Ballantine Books.

Epstein, D. (2019). *Range: Why generalists triumph in a specialized world*. Riverhead Books.

Fleming, A. (1928). *Discovery of penicillin*.

Fogg, B. J. (2019). *Tiny habits: The small changes that change everything*. Houghton Mifflin Harcourt.

Foster, R. J. (1978). *Celebration of discipline: The path to spiritual growth*. HarperOne.

Godin, S. (2008). *Tribes: We need you to lead us*. Portfolio.

Godin, S. (2020). *The practice: Shipping creative work*. Portfolio.

Hardy, B. (2022). *Be your future self now: The science of intentional transformation*. Hay House.

Holt, J. (2018). *When Einstein walked with Gödel: Excursions to the edge of thought*. Farrar, Straus and Giroux.

Kahneman, D. (2011). *Thinking, fast and slow*. Farrar, Straus and Giroux.

Kellerman, B. (2014). *Hard times: Leadership in America*. Stanford University Press.

Kounios, J., & Beeman, M. (2015). *The eureka factor: Aha moments, creative insight, and the brain*. Random House.

Kouzes, J. M., & Posner, B. Z. (1987). *The leadership challenge: How to make extraordinary things happen in organizations*. Jossey-Bass.

Magness, S. (2022). *Do hard things: Why we get resilience wrong and the surprising science of real toughness*. HarperOne.

Maxwell, J. C. (1998). *The 21 irrefutable laws of leadership: Follow them and people will follow you*. Thomas Nelson.

Medcalf, J. (2015). *Chop wood carry water: How to fall in love with the process of becoming great*. Train to Be Clutch.

Navarro, J., & Karlins, M. (2008). *What every body is saying: An ex-FBI agent's guide to speed-reading people*. William Morrow Paperbacks.

Nixon, N. (2020). *The creativity leap: Unleash curiosity, improvisation, and intuition at work*. Berrett-Koehler Publishers.

Sinek, S. (2009). *Start with why: How great leaders inspire everyone to take action*. Portfolio.

Sire, J. W. (1976). *The universe next door: A basic worldview catalog*. IVP Academic.

Sun Tzu. (1910). *The art of war* (L. Giles, Trans.). Various editions.

Taleb, N. N. (2012). *Antifragility: Things that gain from disorder*. Random House.

Zohar, D. (2016). *The quantum leader: A revolution in business thinking and practice*. Prometheus.

# ACKNOWLEDGMENTS

Thank you most of all to my readers. Without you, there is no book!

To my mentors and friends, you know who you are—your help, encouragement, and support is priceless and beyond words.

To Angie, the love of my life and best friend—thank you. I love you! You are the epitome of EPIC.

# OTHER BOOKS BY MATTHEW R. KUTZ, PHD

*Contextual Intelligence: How Thinking in 3D Can Help Resolve Complexity, Uncertainty, and Ambiguity*

*Building a Marriage That Is in FOCUS: Bringing Clarity to the Five Things That Cause the Most Conflict in Your Marriage (Finances, Others, Children, Use of Time, and Sex)*

*They Were Sent: Exploring the Apostolic Assignment of Biblical Leaders from the Old Testament*

*42 Leadership Insights: Curated Ideas to Help You Become a Better Leader*

*Leadership Questions for Health Care Professionals: Applying Theories and Principles to Practice*

**CONTACT MATT KUTZ AT WWW.MATTHEWKUTZ.COM OR INFO.MATTHEWKUTZ@GMAIL.COM.**